CHOICES FOR COLLEGE SUCCESS

third edition

CHOICES
For College Success

STEVE PISCITELLI

PEARSON

Boston • Columbus • Indianapolis • New York • San Francisco • Upper Saddle River
Amsterdam • Cape Town • Dubai • London • Madrid • Milan • Munich • Paris • Montreal • Toronto
Delhi • Mexico City • Sao Paulo • Sydney • Hong Kong • Seoul • Singapore • Taipei • Tokyo

Editor-in-Chief: Jodi McPherson
Acquisitions Editor: Katie Mahan
Managing Editor: Karen Wernholm
Senior Development Editor: Shannon Steed
Editorial Assistant: Erin Carreiro
Executive Marketing Manager: Amy Judd
Senior Production Project Manager: Peggy McMahon
Senior Manufacturing Buyer: Roy Pickering
Senior Author Support/Technology Specialist: Joe Vetere
Full-service Vendor: Electronic Publishing Services Inc., NYC
Program Design Lead: Beth Paquin
Associate Director of Design, USHE EMSS/HSC/EDU: Andrea Nix
Image Manager: Rachel Youdelman
Permissions Liaison Manager: Joseph Croscup
Cover Design: Studio Montage
Cover Photos: (top) Adam Kazmierski/E+/Getty Images; (bottom) Digital Skillet/E+/Getty Images

Credits and acknowledgments borrowed from other sources and reproduced, with permission, in this textbook appear on the appropriate page within text or on page 281, which is hereby made part of this copyright page.

Library of Congress Cataloging-in-Publication Data

Piscitelli, Stephen.
    Choices for college success/Steve Piscitelli. — Third edition.
        pages cm
    Includes bibliographical references.
    ISBN 978-0-321-90869-8
    1. College choice.   I. Title.
    LB2350.5.P57 2015
    378.1'98—dc23

                                        2013030201

10 9 8 7 6 5 4 3—RRD—16 15 14

ISBN-10: 0-321-90869-4
ISBN-13: 978-0-321-90869-8

Dedication

For every student who dares
to *dream*, *act*, and *create*
a better world.

Steve Piscitelli understands, applies, and builds upon basic principles of student success. He helps students visualize their dreams and prioritize their resources on the way to a life of well-being and balance.

In addition to this third edition of *Choices for College Success*, Pearson Education published *Study Skills: Do I Really Need This Stuff?* (third edition, 2013). Steve has also written, recorded, and produced two music CDs. He maintains a YouTube Channel and posts a weekly blog on life success issues and strategies. His classroom and nationally known workshops combine energy, inter-action, music, video, and humor to connect students and faculty with practical strategies. Steve earned degrees from Jacksonville University, the University of North Florida, and the University of Florida. He brings more than thirty years of classroom teaching experience to this edition of *Choices*.

Steve lives with his wife, Laurie, and canine companion, Buddy, in Atlantic Beach, Florida. You can learn more about Steve at www.stevepiscitelli.com.

BRIEF CONTENTS

CONTENTS

Chapter 4
INFORMATION LITERACY 57

Chapter 5
MOTIVATION AND ACHIEVING YOUR GOALS 77

Chapter 6
LEARNING STYLES   95

Chapter 7
CLASS-TIME LISTENING AND NOTE TAKING   111

Chapter 8
MEMORY AND STUDYING   131

Chapter 9
READING   151

Chapter 10
TEST PREPARATION AND TEST TAKING   169

Chapter 11
CIVILITY   191

Chapter 12
TREATING YOURSELF WITH RESPECT 209

Chapter 13
FINANCIAL LITERACY 229

Chapter 14
EXPLORATION OF MAJORS AND CAREERS 249

Choices for College Success, 3rd edition emphasizes the power of personal choice and responsibility. It integrates two models to help students create the life of their dreams:

1. The R.E.D. Model for critical thinking presents an eloquently simple and practical model to carefully analyze and address school and life challenges.

2. A multi-dimensional model for personal well-being and balance helps students navigate the transitions and adjustments to college life.

These models, combined with reflective exercises throughout the book, enable students to build a sense of self-efficacy by managing their priorities and leading a balanced life.

Both students and instructors will find coherent strategies and practical exercises for immediate use.

NEW TO THE THIRD EDITION

■ **The R.E.D. Model* is introduced in topic 2 and integrated throughout the book.** This model serves as the basis for opening and ending-of-topic activities. Its use throughout the book helps students see that critical thinking provides a foundation for academic, career, and life success.

■ **Each topic begins with a student vignette.** These scenarios incorporate typical and specific challenges that students encounter. For example, in the chapter addressing information literacy (#4), the student vignette focuses on issues of personal privacy and integrity in the world of social media. All vignettes end with a challenge so that students can apply their learning.

■ **Each topic ends with a section titled "Critically Thinking: What Have You Learned?"** Students must apply the learning outcomes, key terms, strategies, and the R.E.D. Model to offer a plan of action for the student featured in the opening vignette.

■ **Topics are reorganized to reflect today's classroom and student needs.** Reorganizing topics in this edition reflects immediate needs of most students.

- Critical Thinking (#2) and Learning Styles (#6) are now standalone chapters (rather than combined in one chapter).

- Given the importance and prevalence of social media, online personal profiles, and personal reputation issues, information literacy is now the fourth topic in this edition (it had been topic 9 in the previous edition).

- The topic of memory is paired with studying (#8).

*Watson-Glaser Critical Thinking Appraisal, Forms A/B (WGCTA). Copyright ©2007 NCS Pearson, Inc. Reproduced with permission. All rights reserved. "Watson-Glaser Critical Thinking Appraisal" is a trademark, in the US and/or other countries, of Pearson Education, Inc. or its affiliates(s).

- **Topic 4, Information Literacy, is restructured and updated.**
  - The first half of this topic addresses "traditional information literacy" of finding, evaluating, and using information. The second part of this chapter has a more in-depth focus on social media and communication in the Internet Age.
  - The topic of communication is rewritten to include tips for creating and posting appropriate social media updates, as well as establishing (or not) an online profile. Privacy issues are explained and the concept of a "digital tattoo" is emphasized.
  - A quick-reference plagiarism table is new to this edition. Typical student questions are posed about plagiarism. A strategy on how to avoid plagiarism follows.

- **The VAK Survey has replaced the VARK Questionnaire (topic #6).**

- **Reading is a standalone topic in this edition.** This topic includes information on strategic highlighting (topic #9).

- **The "forgetting curve" is explained and connected to memory strategies (topic #8).**

- **The topic on testing has been re-organized.** It still examines the distinction between two separate processes: test *preparation* and test *taking*. In this edition, both topics are combined into one chapter **(topic #10)**.

- **A Glindex replaces the subject index.** This feature provides a glossary for every keyword from each chapter. This is a concise and easy reference for students and instructors.

FEATURES OF THE THIRD EDITION

The activities and strategies in this book focus on three core principles—critical thinking, priority management, and personal well-being. These form the foundation for student, career, and life success. In addition to new and updated coverage, students and instructors will also find the following features in this edition:

- Each topic starts with the same learning components:
  - Student vignette and a challenge to the reader to "think critically" about the student situation
  - Learning outcomes
  - Key terms
  - Introduction
  - An assessment activity for students to reflect on their level of skill with the chapter topic

- The R.E.D. Model icon appears throughout the book to signal when students need to apply their critical thinking skills.

- Each topic continues to have activities to reinforce the chapter study skills introduced.

- The well-being and balance emphasis introduces students to strategies they can apply to all areas of their lives.

- Topics end with a "Critically Thinking: What Have You Learned?" It consists of a review of the chapter outcomes and a final chance to think critically through the student situation presented in the opening scenario.

- Over the course of the book, students have the opportunity to complete a number of reflective activities. They can compile these into a portfolio of strategies. In this way, they will be able to answer the question, "What am I doing to get what I want from college and life?"

- Citations are provided for each chapter (and references can be found at the end of the book) for instructors and students to conduct further research as desired.

INSTRUCTOR RESOURCES

- *Online Instructor's Manual.* This manual provides a framework of ideas and suggestions for activities, journal writing, thought-provoking situations, and online implementation including MyStudentSuccessLab recommendations.

- *Online PowerPoint Presentation.* A comprehensive set of PowerPoint slides that can be used by instructors for class presentations and also by students for lecture preview or review. The PowerPoint presentation includes summary slides with over-view information for each chapter. These slides help students understand and review concepts within each chapter.

ACKNOWLEDGEMENTS

As the author, I put words to paper. The final product, though, is the work of a larger team. At every step of the writing process, nurturing friendships, honest critiques, and professional guidance helped me on this journey. Thanking everyone is impossible; however, I would like to mention a few of the key people who have added immeasurably to the book you are reading.

- *Pearson Education.* Jodi McPherson, Editor in Chief, saw the wisdom in this revision and provided the resources for it to come to fruition. Shannon Steed, Senior Development Editor, reviewed my submissions and kept me abreast of guidelines and expectations throughout the project. Katie Mahan, Acquisitions Editor, provided steady guidance and encouragement during the manuscript development. Erin Carreiro, Editorial Assistant, patiently took time to help maneuver the final manuscript into and through the production process. Thanks to Amy Judd (Executive Marketing Manager for Pearson) and her entire team for their continuous support. Amy has always been there for me with encouragement, guidance, mentoring, and validation. Moreover, I have nothing but respect and gratitude for the Pearson representatives throughout the nation who match instructors with the appropriate books and resources for their students.

- *Those professionals who put the final product together.* Thank you to everyone who had input from copyediting, to proofing, to layout, to printing. Content is one piece of the process. Production is another. A huge thank you to Joe Vetere, Senior Author Support/Technology Specialist, and Peggy McMahon, Senior Production Project Manager. They patiently answered emails and phone calls to help me with review and formatting guidelines. Their team helped to make this final product "pop"! Thanks to Melinda Durham, Content Project Manager, and Electronic Publishing Services, Inc. for their guidance as well.

■ *Students.* More than a kernel of truth exists in the adage that teachers learn as much from their students as they teach their students. I am a better teacher and writer for working with them.

■ *Student Services Professionals.* I have been fortunate to learn from caring and insightful advisors and counselors, both on my campus and throughout this nation. Their continued collaboration with the "academic side of the house" is a critical component to student success. It takes a whole college to nurture a total student.

■ *Teaching Colleagues.* I am grateful to every teacher I have met during my career. Each one has helped me grow. Special thanks to my campus colleagues who always encourage and validate me as a person and a teacher. Thanks as well to the reviewers of this edition for their time and considered responses: Sara Marchessault, Tallahassee Community College; Patrick D. McDermott, Tallahassee Community College; Carolyn D. Sotto, University of Cincinnati; and Eunice Walker, Southern Arkansas University. The final product benefited from their scrutiny and suggestions.

■ *My best friend.* Again, my wife, Laurie, unselfishly sacrificed weekends, holidays, and evenings as I worked on this project. Without her love, support, understanding, and friendship, I would not have completed this book.

■ *Buddy.* Finally, Buddy, my canine companion. Whether lying beside my desk as I typed, reminding me to take a break with a howl by the door, or leading me down the beach at sunrise, he reminds us all to find the joy in the simple things in life.

I continue to be a fortunate man!

Steve Piscitelli
Atlantic Beach, Florida

BREAKTHROUGH
To better results

Give your students what they need to succeed.

As an instructor, you want to help your students succeed in college. As a mentor, you want to make sure students reach their professional objectives. We share these goals, and we're committed to partnering with educators to ensure that each individual student succeeds—in college and beyond.

Simply put, Pearson creates technologies, content, and services that help students break through to better results. When a goal as important as education is at stake, no obstacle should be allowed to stand in the way.

The following pages detail some of our products and services designed to help your students succeed. These include:

- Pearson Course Redesign
- MyFoundationsLab for Student Success
- MyStudentSuccessLab
- CourseConnect™

- Custom Services
- Resources for Students
- Professional Development for Instructors

Pearson Course Redesign
Collect, measure, and interpret data to support efficacy.

Rethink the way you deliver instruction.

Pearson has successfully partnered with colleges and universities engaged in course redesign for over 10 years through workshops, Faculty Advisor programs, and online conferences. Here's how to get started!

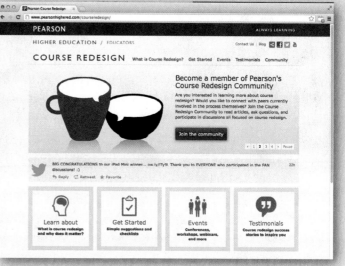

- Visit our course redesign site at **www.pearsoncourseredesign.com** for information on getting started, a list of Pearson-sponsored course redesign events, and recordings of past course redesign events.

- Request to connect with a Faculty Advisor, a fellow instructor who is an expert in course redesign, by visiting **www.mystudentsuccesslab.com/community**.

- Join our Course Redesign Community at **www.community.pearson.com/courseredesign** and connect with colleagues around the country who are participating in course redesign projects.

Don't forget to measure the results of your course redesign!

Examples of data you may want to collect include:

- Improvement of homework grades, test averages, and pass rates over past semesters

- Correlation between time spent in an online product and final average in the course

- Success rate in the next level of the course

- Retention rate (i.e., percentage of students who drop, fail, or withdraw)

Need support for data collection and interpretation?

Ask your local Pearson representative how to connect with a member of Pearson's Efficacy Team.

MyFoundationsLab®

Built on the success of MyMathLab, MyReadingLab, and MyWritingLab, **MyFoundationsLab** is a comprehensive online mastery-based resource for assessing and remediating college- and career-readiness skills in mathematics, reading, and writing. The system offers a rich environment of pre-built and customized assessments, personalized learning plans, and highly interactive activities that enable students to master skills at their own pace. Ideal for learners of various levels and ages, including those in placement test prep or transitional programs, MyFoundationsLab facilitates the skill development students need in order to be successful in college-level courses and careers.

New! MyFoundationsLab for Student Success

In response to market demand for more "non-cognitive" skills, Pearson now offers **MyFoundationsLab for Student Success**, which combines rich mathematics, reading, and writing content with the 19+ MyStudentSuccessLab modules that support ongoing personal and professional development. To see a complete list of content, visit **www.mystudentsuccesslab.com/mfl.**

If you're affiliated with boot camp programs, student orientation, a testing center, or simply interested in a self-paced, pre-course solution that helps students better prepare for college-level work in basic skills, contact your Pearson representative for more information.

"Students like learning at their own pace; they can go as fast or as slow as they need. MyFoundationsLab facilitates this structure; it's more driven by mastery learning, not by what the teacher says a student should be doing."

—Jennifer McLearen, Instructor, Piedmont Virginia Community College

Data from January 2007 through June 2008 offers solid evidence of the success of MyFoundationsLab:

91% of students who retested in reading improved at least one course level

70% of students who retested in writing improved at least one course level

43% of students who retested in math improved at least one course level

MyStudentSuccessLab

Help students start strong and finish stronger.

MyStudentSuccessLab™

MyStudentSuccessLab helps students acquire the skills they need for ongoing personal and professional development. It is a learning-outcomes-based technology that helps students advance their knowledge and build critical skills for success. MyStudentSuccessLab's peer-led video interviews, interactive practice exercises, and activities foster the acquisition of academic, life, and professionalism skills.

Students have access to:

- Pre- and Post-Full Course Diagnostic Assessments linked to key learning objectives

- Pre- and Post-Tests dedicated to individual topics in the Learning Path

- An overview of objectives to build vocabulary and repetition

- Videos on key issues that are "by students, for students," conveniently organized by topic

- Practice exercises to improve class prep and learning

- Graded activities to build critical-thinking and problem-solving skills

- Student resources, including Finish Strong 24/7 YouTube videos, professionalism tools, research aids, writing help, and GPA, savings, budgeting, and retirement calculators

- Student Inventories designed to increase self-awareness, including Golden Personality and Thinking Styles

Students utilizing MyStudentSuccessLab may purchase Pearson texts in a number of cost-saving formats—including **eTexts, loose-leaf Books à la Carte editions**, and more. Contact your Pearson representative for more information.

Topics and features include:

- College Transition
- Communication
- Critical Thinking
- Financial Literacy
- Goal Setting
- Information Literacy
- Interviewing
- Job Search Strategies
- Learning Preferences
- Listening and Taking Notes in Class
- Majors/Careers and Resumes
- Memory and Studying
- Problem Solving
- Reading and Annotating
- Self-Management Skills at Work
- Stress Management
- Teamwork
- Test Taking
- Time Management
- Workplace Communication
- Workplace Etiquette

Assessment

Beyond the Pre- and Post-Full Course Diagnostic Assessments and Pre- and Post-Tests within each module, additional learning-outcome-based tests can be created using a secure testing engine, and may be printed or delivered online. These tests can be customized to accommodate specific teaching needs by editing individual questions or entire tests.

Reporting

Measurement matters—and is ongoing in nature. MyStudentSuccessLab lets you determine what data you need, set up your course accordingly, and collect data via reports. The high quality and volume of test questions allows for data comparison and measurement.

MyLabsPlus service is a teaching and learning environment that offers enhanced reporting features and analysis. With powerful administrative tools and dedicated support, MyLabsPlus offers an advanced suite of management resources for MyStudentSuccessLab.

Content and Functionality Training

Organized by topic, the **Instructor Implementation Guide** provides grading rubrics, suggestions for video use, and more to save time on course prep. Our **User Guide** and "How do I…" **YouTube videos** indicate how to use MyStudentSuccessLab, and show scenarios from getting started to utilizing the Gradebook.

Peer Support

The **Student Success Community** site is a place for you to connect with other educators to exchange ideas and advice on courses, content, and MyStudentSuccessLab. The site is filled with timely articles, discussions, video posts, and more. Join, share, and be inspired!
www.mystudentsuccesscommunity.com

The **Faculty Advisor Network** is Pearson's peer-to-peer mentoring program in which experienced MyStudentSuccessLab users share their best practices and expertise. Our Faculty Advisors are experienced in one-on-one phone and email coaching, webinars, presentations, and live training sessions. Contact your Pearson representative to connect with a Faculty Advisor or learn more about the Faculty Advisor Network.

Integration and Compliance

You can integrate our digital solutions with your learning management system in a variety of ways. For more information, or if documentation is needed for ADA compliance, contact your local Pearson representative.

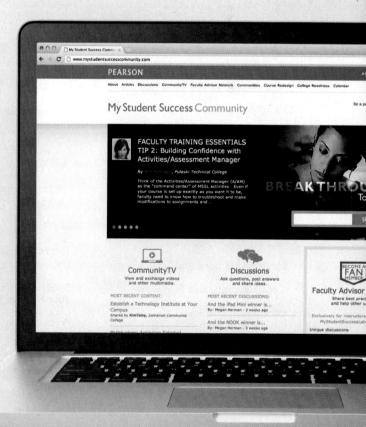

CourseConnect™

Trust that your online course is the best in its class.

Designed by subject matter experts and credentialed instructional designers, **CourseConnect** offers award-winning customizable online courses that help students build skills for ongoing personal and professional development.

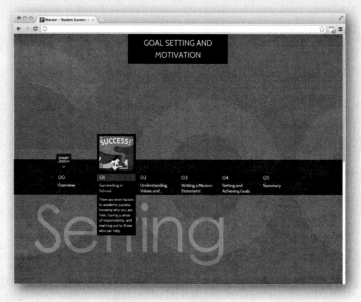

CourseConnect uses topic-based, interactive modules that follow a consistent learning path—from introduction, to presentation, to activity, to review. Its built-in tools—including user-specific pacing charts, personalized study guides, and interactive exercises—provide a student-centric learning experience that minimizes distractions and helps students stay on track and complete the course successfully. Features such as relevant video, audio, and activities, personalized (or editable) syllabi, discussion forum topics and questions, assignments, and quizzes are all easily accessible. CourseConnect is available in a variety of learning management systems and accommodates various term lengths as well as self-paced study. And, our compact textbook editions align to CourseConnect course outcomes.

Choose from the following three course outlines ("Lesson Plans")

Student Success

- Goal Setting, Values, and Motivation
- Time Management
- Financial Literacy
- Creative Thinking, Critical Thinking, and Problem Solving
- Learning Preferences
- Listening and Note-Taking in Class
- Reading and Annotating
- Studying, Memory, and Test-Taking
- Communicating and Teamwork
- Information Literacy
- Staying Balanced: Stress Management
- Career Exploration

Career Success

- Planning Your Career Search
- Knowing Yourself: Explore the Right Career Path
- Knowing the Market: Find Your Career Match
- Preparing Yourself: Gain Skills and Experience Now
- Networking
- Targeting Your Search: Locate Positions, Ready Yourself
- Building a Portfolio: Your Resume and Beyond
- Preparing for Your Interview
- Giving a Great Interview
- Negotiating Job Offers, Ensuring Future Success

Professional Success

- Introducing Professionalism
- Workplace Goal Setting
- Workplace Ethics and Your Career
- Workplace Time Management
- Interpersonal Skills at Work
- Workplace Conflict Management
- Workplace Communications: Email and Presentations
- Effective Workplace Meetings
- Workplace Teams
- Customer Focus and You
- Understanding Human Resources
- Managing Career Growth and Change

Custom Services
Personalize instruction to best facilitate learning.

As the industry leader in custom publishing, we are committed to meeting your instructional needs by offering flexible and creative choices for course materials that will maximize learning and student engagement.

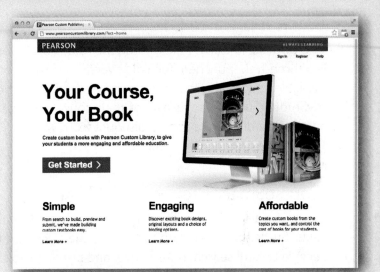

Pearson Custom Library

Using our online book-building system, create a custom book by selecting content from our course-specific collections that consist of chapters from Pearson Student Success and Career Development titles and carefully selected, copyright-cleared, third-party content and pedagogy. **www.pearsoncustomlibrary.com**

Custom Publications

In partnership with your Custom Field Editor, modify, adapt, and combine existing Pearson books by choosing content from across the curriculum and organizing it around your learning outcomes. As an alternative, you can work with your Editor to develop your original material and create a textbook that meets your course goals.

Custom Technology Solutions

Work with Pearson's trained professionals, in a truly consultative process, to create engaging learning solutions. From interactive learning tools, to eTexts, to custom websites and portals, we'll help you simplify your life as an instructor.

Online Education

Pearson offers online course content for online classes and hybrid courses. This online content can also be used to enhance traditional classroom courses. Our award-winning CourseConnect includes a fully developed syllabus, media-rich lecture presentations, audio lectures, a wide variety of assessments, discussion board questions, and a strong instructor resource package.

For more information on custom Student Success services, please visit **www.pearsonlearningsolutions.com** or call **800-777-6872**.

Resources for Students

Help students save and succeed throughout their college experience.

Books à la Carte Editions

The Books à la Carte (a.k.a. "Student Value" or "Loose Leaf") edition is a three-hole-punched, full-color version of the premium text that's available at 35% less than the traditional bound textbook. Students using MyStudentSuccessLab as part of their course materials can purchase a Books à la Carte edition at a special discount from within the MyLab course where "Click here to order" is denoted.

CourseSmart eTexbooks

CourseSmart eTextbooks offer a convenient, affordable alternative to printed texts. Students can save up to 50% off the price of a traditional text, and receive helpful search, note-taking, and printing tools.

Programs and Services

As the world's leading learning company, Pearson has pledged to help students succeed in college and reach their educational and career aspirations. We're so dedicated to this goal that we've created a unique set of programs and services that we call **Pearson Students**. Through this program, we offer undergraduate students opportunities to learn from, and interact with, each other and Pearson professionals through social media platforms, internships, part-time jobs, leadership endeavors, events, and awards. To learn more about our Pearson Students programs and meet our Pearson Students, visit **www.pearsonstudents.com**.

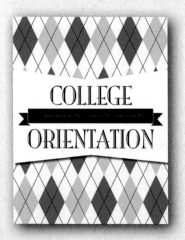

Orientation to College

In Bendersky's *College Orientation,* students learn how to adapt to college life and stay on track towards a degree—all while learning behaviors that promote achievement after graduation. This reference tool is written from an insider's point of view and has a distinct focus on promoting appropriate college conduct. It covers topics that help students navigate college while learning how to apply this knowledge in the workplace.

Help with Online Classes

Barrett's *Power Up: A Practical Student's Guide to Online Learning, 2/e* serves as a textbook for students of all backgrounds who are new to online learning, and as a reference for instructors who are also novices in the area or who need insight into the perspective of such students.

Effective Communication with Professors

In Ellen Bremen's *Say This, NOT That to Your Professor*, an award-winning, tenured communication professor takes students "inside the faculty mind," and guides them to manage their classroom experience with confidence. This book aims to facilitate improved relationships with professors, better grades, and an amazing college experience.

Expert Advice

Our consumer-flavored *IDentity* series booklets are written by national subject-matter experts, such as personal finance specialist, author, and TV personality, Farnoosh Torabi. The authors of this series offer strategies and activities on topics such as careers, college success, financial literacy, financial responsibility, and more.

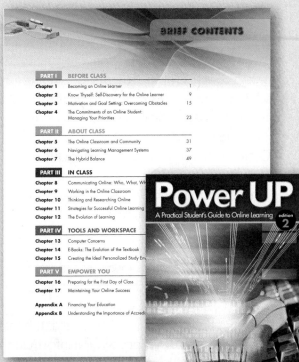

Power UP
A Practical Student's Guide to Online Learning edition 2

Stacey Barrett • Catrina Poe • Carrie Spagnola-Doyle

Quick Tips for Success

Our *Success Tips* series provides one-page "quick tips" on six topics essential to college or career success. The *Success Tips* series includes MyStudentSuccessLab, Time Management, Resources All Around You, Now You're Thinking, Maintaining Your Financial Sanity, and Building Your Professional Image. The *Success Tips for Professionalism* series includes Create Your Personal Brand, Civility Paves the Way Toward Success, Succeeding in Your Diverse World, Building Your Professional Image, Get Things Done with Virtual Teams, and Get Ready for Workplace Success.

Professional Development for Instructors
Augment your teaching with engaging resources.

Foster Ownership

Student dynamics have changed, so how are you helping students take ownership of their education? Megan Stone's *Ownership* series offers online courses for instructors, and printed booklets for students, on four key areas of professional development: accountability, critical thinking, effective planning, and study strategies. The instructor courses, in our CourseConnect online format, include teaching methods, activities, coaching tips, assessments, animations, and video. Online courses and printed booklets are available together or separately.

Promote Active Learning

Infuse student success into any program with our *Engaging Activities* series. Written and compiled by National Student Success Institute (NSSI®) co-founders Amy Baldwin, Steve Piscitelli, and Robert Sherfield, the material provides educators strategies, procedural information, and activities they can use with students immediately. Amy, Steve, and Robb developed these practical booklets as indispensable, hands-on resources for educators who want to empower teachers, professional development coordinators, coaches, and administrators to actively engage their classes.

Address Diverse Populations

Support various student populations that require specific strategies to succeed. Choose from an array of booklets that align with the needs of adult learners, digital learners, first-generation learners, international learners, English language learners, student athletes, and more.

Create Consistency

Instructional resources lend a common foundation for support. We offer **online Instructor's Manuals** that provide a framework of ideas and suggestions for online and in-class activities and journal writing assignments. We also offer comprehensive **online PowerPoint presentations** that can be used by instructors for class presentations, and by students to preview lecture material and review concepts within each chapter.

CHOICES FOR COLLEGE SUCCESS

Transitions,
BALANCE, AND
ORGANIZATION

1

LEARNING OUTCOMES

By the time you finish reading this material and completing its activities, you will be able to do the following:

- Explain two ways a college education will be valuable for you.

- Describe two college transition issues you have already experienced or you think you will have to experience before the end of this term.

- Provide two examples of how knowledge of your life dimensions will help you be successful in school and/or balanced in your personal life.

- Identify two organizational strategies you can use immediately that will help you achieve academic success.

The First Day of CLASS

It is the first day of the college term. Your instructor asks you to take out a piece of paper and respond to the following statements:

1. You have been placed in a first-year, orientation-to-college course this term. Explain why you do NOT really need this stuff! There must be some mistake. After all, you have spent many years in classrooms, and you have plenty of life experiences. You know what to do and how to do it.

Key Terms

- Balance
- C.A.P. Principle
- Critical thinking
- Habit
- Integrity
- Opportunity costs
- Priority management
- Six dimensions of well-being
- Transitions

Chapter INTRODUCTION

You have made it! You have purchased your books and hold the class schedule in your hand. With confidence from your prior experiences—and, yes, perhaps a bit of anxiety—you have arrived for the first week of classes. Your road to this point may have been short, leading directly from high school graduation to the college campus. Or perhaps the road first carried you through significant life events such as marriage, children, military service, or a stint in the workforce. Whatever the route, you are here and ready for a fascinating and challenging new stage of life.

2. You have been placed in a first-year, orientation-to-college course this term. Explain why you DO really need this stuff! Even though you have spent many years in classrooms and have life experiences, there are some areas you need to improve on as you begin the term.

CRITICALLY THINKING
about *Your* situation

Take a quiet moment to reflect on the statements just presented:

1. What reasons come to mind as to why you feel you do *not* need to be in this type of course?
2. What reasons explain why this course is the *correct* placement for you this term? (Piscitelli, 2013).

Regardless of your personal history, your life experiences can serve you well in college. Reflect and draw upon those skills as you tackle the new challenges in front of you and discover how much you have to offer yourself and those around you.

Success in any endeavor involves work on our part. The question "What are you doing to get what you want?" reminds us that we have to work to reach our dreams. Success is a journey that requires dedication. Obviously, students do not purposefully start their days saying, "I will look for ways to

MyStudentSuccessLab

MyStudentSuccessLab (www.mystudentsuccesslab.com) is an online solution designed to help you 'Start strong, Finish stronger' by building skills for ongoing personal and professional development.

be disorganized. I want to be unhealthy and unhappy." But even students who think they know what to do to be successful may make ill-advised choices that create frustration and difficulties. Like all students, you must navigate and make choices about a series of transitions when you walk on campus.

A **transition** is a change that occurs as you move from one phase of your life to another. Enrolling in college is one of those transitions. Each school term will introduce you to new instructors, course work, and classmates. It will be exciting and, at times, anxiety producing. Your school offers many resources to help you get the most from your college experiences. However, before you can identify the correct resources, it will be helpful to ask yourself two questions: "What do I want from school?" and "What am I willing to do to get what I want?"

Choices for College Success will demonstrate how organized action and critical thinking on your part will help you achieve academic success, create a healthy and balanced life, and reach your dreams.

In short, this is a book that will help you get what you want from school and life.

CORE PRINCIPLES

You will find three core life-skill principles present throughout this book: Critical thinking, priority management, and personal well-being. Each principle integrates with and complements the other two.

CRITICAL THINKING

When we critically think, we gather information, weigh it for accuracy and appropriateness, and then make a rational decision based on the facts we have gathered. Critical thinkers are active learners who seem to never stop asking questions about whatever is before them. As you read each of the topics, apply your **critical thinking** skills to determine how you can best use the strategies to help you become successful in the classroom and make connections that go beyond the classroom.

PRIORITY MANAGEMENT

Since priorities are those things that are important in your life (those things that help you get what you want), it makes sense to practice **priority management**. When you do this, you are critically thinking about what important things you need to do each day to move closer to your dreams. When you manage your priorities, you will decrease your stress—and improve the balance and health in your life (Winget, 2004). Effective priority management is another essential life skill (Urban, 2003).

PERSONAL WELL-BEING

When we speak of well-being, we look at the habits of our lives that lead to steadiness, stability, and equilibrium. How you handle the transitions in front of you will have an impact on your health and well-being. The reverse, also, is true. The level of your health and well-being will have an impact on how you handle your college experiences. *Choices for College Success* will show you how to critically examine those habits that may cause instability and disequilibrium in your life. Do you show respect for yourself by caring for your mind, body, and spirit? Do your priorities reflect honesty, fairness, and trustworthiness? The pages ahead will help you critically examine the various dimensions of your life.

Activity 1.1

Critically Thinking about Your Ability to Handle Transitions

Before you answer the items below, reflect on how you currently handle change in your life. Think of how well (or poorly) you have been able to make transitions from one way of doing something to a new way.

There are no "right" answers for the questions below. As with all of the reflective activities in this book, write from your heart. This exercise is not meant for you to answer just like your classmates—or to match what you may think the instructor wants to see. Take your time to give a respectful and responsible general accounting of your experiences with transitions. A truthful self-assessment now will help you build on skills you have while developing those you lack.

For the following items, circle the number that best describes your typical experience with transitions. The key for the numbers is:

0 = never, 1 = almost never, 2 = occasionally, 3 = frequently, 4 = almost always, 5 = always

When considering your past successes and challenges with transitions, how often:

1.	Were you able to identify habits that created problems for you reaching a goal?	0	1	2	3	4	5
2.	Were you able to take action to change habits that created problems for you reaching a goal?	0	1	2	3	4	5
3.	Have you carefully considered all of the "costs" (money, time, relationships, and health) before taking action?	0	1	2	3	4	5
4.	Did you prioritize a series of tasks so that you could concentrate on the important issues in your life?	0	1	2	3	4	5
5.	Have you faced the prospect of change with excitement and enthusiasm?	0	1	2	3	4	5
6.	Have you followed a responsible diet and exercise routine?	0	1	2	3	4	5
7.	Have you managed and expressed emotions appropriately?	0	1	2	3	4	5
8.	Have you carefully examined all information and weighed all options before making a decision?	0	1	2	3	4	5

Add up your scores for items 1, 2, and 5. Divide by 3. Write your answer here: _____

Using the key explanations above for each number (0, 1, 2, 3, 4, 5), complete this sentence: When it comes to handling transitions, I _____ handle change effectively.

Add up your scores for items 3, 4, and 8. Divide by 3. Write your answer here: ....

Using the key explanations above for each number (0, 1, 2, 3, 4, 5), complete this sentence: When it comes to critical thinking, I _____ gather and evaluate information effectively.

Add up your scores for items 3, 6, and 7. Divide by 3. Write your answer here: ....

Using the key explanations above for each number (0, 1, 2, 3, 4, 5) for this activity, complete this sentence: When it comes to my health and well-being, I _____ treat myself with respect physically and emotionally.

Based on your answers, what insights do you have about your experiences with transitions, critical thinking, and personal well-being?

THE VALUE OF A COLLEGE EDUCATION

A college education represents a huge investment of time, money, and emotion. When you made the choice to enroll in school, you sacrificed something. To be here, you have given up the opportunity to be somewhere else or do something else with your precious resources.[1]

Economists frequently refer to the concept of **opportunity costs**. Each time you make a choice to do one thing, you eliminate, or at the very least, postpone, another option. For instance, if a student decides to drop out of school so that he can get a job, earn money, and buy a car, the opportunity cost of buying the car is the loss (or postponement) of his school graduation.

For everything we do, there is a cost of some sort. It is not always directly related to dollars and cents—but something is gained and something is lost.

When you are sitting in class or completing a homework assignment, you could have chosen, instead, to earn money in the workforce. The amount of money you are *not* making because you are in school is an opportunity cost. If you could be earning $10,000 a year and stay in college for four years (instead of earning income), your opportunity cost equates to $40,000—the amount of money you could have earned in that same period of time. When you consider other educational costs, such as tuition, books, transportation, room, board, and fees, the cost to attend college is considerable.

With those kinds of numbers to consider, why do people decide to attend college? One explanation is because the value of a college education is greater in

---

[1]Innumerable sources tout "value of a college education." A recent Google search (August 26, 2012) found about 710,000 sites! A few have been referenced in this section for your continued reading.

the long term. Whenever you feel emotionally drained or may be thinking of giving up on college, consider that the opportunity cost of a college education is an investment in you. What you are doing now will help you get what you want in the future.

DOLLARS AND CENTS

Consider the opportunity costs of not pursuing a college degree. According to the *U.S. Census Bureau News*, full-time workers with a bachelor's degree earn on average about $52,200 per year. High school graduates (no college) earn about $22,000 less per year (Ewert).

Even as income figures change from year to year, the positive relationship between years of schooling and potential income remains. Do the math (see Table 1.1). If the "accumulated earnings" (the amount that would be earned over the career span of a worker) are considered, the numbers are staggering. A person with a four-year college degree can expect to earn nearly one million dollars *more* than someone without a degree. Calculate the additional value of graduate degrees, and the money differential continues to widen. That might make all those college tests and term papers seem a little bit more bearable!

BEYOND DOLLARS AND CENTS

A college education has value beyond your savings account. A liberal arts education, for example, provides a broad base of knowledge to prepare you for many types of jobs. It exposes you to differing viewpoints, and it helps you critically analyze what you read and what you hear. Higher education provides advanced knowledge of history, politics, and culture. You discuss issues with like-minded individuals as well as debate issues with those who hold opposing beliefs. A college education allows you to broaden your knowledge base, reaffirm your beliefs, and, at times, change your positions.

The value of a college education is dollars and cents—but it is so much more.

Table 1.1 **U.S. Census Bureau: Income Differential* According to Level of Education (full-time workers) (*Ewert, 2009*)**

	Less Than a High School Diploma	High School Diploma	Associate Degree	Bachelor's Degree	Master's Degree	Doctoral Degree
Median Income	$24,000	$30,600	$41,472	$52,260	$65,004	$81,996
Income Earned in 40 Years	$960,000	$1,224,000	$1,658,880	$2,090,400	$2,600,160	$3,279,840

*The numbers do not take into account pay raises or inflation.

Activity 1.2

Critically Thinking about What You Want from College and What You Can Do to Get What You Want

(A note to the student: You will find reflective activities throughout the book. Use these as journaling exercises to help you reflect on your personal choices concerning your education and your life. Please take your time. In other words, slow down and concentrate. In this way, you will help yourself to critically think about what you are doing with different aspects of your life—and evaluate what you still need to do to stay balanced and healthy while moving toward your dreams. Place your answers in your class notebook or personal journal, or keep a computer file of all your reflections.)

Students enroll in college for a variety of reasons. Some students come to:

- Advance in a current job
- Develop a sense of independence
- Earn a lot of money
- Explore areas of interest
- Find a job
- Fulfill a lifetime dream
- Train for a skill

- Learn about the world
- Make a better life for family and self
- Reach specific goals
- Participate in intellectual discussions
- Play college-level athletics
- Socialize with peers

Consider what you want from college and reflect on why you have decided to spend your time and money in college at this point in your life. List the top three reasons you came to college. That is, what do you want from college? What are your dreams?

For each of the three items you listed, what is one action (beyond enrolling in college) you can take right now that will help you get closer to what you want?

KEY TRANSITIONAL ISSUES

People experience change when they move into their first job, when they move into their first apartment, or when they become involved in their first serious relationship. Life brings change—transitions from one place to another.

At times, change can cause fear of the unknown. It, also, can be quite energizing as it brings elements of excitement and vitality to your life. Change, therefore, can bring life. Change is invigorating and passion producing.

Where you are now physically, intellectually, emotionally, and socially is different from where you were at this time last year. Whether you are a full-time student fresh from high school or a part-timer taking classes after work a couple of nights a week, your new surroundings—the campus, the classrooms, the diverse mix of students and instructors—may look and feel different compared to what you are used to in your life.

As you face new challenges, you may be anxious about stepping outside of your comfort zone. Be willing to use your old skills in new situations—adjust and change as needed—but never forget that you have a great deal of experience from which to draw.

For instance, you can use note-taking skills developed in previous classes while also experimenting with new strategies. Or if you already know how to juggle a busy social or family calendar, you can apply your priority management skills to your course assignments.

PHYSICAL TRANSITIONS: Diet, Exercise, and Stress Release

You may have heard of the "Freshman 15." It refers to the fifteen pounds students reportedly gain in their first year of college. Whether because they consume fatty fast foods, alcohol, or late-night snacks, students often find their waistlines expanding. Exercise, also, may suffer when getting used to a new college routine (*Freshman 15*). For others, increased stress levels might even cause weight loss. Whether you gain, lose, or maintain a healthy weight, the college environment can present temptations that may lead to unhealthy habits—habits that can create challenges for the rest of your life.

Making the time to balance class expectations and a workout regimen will require discipline on your part.

INTELLECTUAL TRANSITIONS: What You Can Do Right Now

Many non-academic reasons are responsible for students dropping out (leaving with no plans to return to college) or stopping out (leaving with plans to return in the near future) of college. Finances, time factors, family concerns, and emotional issues can cause a student to withdraw from school (Whitbourne, n.d.; *News Blaze*, 2007).

Having said that, college success *will* depend on how well you do in the classroom. Even with appropriate finances, time, and family support, you will need to perform academically if you expect to remain in college. And that performance begins at the start of the school term. It is not unusual to feel overwhelmed at the beginning of a new school term. Use the following basic academic organizational checklist now to start on a positive note.

- Read each class syllabus carefully (and regularly) and transfer due dates to your calendar (paper or electronic).
- Begin to build a positive relationship with each instructor. Visit your instructors during office time for clarification of course material and expectations.
- Come prepared each class to ask appropriate questions and participate in discussions.
- Complete all assignments on time.
- Review your class notes immediately after each class. You can do this on your own or as part of a study group.
- Find and explore the campus library.
- Be curious! Ask questions; seek answers.

EMOTIONAL TRANSITIONS: Managing the Freedom and Responsibility of College

College life provides a great deal of personal independence but also requires a corresponding level of emotional responsibility. The emotionally mature (or emotionally intelligent) person is aware of her emotions, can manage her emotions, understands the emotions of others, and can have an "adult" relationship with another person (Goleman).

College life demands that you attend classes, read extensive assignments, complete research projects, involve yourself in lab work, and, possibly, engage in community service activities. Additionally, you may have to balance family, work, and/or cocurricular responsibilities. At times, it may seem as though there are not enough hours in the day.

In many ways, college life is different from high school and the world of work. Even though rules and procedures vary from college to college and from instructor to instructor, the responsibility for getting to class and completing assignments rests squarely on the student's shoulders. If you miss an 8:00 a.m. psychology class every Monday, there is a better than average chance that no one on the campus will come looking for you. You will have to make it to the class or scramble to get the notes and instructions you may have missed.

Perhaps you are taking only one course, slipping away during your lunch break at work to take an English class. If your boss requires you to take a different lunch shift and it interferes with your schooling, it will be your responsibility—not your instructor's—to handle the conflict. There will not be a counselor or some other person to intervene on your behalf. Moreover, when it comes to absences, you will encounter instructors who will not make a distinction between "excused" and "unexcused" absences. Their view holds that a missed day of class participation is a *missed* day—there is no way to make that up. The class discussion occurred and cannot be repeated. Also, remember that the dynamics of the class will change without your presence. Your input will add an important dimension to class discussions.

Family life, also, will have an impact on how a student adjusts in college. Consider the different circumstances of the following students—and what they will need to do in order to adjust to college demands.

- **Student #1.** Coming from a family where rigidly enforced rules were common, this student can go in a couple of directions. On the one hand, always having had the rules explicitly stated and enforced, he may not know what to do in college because no one is directing his every move; he is not used to making his own decisions. On the other hand, once away from the strict family rules, he might "go wild" with his newfound independence.

- **Student #2.** This student has enjoyed more freedom than the student described above, but still had somebody always available to help in times of difficulty. For instance, her parents were constantly on the phone to the high school guidance counselor, seeking assignment extensions. It comes as quite a shock when she enters college and must live with the consequences of her actions that cannot be "fixed" by someone calling the school. In fact, due to confidentiality laws, schools face some restrictions as to the information they can release without student permission (FERPA).

- **Student #3.** Our third student has had a great deal of responsibility placed upon him to raise siblings, care for an elderly relative, or work to help support the family. Such responsibilities may continue during college. He will still be accountable for his home-based duties while finding time to tackle the expectations of college. This overly responsible student may have a stressful time balancing everything he must do.

- **Student #4.** This student has come to college more than a decade after graduating from high school. She (or he) works full-time to support her (or his) two children. Daily life is a challenge between arranging daycare, getting to and from work, taking care of a household, and completing college assignments. She (or he) is very responsible, yet wonders if college will be too much to handle.

SOCIAL TRANSITIONS: A Balancing Act

You might be actively involved in cocurricular activities like student government or intramural sports. Alternatively, you may only be on campus a short time each day, leaving campus immediately after class in order to go home or to work. The time you spend with family and friends may need to be adjusted so you can meet your academic obligations. You might find the following general strategies helpful now:

- On average, budget two hours of study time for each hour spent in a class.
- Commit to work and cocurricular activities once you have scheduled appropriate time for class, study, and sleep. Critically think and distinguish between priorities and non-priorities.
- Consider how you will maintain your health.
- Be sure to schedule time for physical, emotional, and social renewal.

How you use time is your choice.

Developing supportive relationships. A successful transition to college can be enhanced by the right people—and there are many on campus waiting to help you. To name all of the key people on campus would require its own chapter. Moreover, a key person to one student might not be a key person to another student. For instance, a student needing financial assistance (grants, scholarships, or an on-campus job) may find the financial aid office initially to be the most important stop on campus. An athlete might find his coach to be the key contact.

Educators often mention the same "top three people to know" for a student to have an increased chance of college success.

- **C**lassmate
- **A**dvisor or counselor
- **P**rofessors

Note that the first letter of each name forms the acronym *C.A.P.* When you follow the **C.A.P. Principle**, you form relationships with three key people who can help you connect with the physical campus, adjust to the college experience, and persist to graduation. In fact, do not settle for knowing just one of each; get to know as many as you possibly can.

WELL-BEING AND SUCCESS

Think of well-being as being a condition of **balance** or contentment when you feel intellectually alert, emotionally stable, and physically strong. Maintaining a healthy lifestyle will help you adapt and thrive in your new environment. In short, your balance (or lack of it) will have a major impact on the quality of your college and life experiences.

DIMENSIONS OF WELLNESS

Dr. Bill Hettler, cofounder of the National Wellness Institute (NWI), developed the *Six Dimensional Wellness Model.* This very simple yet powerful model reminds us that a balanced life needs more than three good meals and a restful night's sleep. Each of the **six dimensions of well-being** has an impact on the other five. According to the NWI, no single category operates by itself; all six—social, occupational, spiritual, physical, intellectual, and emotional—impact each other for a balanced *or* unbalanced life (Hettler).

The transitions we reviewed previously match up with Hettler's dimensions. That means successfully navigating each of the transitions you face is critical not only to your success in college but also to your overall sense of balance in life. Your health and well-being will have an impact on how well you handle each transition you encounter. As you review each category below, think how your daily activities and lifestyle measure up to each description.

Table 1.2 Dimensions of Wellness

Dimension	Description of a "Balanced Person"
Physical	You maintain a healthy lifestyle (diet, rest, exercise, strength, and muscle flexibility). You are able to recognize and appropriately respond to warning signs of ill health.
Intellectual	You actively seek to expand your knowledge base and skill base and to develop your creativity and critical thinking skills.
Emotional	You have the ability to manage and express emotions appropriately and handle stress effectively.
Social	You maintain positive relationships with people around you and build a support network of family, friends, classmates, and/or coworkers. You have an awareness of your impact on society and the environment—and their impact upon you.
Occupational	You are involved in a profession or course of study that is personally satisfying. You learn new skills and develop career-oriented goals.
Spiritual	You stress the importance of finding your life's purpose by reflecting (meditating, praying) on the purpose of life, and then you act on your beliefs and values to reinforce your discovered purpose. You acknowledge and understand that you are part of a larger universe.

Source: Adapted from "The Six Dimensional Wellness Model," National Wellness Institute, http://www.nationalwellness.org/?page=Six_Dimensions (accessed June 19, 2013).

One way to think of this model is to visualize a six-string guitar (Figure 1.1). The guitar (you) will be able to make harmonious music with properly tuned strings (life dimensions). If one of the six strings (life dimensions) falls out of tune or breaks, the guitar will still play, but the song will not be as pleasing. As more strings weaken or break from undue stress, the guitar loses its ability to play music. The remaining strings will not be able to carry the tune, possibly leading to the total collapse of the guitar (mind, body, spirit).

Whatever metaphor or image you use, it may help to remember that each life dimension is intimately related to your growth as an individual. By taking notice and care of each dimension of your life, you will take important steps toward turning your dreams into realities. If ignored, however, any one of the dimensions can have a detrimental effect on the others. For instance, if you consistently operate on too little sleep, eat less than nutritious food, associate with negative people, or depend on the "help" of drugs and alcohol to cope with life's challenges, your life dimensions will eventually weaken. The small consistent choices you make and carry out have huge consequences.

Early in the college experience, you may face any number of stressors that will weaken one or more of your life dimensions. If this happens to you, draw on your experiences, college resources, and the healthy ways you already possess to strengthen each dimension in your life. Strategies to help balance your new expectations will

Figure 1.1

Tuning Your Life-Strings

social
occupational
spiritual
physical
intellectual
emotional

balance and wellness

help you maintain your health. Care for your life dimensions, and you will continue to play rich music.

BALANCE IS NOT NECESSARILY "EVEN"

When thinking of the concept of *balance*, you may envision something with equal parts. For instance, a balanced wheel might have six evenly spaced spokes. Or if you had two book bags, you would consider them balanced if they each weighed the same. That thinking does not necessarily hold true when examining your life dimensions.

One of your dimensions probably looms as the most significant in your life. It is the strongest or the one that serves as the "rock"—the foundation, the base—for your life. For some people, the spiritual dimension is their guiding light. In times when their entire world seems to be crumbling around them, they can draw on their spiritual strength to maintain balance and safely weather the turbulence.

For you, the physical dimension may be the part of life that provides a strong foundation. In times of stress, you might find that physical exercise, yoga practice, or a cup of green tea helps you stay calm.

Whatever dimension is your strength, it may well overshadow all the other dimensions of your life. Moreover, your "base" dimension might very well change over the course of your semester—and life.

Activity 1.3

Critically Thinking about Personal Well-Being

WHAT DOES THIS MEAN FOR YOU AND YOUR ACADEMIC SUCCESS?

Reread the descriptions in Table 1.2 and then rank (place in order of importance) each according to its strength in your life. In your notebook or personal journal, write the numbers 1 through 6. Next to the number 1 write the name of the life dimension that you consider the strongest in your life. For the purpose of this activity, consider "strongest" to mean that which helps you maintain health and balance (a feeling of wellness and stability) in your life. In the second column, explain how you think the dimension will help you be successful in school. Then next to the number 2 write the dimension that is the second strongest in your life, and so on for the rest of the items.

WELL-BEING AND INTEGRITY

Often, architecture will be described in terms of structural integrity. Such a description indicates to what extent the structure is doing what it is *supposed* to do. A bridge that has structural integrity does what it was built to do—provide for safe transportation from one point to another. Likewise, a tall office building that safely houses its occupants also has structural integrity.

A similar description applies to people. Our beliefs and values are at the center of our moral code. When they guide us—motivate us—to act with integrity, to do what is right and avoid what violates our code, then we do what we are supposed to do.

HONESTY, RESPONSIBILITY, AND RESPECT

In its broadest sense, **integrity** means conducting oneself in an honest, responsible, and respectful fashion. If you say you will do something, you do it. When you do something wrong, you admit your errors. Your actions show respect for yourself as well as for those around you. Living a life of integrity is more than a series of strategies and techniques; it requires a specific mindset and value structure to do what is right for you and for others. There are no shortcuts or cram courses on how to be a person of integrity. You do not practice integrity for part of the day; it is woven into your life.

The manner in which you take care of, or neglect, the dimensions of your life has an impact on your health and well-being. In reality, when you develop and practice a healthy lifestyle, you act with integrity. That is, each of your six life dimensions becomes stronger when you act honestly, responsibly, and respectfully within each dimension. Table 1.3 explains this relationship between integrity and well-being.

Table 1.3 **Connection between Integrity and the Dimensions of Well-Being**

Dimension	Connection to Your Integrity
Social	You respectfully enter—and maintain—relationships.
	You speak with honesty when talking with or about other people.
	You do not put yourself or another person in foolishly risky situations.
Occupational	On the job (or in the classroom) you take care of your responsibilities in an honest fashion.
	You are honest with yourself about why you do (or will do) what you do for work.
Spiritual	You respectfully attempt to understand differing spiritual beliefs.
	You seek to live your life according to a higher purpose.
Physical	You treat your body with respect.
	You follow a responsible diet and exercise regimen.
Intellectual	You do not engage in acts of academic dishonesty.
	You continuously feed your mind with responsible thought-provoking material.
	You respectfully listen to and discuss differing points of view.
Emotional	You find healthy and responsible ways in which to handle stressful situations.
	You are respectful of your emotional needs as well as the needs of those around you.
	You understand how your emotional well-being affects other dimensions of your life.

PRIORITY MANAGEMENT AND PERSONAL WELL-BEING

HABITS

Once a day, an hour, or a minute goes by, we can never get it back. It is gone forever. If we want to use time effectively, we have to build good habits. This book will help you examine how you can prioritize your time to improve the physical, intellectual, emotional, and social areas of life while helping yourself succeed in your studies. In addition, you will learn how building habits of organization now (or improving on the effective ones you already have) will have a positive impact on your life outside of college. If you can concentrate on your priorities, you will have a better chance of mastering your life.

A **habit** is something we repeat with such frequency that it becomes an involuntary act. It seems as though we cannot help but do it. If each day finds you mindlessly drifting from one activity to the other, it will be difficult to build a life with disciplined habits. Waste time on a regular basis and it will become a habit—a bad habit. Effective organization requires critical thought and practice—and good habits. It is a skill that, when mastered, can improve many aspects of your life.

Organization, however, involves more than time. For instance, some students may drop out of college because they find it difficult to use their time and their financial resources effectively. Whether they run out of time or run out of cash, the shortfall has a negative impact upon their continued enrollment.

DISORDER

Habits of disorganization can create stress, which in turn can threaten your well-being. For instance, the disorganized student can experience any or all of the following:

- Clutter
- Debt
- Discouragement
- Illness
- Loss of financial aid
- Lost opportunities
- Lowered GPA
- Missed assignments
- Missed exams or quizzes
- Missed interviews or appointments
- Relationship difficulties
- Reputation as someone not dependable
- Stress
- Suspension from school
- Tardiness to class

ORDER

Now, look at how organization can positively affect your life:

- Financial responsibility
- Goal attainment
- Health
- Increased chances of landing the job you want
- Greater likelihood of securing and maintaining financial aid
- Higher GPA
- Improved opportunities
- Meaningful relationships

- Peace and calm
- Regular punctuality
- Reputation as being dependable
- Success on exams and quizzes
- Smooth progress in academic programs
- Timely completion of assignments

On which person—the disorganized and chaotic or the organized and orderly—would you want to depend? Sound organizational habits weave their way throughout your life by enabling a positive work ethic and helping you develop healthy habits of balance and wellness. To build these practical habits, you will need to critically evaluate how you organize your life (or not).

WHAT YOU CAN DO NOW TO GET STARTED

Consider the following "just-in-time" organizational tips shown in Table 1.4 to help you now with your studies.

Table 1.4 Organization Creates a Foundation

If You Want To...	Then...
Remember all important due dates (assignments, payment deadlines)	Review all your syllabi now and place the assignment due dates on a calendar.
Reach your educational dreams	Establish clear goals and take action each day to move closer to your goals.
Earn "respectable" grades—and eventually make the dean's list	Create a study schedule that blocks out at least two hours a week for each hour spent in the classroom.
Finish course work quickly and with quality results	Sign up for a class schedule that fits your lifestyle. Be realistic.
Work or play sports or join the band	Make a list of all your obligations (work, family, cocurricular activities)—and determine how much quality time you have for class. Do not overextend yourself.
Finish lengthy reading assignments—and remember what you have read	For each reading assignment, read a few pages a night rather than waiting and wading through the entire chapter the night before it is due.
Better understand classroom lectures	Ask whether your instructor posts outlines or notes online for student use.
Understand your notes	Set up a schedule so that you can review your notes nightly. Jot down any questions you might have, and ask your instructor the next class session.
Get notes for the class sessions you miss	Early in the semester identify a study partner and consider exchanging phone numbers and/or e-mail addresses.
Perform as well as possible on all of your exams	Develop a study schedule so that you can begin a nightly review rather than waiting for a night-before cram session. You might want to explore the possibility of joining a study group.
Be healthy	Schedule a specific amount of time each day for healthy physical activity and appropriate sleep each night.

Chapter SUMMARY

Life as a college student will have moments of exhilaration and challenge. You will be able to maximize the highpoints and minimize the anxiety if you build habits that will help you navigate the transitions you will encounter.

Before leaving this material, keep the following points in mind:

- Whenever you feel emotionally drained or may be thinking of giving up on college, consider that the opportunity cost of a college education is an investment in you.

- Be willing to use your old skills in new situations—adjust and change as needed—but never forget that you have a great deal of experience from which to draw.

- Develop healthy and respectful relationships with classmates and college staff to help you transition successfully.

- Maintaining a healthy lifestyle will help you adapt and thrive in your new environment.

CRITICALLY THINKING

What Have You Learned?

Return to the situation that was described (and you wrote about) at the beginning of this topic. Specifically, look at the second part of that scenario, which stated:

> You have been placed in a first-year, orientation-to-college course this term. Explain why you DO really need this stuff! Even though you have spent many years in classrooms and have life experiences, there are some areas you need to improve on as you begin the term.

Reflect on the answer you wrote to that statement. After you complete that, review your notes from this chapter, the learning outcomes, the key terms, bold-faced headings, and the figures.

Based on what you have read in this material, write a revised response to the situation above. Please describe what has caused you to adjust (or maintain) your evaluation. In what ways do you see a first-year, orientation-to-college course in a different way than when you started reading this material? How will you use your strengths to minimize your challenges?

Critical
THINKING
2

LEARNING OUTCOMES

By the time you finish reading this material and completing its activities, you will be able to do the following:

- Define critical thinking.

- Use the R.E.D. Model to establish a clear and precise plan to minimize (or eliminate) an academic problem you have.

- Understand the language of critical thinking.

- Explain how critical thinking skills can help you maintain balance and wellness in your life.

The Case of RICKY

Ricky is a first-semester student. His initial excitement about attending college has turned to panic. His first shock hit when he went to the bookstore to get his books. Besides the "sticker shock" of how much the books cost, he was overwhelmed by the sheer number of books he had to buy for each class. Initially, he thought, "There is no way the instructors will expect us to read all of these books. I'll wait until the first day of class to see if there has been some sort of mistake."

Key Terms

Accuracy
Analyzing
Assumption
Brainstorm
Clarity
Confirmation bias
Creative thinking
Critical thinking
Evaluate
Higher-order thinking skills
Logic
Lower-order thinking skills
Problem solving
Problem-solving trap
R.E.D. Model
Relevance

Chapter INTRODUCTION

"But it's my opinion! How can it be wrong?" You may have heard someone blurt out some such statement. Perhaps the person wanted to support an argument with a degree of certainty that would make the point sound reasonable and logical. Unfortunately, such a statement will not meet the test of *critical thinking*—a skill that your instructors will expect you to demonstrate on assignments, on tests, and in class discussions. While "But it's my opinion!" might work with a friend or a status update on social media or a sound bite on television, it will not carry much weight in an intellectual discussion.

The first day came—and sure enough, there was no mistake. Each instructor plopped a large syllabus and reading-assignments page at his seat. He then learned that each instructor required the students to critically read each assignment. Ricky's idea of reading has been to skim the chapter for words that might be on a quiz, memorize them, and spit them back when asked. Now, he will have to write or orally explain his readings. He has very little experience doing this.

Ricky is considering quitting school.

CRITICALLY THINKING
about *Ricky's* situation

You are Ricky's best friend. What advice would you give your friend?

This topic provides strategies to use throughout this book, in your classes, and during the rest of your life. You will learn to use the R.E.D. Model, which will help you logically think through both academic and personal issues.

As you move through each topic in your course, you will critically assess your skill level as it exists at the beginning of each topic. From there, you will have the opportunity to build a selection of strategies that will improve your chances for achieving academic and life successes. Activity 2.1 is the first of these assessments.

MyStudentSuccessLab

MyStudentSuccessLab (www .mystudentsuccesslab.com) is an online solution designed to help you "Start strong, Finish stronger" by building skills for ongoing personal and professional development.

Activity 2.1

Reflecting on Your Current Level of Critical-Thinking Skills

Before you answer the items that follow, reflect on your school experiences. Maybe it was last year—or as long as 20 years ago. Can you remember the types of questions your teachers asked you? Not the content of the questions but rather the difficulty level of the questions? Were you asked to memorize lists of terms and "spit them back" (known as a lower-order thinking skill), or did you have to *understand* and *analyze* and *evaluate* terms and concepts (known as higher-order thinking skills)?

There are no right answers for the questions below. It's okay if you cannot recall exactly which type of questions you most often faced; remember as best as you can. As with all of the reflective activities in this book, write from your heart. This exercise is not meant for you to answer just like your classmates—or to match what you may think the instructor wants to see. Take your time to give a respectful and responsible general accounting of your experiences with critical thinking. A truthful self-assessment now will help you build on skills you possess while developing those you lack.

For each of the following items, circle the number that best describes your typical experience with critical thinking. The key for the numbers is as follows:

0 = never, 1 = almost never, 2 = occasionally, 3 = frequently, 4 = almost always, 5 = always

When considering your past schoolwork, how often:

1.	Did you have to memorize things such as terms, dates, and formulas?	0	1	2	3	4	5
2.	Were you rewarded (with a good grade) for "spitting back" nearly exact wording from textbooks, definitions, or lectures?	0	1	2	3	4	5
3.	Did you have to summarize a passage in your own words?	0	1	2	3	4	5
4.	Were you assigned to read a chapter (or book or essay or Internet site) and then asked to evaluate (judge) what you read according to specific standards or criteria?	0	1	2	3	4	5
5.	Did your teachers ask you to develop (create) your own theory or explanation for an event?	0	1	2	3	4	5
6.	Did your teachers expect you to apply (use) the knowledge you learned in class to solve a problem you had never seen before?	0	1	2	3	4	5
7.	Were you encouraged and rewarded for developing new and unusual solutions to a problem?	0	1	2	3	4	5
8.	Did you have to answer questions simply by searching for the correct answers in the textbook or lecture notes?	0	1	2	3	4	5

Lower-order thinking skills experience. Add up your scores for items 1, 2, 3, and 8. Divide by 4 and write your answer here:

Using the key explanations provided for each number (0, 1, 2, 3, 4, 5) for this activity, complete this sentence: When it comes to thinking, I have _____ used lower-order thinking skills.

Higher-order thinking skills experience. Add up your scores for items 4, 5, 6, and 7. Divide by 4 and write your answer here: ....

Using the key explanations provided for each number (0, 1, 2, 3, 4, 5) for this activity, complete this sentence: When it comes to thinking, I have _____ used higher-order thinking skills.

Based on your answers, what insights do you have about your experiences with higher-order (critical) thinking skills?

DEFINING CRITICAL THINKING

Critical thinking is gathering information, weighing it for accuracy and appropriateness, and then making a rational decision based on facts you gathered. When your instructors ask you to think, read, write, or discuss an issue critically, they want you to examine, argue, analyze, evaluate, or create something.

Critical thinkers demonstrate command of basic information about an issue as they logically, precisely, and systematically examine the issue from many sides—even if that examination may uncover information that differs from a deeply held personal belief. College life exposes you to situations that will challenge what you already "know" to be certain. For instance, your opinion may tell you there is no need to read textbook assignments or come to class every day. However, as you gain experience—such as failing quizzes or exams—you may revisit and then change that mindset. You may also "know" that you can exist on minimal sleep. But a few weeks into the semester, you may question that "truth."

You have no doubt encountered similar revelations in your life outside college. At the writing of this topic, loud debates can be heard about the issues of national health care reform and the economic direction of our nation. On television, on the floor of the U.S. Congress, and in state legislatures across the country, people are voicing their opinions. Unfortunately, there have been times when critical thinking has given way to shouting, name-calling, and questionable logic. While it might seem impossible in the midst of the shouting, having critical-thinking skills can help to distinguish between accuracies and inaccuracies regarding these important issues.

Active learning involves many forms of thinking. Some people use the terms *critical thinking*, *problem solving*, and *creative thinking* interchangeably, freely substituting one term for another.

One view would be to think of each as a distinct thinking process; one leads to the other; one builds on the previous and uses deeper thinking skills. Each will be described and demonstrated in this topic. Critical thinking, as you will see, is part of all reasoning and reflective thinking.

THE R.E.D. MODEL*

It is difficult to imagine a decision that you make that doesn't involve critical thinking. Even buying a cup of coffee at the local coffee shop requires a degree of critical thinking. What size will it be? Is it so strong you will need extra sweetener? Is it a better deal to buy the large or small size?

If you drive a car, have you ever had to stop at a four-way stop sign intersection? Determining when to tap the accelerator and move through the intersection required critical thinking.

If you have a Facebook account and have ever received a "friend" request, you were using critical-thinking skills to make your decision to "confirm" or quietly "ignore."

We all have done this. Critical thinking is not new. But still, aren't you amazed by the number of people who seem to stumble through life making one uninformed decision after another? (And it is even more worrisome to think that there are people who vote without using critical-thinking skills!)

Let's examine a model that will help you *make sure* you are thinking critically and not, in fact, using noncritical thinking.

Models provide a systematic, step-by-step way to accomplish a task. The **R.E.D. Model** does just that for your critical thinking. The easy-to-remember acronym will help you remember the process steps. (An *acronym* is formed by taking a letter or two from a series of words. It creates another word—one that will help you remember the original series.)

Mark this page with a sticky note, bookmark, or paper clip so that you can easily refer to it. You will draw on the concepts presented throughout this course. Whenever you see the R.E.D. Model icon, it will be your reminder to apply your critical-thinking skills.

Step #1. STOP AND THINK

This is old yet sage advice. Before you can start the critical-thinking process, you have to stop all of the chatter and distractions in your mind. Prior to diving into an issue, pause, take a breath, and focus your thoughts. Make sure you know what the issue before you is—or is not.

Step #2. RECOGNIZING ASSUMPTIONS: Separating Fact from Fiction

Keys to CRITICAL THINKING

- Stop and Think
- **R** ecognize Assumptions
- **E** valuate Information
- **D** raw Conclusions
- Plan of Action

Think about this: One of our First Amendment rights is freedom of speech. Is this an absolute right? Can we say anything we want? Can we utter statements that are deemed as cruel, hurtful, and even hateful to and by others?

When we assume (make an **assumption**), we make a decision based on many things—but not necessarily facts. Consider an assumption to be a theory, paradigm, or one's view of the world. When we *assume*, we accept something to be correct. We may or may not have actual proof, but we believe the opinion or position to be accurate. When we question assumptions, we **evaluate** whether what we assume to be true is actually true. When you read the questions above about the First Amendment, do you immediately form an opinion—an assumption—about what freedom of speech really means? What makes you sure that *you* are correct?

We may *assume*, for example, a political candidate is telling the truth because he belongs to the political party we belong to. Or we *assume* posting a comment on a social media site will never be seen by anyone except our "friends." Or maybe a student *assumes* she cannot be an engineer because no one in her family can "do" math.

Each of these assumptions is based on an opinion. Sometimes that opinion comes from past experience; other times it evolves from personal prejudices and biases. The problem with assumptions is that they can very easily be more fiction than fact.

Critical thinking requires you to understand the issue or situation in front of you. Thinking critically requires you to question your own positions, theories, and assumptions.

Step #3. EVALUATING INFORMATION: Remaining Objective and Unemotional

Think about this: In the case of *Snyder v. Phelps* (2011), the Chief Justice of the Supreme Court of the United States issued an opinion that said the United States has a history of protecting hurtful speech in order to protect public debate. Another judge stated in a dissenting opinion that free debate and speech does not give permission for mean-spirited discourse. The final 8–1 decision held that the First Amendment does in fact protect hurtful speech in public.

When you read what the two justices believe, do you automatically gravitate to one side of the debate? More than likely, you probably do. (NOTE: The previous sentence is an assumption!) Be careful in this step. Avoid **confirmation bias**. That is, don't let your preconceived ideas get in the way of an unbiased decision.

Can you see beyond the emotion and objectively judge the information that is before you? Did the judges actually say these things? Do you understand the vocabulary? Do you need additional facts? Once you have determined that the information presented is actually factual, you are on your way to understanding whether an argument is credible or not.

Step #4. DRAWING CONCLUSIONS: Making a Decision

The next step of our critical-thinking model logically follows the preceding two. Once you have separated fact from fiction and have objectively analyzed and evaluated the information presented, you are in a good position to make a decision about what you have before you.

Based on the information presented, you are now in a position to arrive at a conclusion.

If you think about it, this is what learning is all about (or, at least, it should be). We have an experience or gain some knowledge and draw a conclusion based on the experience or knowledge. Perhaps what we have learned reinforces our behavior, or maybe we change how we act. In either case, we have made an evaluation that to act or not act a certain way works or does not work for us.

Figure 2.1

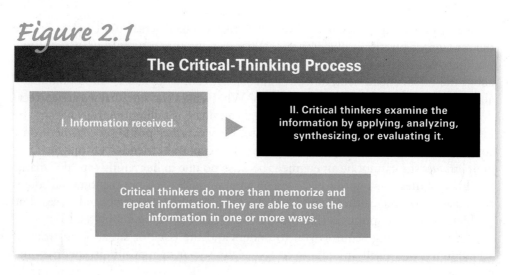

The Critical-Thinking Process

I. Information received.

▶

II. Critical thinkers examine the information by applying, analyzing, synthesizing, or evaluating it.

Critical thinkers do more than memorize and repeat information. They are able to use the information in one or more ways.

Step #5. PLAN OF ACTION

Once you have a basic understanding of the facts and have formed your educated opinion about the issue at hand, you are ready to plan your next step. This could range from thinking about the findings to sharing them with someone else to using the information to solve a problem.

The critical-thinking process is illustrated in Figure 2.1.

Activity 2.2

Critically Thinking about Academic Challenges

R
E
D

Identify one academic challenge you have had in school, such as effectively remembering material for your tests. Using the R.E.D. Model for critical thinking, examine the cause of this challenge.

THE LANGUAGE OF CRITICAL THINKING

When it comes to understanding a problem and moving toward a solution, critical thinkers have to set aside emotion. They must examine the issue on a number of intellectual levels. And they can tell when someone else's argument lacks the basic standards of critical thinking.

USING C.A.R.L. TO UNDERSTAND CRITICAL THINKING

Certain terms and concepts constantly pop up when talking about critical thinking. Here are four such terms:

- **Clarity.** Facts and arguments are presented clearly and unambiguously.
- **Accuracy.** The information presented is factual.

- **Relevance.** The information presented relates to the argument or problems at hand.
- **Logic.** The position makes sense.

Table 2.1 provides a quick example of how to judge the merit of an argument using commonly accepted standards.* For this example, let's return to the case of Ricky you read about earlier.

Table 2.1 Applying Standards of Critical Thinking

Critical Thinking Standard	Application to Ricky's Situation
Clarity	Can you clearly state Ricky's assumptions and surprises about college?
Accuracy	How do you know this analysis is accurate? What facts can you present to support your interpretation of the arguments?
Relevance	How is Ricky's situation similar or dissimilar to your academic life, your well-being, and the choices you make—or will make?
Logic	Based on your evidence, in what ways do Ricky's reactions make sense to you? In what ways do you disagree with him?

In 1956, educational pioneer Benjamin Bloom developed a six-tier thinking skills model that has become the backbone of the critical-thinking process. Again, these terms, listed in Table 2.2, are commonly used with critical thinking. Become familiar with them.

Table 2.2 The Language of Bloom

Steps in Critical Thinking	At This Step, You Can
Remembering	Define, memorize, and recall facts, names, or dates.
Understanding	Describe, explain, paraphrase, and put things into your own words.
Applying	Demonstrate or use something you have learned in a new situation.
Analyzing	Compare, contrast, examine, and break down information into smaller pieces.
Evaluating	Criticize, defend, or judge the worth of information.
Creating	Design, develop, or put together something new (an idea, product, service).

*The intellectual standards used here—clarity, accuracy, relevance, and logic—are commonly cited in the literature. Three other standards may be used as well: precision, breadth, and depth. See Linda Elder and Richard Paul, "Universal Intellectual Standards," The Critical Thinking Community. Retrieved from http://www.criticalthinking.org/pages/universal-intellectual-standards/527.

LOWER-ORDER THINKING SKILLS

Remembering facts or names is the most basic level of thinking. When you memorize a list of vocabulary words and then repeat those words on a classroom quiz, you have recalled the information from your memory. These **lower-order thinking skills** are basic building blocks in the learning process, as they help lay the foundation for the higher-level thinking skills.

The next thinking step—understanding—indicates that you comprehend the information presented. When you can read or hear something and then put it into your own words, you have an increased chance of remembering it.

HIGHER-ORDER THINKING SKILLS

To make the most appropriate use of the **higher-order thinking skills**, you must master the smaller details noted earlier. Your ability to think critically, problem solve, and think creatively will be significantly reduced if you do not understand the basics.

The first two categories (remembering and understanding) exhibit *noncritical thinking characteristics*, but the last four levels describe forms of *critical thinking*. Table 2.3 outlines Bloom's levels of higher-order thinking and suggests that a critical thinker is actively and deeply involved in processing information by applying, analyzing, evaluating, and/or creating information and ideas.

Table 2.3   Using Higher-Level Thinking Skills

Type of Thinking	Example	Why It Is Critical Thinking
Applying	Using your priority management skills, you transfer all of the syllabus assignment and test dates to your calendar. You put yourself on a schedule so that all assignments will be completed on time.	You understand the information and can use it in a new situation.
Analyzing	Once you have all of the due dates on your calendar, you classify your assignments according to which ones will take the most/least time to complete. You ask yourself, "Which items will I need help with?"	You understand the information and demonstrate this understanding by separating or splitting the information into its pieces or parts. With this skill, you can see the essential features of an argument, issue, or process. You are able to recognize assumptions.
Evaluating	After completing the first three weeks of the course, you make a judgment as to how useful your scheduling has been. What worked? What did not work?	You have the ability to judge or critique the value of the information. This is where reflective judgment takes place. In essence, you consider the information before you.
Creating	You understand all of the individual requirements of the course, and you start to see the "whole picture" of how much time you will need to devote to this course to earn an A.	You understand the information and then bring the pieces of the information together to form a "big picture" or new idea. You create a new weekly schedule for yourself. You have synthesized (created) a plan based on your examination of the situation.

Activity 2.3

Using the R.E.D. Model to Examine Your Study Skills

R E D Consider your academic skills, and identify one area of challenge. Using the R.E.D. Model, clearly and precisely state what your specific problem or challenge is with the study skill you identified. For example, perhaps you have difficulty taking notes in class or from reading assignments. Or maybe you run out of time and do not complete assignments.

STOP AND THINK. Identify and write a summary of your study skill challenge.

....

....

RECOGNIZE ASSUMPTIONS. How do you know this is actually a challenge for you? Has anyone ever pointed this out to you? Or perhaps you might say, "I am no good at math because everyone in my family is bad at math. It is genetic!"

....

....

EVALUATE INFORMATION. Why do you have this challenge? What evidence exists? Is the problem a study skills problem—or something else? For instance, you may say, "I do poorly on tests because I am a poor test taker." The reality might be that you never get enough sleep before tests and are, therefore, too tired to perform effectively.

....

....

DRAW CONCLUSIONS. If you can do this step well, you are able to bring together all pieces of the situation and logically use the evidence to come to a reasonable conclusion. For instance, after you have reviewed the evidence, separated fact from fiction, and put emotion aside, you might find yourself saying something like the following: "I was brought up in a family that feared math. I believe that fear has transferred to me. There is nothing genetic about it! I need to work with a tutor and get a good night's sleep."

....

....

Let's use your class syllabus as an example.

If you can read your syllabus and tell a classmate when the next assignment is due, that is important basic-level knowledge. Knowing the due dates of your course assignments and being able to explain in your own words what each assignment requires are important steps to success. This basic understanding lays the foundation for the higher-level thinking skills—similar to a football receiver who must remember the pass pattern he needs to run before he can catch a football successfully in a game.

PROBLEM SOLVING

Problem solving is a process that requires the use of critical-thinking skills to examine a dilemma, situation, or person that presents us with difficulty—the problem. A proposed solution follows this examination. However, if our critical thinker gathers the information, analyzes the information, and submits a report without a solution, then the problem has not been solved. A problem solver looks at the information and then proposes alternatives and answers.

For an example, let's look at our friend Ricky from the beginning of this topic. A critical thinker must first examine Ricky's assumption that "no way" will his instructors expect him to read all of these books. How does he "know" this? The same holds true for what Ricky "knows" to be true about reading an assignment. Where did he get this information, and how does it relate to his new college reality?

Once Ricky has identified his assumptions (and separates his facts from fiction), he can begin to gather more information about what his instructors expect. He might schedule an appointment with each instructor. He might talk with classmates. Perhaps a trip to his campus advisor might help. All of this requires deep thinking, fact finding, and time.

THE PROCESS OF PROBLEM SOLVING

Problem solving generally involves a series of steps. When done effectively, each step is well thought out and answers a question. These answers methodically lead to a solution. The R.E.D. Model provides a clear path to arrive at a well-thought-out solution. In order to demonstrate this, read and complete Activity 2.4. This will allow you to not only practice critical thinking and problem solving but also to apply these skills to maintaining personal well-being. When we tend to our social, emotional, physical, and social well-being, we use critical-thinking skills.

There may be a point in the school term when you begin to feel overwhelmed—when the weight of all your responsibilities and obligations seem impossible to handle. Especially during those times, your critical-thinking skills will prove valuable. Let's see what course of action you would suggest to help Tina. As you can see in the following activity, she is about ready to call it quits.

Activity 2.4

Critical Thinking, Problem Solving, and Personal Well-Being

USING CRITICAL-THINKING SKILLS TO EXAMINE LIFE'S BALANCE

R E D

For this activity, read about Tina's situation. Then, work with a classmate to complete the items that follow.

Twenty-five-year-old Tina is in her first semester of college. In addition to taking two college classes, she works 20 hours a week as a server in a restaurant. Doing her best to make ends meet, she recently took in a roommate to help with rent. Tina has sole custody of her two little girls (two years old and seven years old). She also faithfully participates in a 12-step program. She is proud that she has been "clean" of all drugs and alcohol for nearly three years.

Tina is determined that her past will not become her future. Having a strong faith and loving her two children have helped her to keep focused. Lately, though, she has been gripped by panic and anxiety. As a child, she was always told that she was not very smart. The few relatives with whom she still stays in contact believe she is wasting her time with college. Today, Tina told one of her instructors she has lost confidence in her ability to do college work—and is considering withdrawing from college.

While Tina's battle with her past "demon" of addiction may not be typical of students you know, her insecurities and doubts reflect the issues that can and do paralyze students. Using the strategies you have learned thus far, help Tina critically examine those dimensions of life that may be out of balance.

1. Stop and Think: Reflect on Tina's dilemma. State Tina's problem or problems as clearly as you can. Identify those that may have an impact on her well-being. Help Tina clearly define her challenge.

2. Recognizing Assumptions: What assumptions might Tina be making? Do you know if the assumptions are factual, fictional, or both?

3. Evaluating Information: What is the accurate information that Tina can work with in this situation? Can you sense that there might be some confirmation bias present in Tina's thinking?

4. Drawing Conclusions: Now that you have separated fact from fiction—and helped Tina put aside emotion—what conclusions can you draw about Tina's thought of withdrawing from college?

5. Plan of Action: What is the next step for Tina? Let's drill down a little deeper with this part of the R.E.D. Model. You want to help Tina avoid the temptation of jumping to the first thought that comes into her mind. Again, reflection will be important here. The following steps will clarify what needs to be done.

BRAINSTORMING. Help Tina **brainstorm** some possible paths to follow. The purpose of a brainstorming session is to come up with as many ideas as possible—without judgment. What possible actions could solve this problem? No evaluation is needed for this step. Be as creative as you possibly can be with this process.

CHOOSING. Once you have listed the possible solutions for Tina, choose the best alternative and establish a plan to carry it out. Whatever solution you decide on needs to address the identified problem (see step 1 of the R.E.D. Model). Evaluate your choice. Why do you consider it to be the best choice? Again, are you making any assumptions?

IMPLEMENTING. Now it is time to move from thinking to doing. Put your planning into motion. This may lead directly to the solution of the problem, or you may experience a series of starts and stops. In other words, you may choose a solution and put it into action—only to discover that it does not work like you had thought it would. At that point, based on your evaluation, you may need to return to brainstorming, then choose another alternative and implement that. It may be helpful to periodically ask yourself, "Is this solution working?"

EVALUATING. Effective problem solvers do this along the way and at the end of the process. As noted above, once Tina implements her solution, she will need to stop every so often to make sure she is moving in the correct direction and make adjustments as needed. Once she has completed all the action steps of her plan, she needs to make a final judgment as to the effectiveness of her choices and actions. Has the problem been solved—or does she need to do something else? Did her choice work—or does she need to make some new choices? What can Tina do to judge how effective the solution is?

THE PROBLEM-SOLVING TRAP

Sometimes we are blinded to new alternatives because we are stuck in a routine or trapped by our assumptions. Perhaps we continue to look at a particular problem from the same point of view. For example, if your quiz grades have been lower than you had hoped for, your response may be, "I will study harder!" After all, that is what you have heard all your life: "If you want to do better, just try harder! Give it more effort. Focus!" Let's examine this assumption—and why it may be a **problem-solving trap** for you.

If you were to base your entire problem-solving strategy on the premise that "studying harder" will bring better grades, you could find yourself going nowhere fast.

While the intent is admirable, "study harder" generally means "I'll continue to use the same study methods that have not worked—but I'll do them longer and with more effort." Think about that. Does that *really* make sense to you? It is limited, because you have not questioned your initial assumption or habits—and thus your alternatives are limited. What you need is some new thinking—some new eyeglasses with which to examine the problem.

CREATIVE THINKING

YOU HAVE TO DO IT DIFFERENTLY IF YOU WANT DIFFERENT RESULTS

Just because you put more effort into preparation for your math exam, for example, does not mean you will see better results on the next test. **Creative thinking**—thinking that develops (creates) a new or different product—requires that we look at situations in new ways—from different angles or unique perspectives.

Let's look at the issue of campus security. Solutions to curbing crime on campus might include hiring more security officers for the campus, improving lighting, or installing more emergency phones in high-risk areas on campus. However, a new approach might be to explore the possibility of developing a campus "citizens watch" program, in which student organizations work with campus security personnel to increase student confidence about campus safety.

By creatively tackling a problem, we become more aware of the greater number of possibilities for solving it. We will become better equipped to broaden our thinking and develop new patterns of problem solving.

LEARNING TO THINK CREATIVELY

While some people seem to be naturally creative, others struggle to come up with an original idea. One strategy is to use what you already know. Let's use the problem-solving process you learned earlier to boost your creativity.

Even when you do not need to solve a dilemma, you can use those same steps. For instance, if you would like to write a short story or compose a song, the process of reflecting, brainstorming, choosing, implementing, and evaluating can be used effectively. Table 2.4 gives some guidance as it focuses on the last step of the R.E.D. Model—Plan of Action.

Activity 2.5

Creative Solutions

CRITICAL THINKING FOR ACADEMIC SUCCESS

Return to the academic challenge you identified and examined earlier in this topic. Brainstorm three possible solutions. Step outside the traditional thinking "box." Review your potential solutions. Come up with at least one creative idea to address the challenge. Take a step. For the purpose of this activity, be bold. Even if your ideas seem silly or outlandish, write them on a separate piece of paper.

As you learned earlier, once you have solutions, you will need to evaluate (a higher-level thinking skill) the potential consequences of each solution. Do that now for your creative ideas.

Finally, based on this exercise, which solution do you favor—and why do you think it will successfully address your study skill challenge?

Table 2.4 **The Creative-Thinking Process**

Steps to Establishing a Plan of Action	Suggestions to Increase Creativity
Reflecting	• Slow down and think about the problem. Do not "solve" it until you understand it. • Be kind to yourself. If you constantly tell yourself, "I would not recognize a creative idea if it hit me in the head," you are establishing a negative attitude. What you "see" in your mind may become what you experience in your life. • Associate with people who seem to be able to "think outside the box." Listen to creative people. Read about creative people. • Challenge any assumptions that might shut down creativity. Silence internal criticism such as "Don't be foolish" or "I'm not creative."
Brainstorming	• Brainstorm effectively. List your ideas on a piece of paper, but do not stop to judge whether they are good or bad. Making judgments will slow down your flow of ideas and inhibit your free thinking. There will be time later to judge practicality. • Accept the fact that there are different ways to look at your problem or situation. Look at it from different perspectives. How would your instructor view the problem? How about a friend? If you can see the issue from different angles, chances are you can find multiple solutions as well. Again, challenge assumptions. • Avoid the temptation to grab the first solution that comes to your mind. Brainstorm as many solutions as you can imagine. Ask a trusted friend to help you. This will give you the opinions of someone who is not personally involved in the problem.
Choosing	• Identify what types of solutions have been used in the past with similar problems. If you can, determine whether the solutions were successful.
Implementing	• Practice. Listen to or read the news. Can you propose a creative solution to a current event? Opportunities are all around. Do this frequently.
Evaluating	• Go beyond thinking about creativity. Feel it, taste it, hear it, and see it. Use every sense you have to understand the world around you.

ADAPTING OLD SKILLS TO NEW SITUATIONS: MAKING CHOICES

You will continually confront situations in which you must apply the skills you have developed over the years. You learn something in one school year or subject area—for example, how to take notes—and you must apply it in another school year or subject area. Occasionally, a new situation presents itself, in which the old skills do not easily work. You must then make some sort of adjustment. In some cases, this may be minor; in others, quite dramatic. Frustration may very likely occur. In such situations, you have four broad choices—and each requires critical thinking:

1. Quit or remove yourself from the situation:
   ■ The new instructor is requiring things that you have either not done before or have done but not done well. Rather than confront the

situation, you drop the class. Think about the assumptions being made here.

- A similar scenario may be a catalyst for someone to quit a job.

2. Stay in the new situation without adjusting your skills and suffer a miserable existence.
   - This situation is the same as the first, except you cannot or will not drop the class. You dislike the class, but you refuse to modify your skills. Consequently, you are one unhappy student!
   - Do you know someone who cannot adapt to a new boss or manager? Rather than look for ways to improve the situation, the person suffers a miserable existence in the job.

3. Modify your skills to get by in the new situation.
   - You are not particularly happy about the new challenge, but you realize you have to make some adjustments. You might not make a dramatic change, but you do enough to get by.
   - The new position at work requires you to develop some new techniques to be successful. You may not like the adjustment, but you realize it is necessary to stay with a job you otherwise like.

4. Change and adapt your old skills so that they better fit the new demands.
   - You take the challenge head on. You may stumble a couple of times, but you make the needed changes in your skills to serve you and the situation better.
   - You want to thrive in the company and move up the promotion ladder. You search for ways to learn and grow each day.

You need to consciously identify and review where you are in your thought process. First ask yourself, "What assumptions am I making?" Then ask yourself, "What can I do?" Sometimes, the first option—quit—is the best. You may be "over placed" in a class (for example, you did not take a prerequisite course that taught the skills needed). Or the job is just not matched to your skills. But don't jump to this choice because it seems like the easy way out. Many times, quitting only postpones the inevitable. You will eventually need the skill in question.

Chapter SUMMARY

In this material, you have examined the critical-thinking process. More specifically, you learned about and practiced the R.E.D. Model for critical thinking.

Before moving on to the next topic, take a moment to reflect on the following points:

- You have been in school before—and you have been successful in school before. Respect the skills you have, and critically think about how you can apply these skills to your new college environment.

- Critical thinking requires reflection and analysis (as well as application and evaluation) of issues or events.

- Problem solving requires the use of critical-thinking skills to examine a dilemma and then propose a solution.

- When solving a problem, use creative-thinking strategies to look at multiple perspectives. This will help you see that problems and issues generally have more than two sides.

- Critical thinking can help you maintain a sense of balance and well-being in your life.

Use the R.E.D. Model to recognize assumptions, evaluate information, and draw conclusions.

CRITICALLY THINKING
What Have You Learned?

At the beginning of this topic, you read about Ricky. You might remember that he had worked himself into such a state that he was considering dropping out of school.

All topics throughout these course materials will end with a section titled *Critically Thinking: What Have You Learned?* You will then use (apply) what you have learned to the opening situation of each section. However, before you dive into Ricky's problem (this topic's situation) and propose your solution, stop and think about the main points of the topic.

Review your notes from this topic, as well as the key terms, learning outcomes, bold-faced headings, figures, tables, and activities. For instance, consider how the learning outcomes may be used to help Ricky:

- Define critical thinking. (Ricky will need to weigh the facts of his situation before he can make a rational decision.)

- Use the R.E.D. Model to establish a plan. (Gathering facts is one of the steps of critical thinking. Ricky will also need to identify any opinions he holds that may lead him to an inappropriate conclusion.)

- Understand the language of critical thinking. (To appropriately use the R.E.D. Model, Ricky will need to understand how to analyze and evaluate information.)

- Explain how critical-thinking skills can help maintain balance and wellness. (Ricky is not in a good place right now. You will be able to offer him ideas on how to solve his problem and maintain his health in the process.)

TEST YOUR LEARNING

Now that you have reviewed the main steps of the critical-thinking and problem-solving processes, reread Ricky's story. Pretend that you are Ricky's best friend. Using the R.E.D. Model for critical thinking, help Ricky critically review his problem before he does something he may regret.

Recognize Assumptions:

Facts: What are the facts in Ricky's situation?

Opinions: What opinions do you find in this situation?

Assumptions: Are Ricky's assumptions accurate?

Evaluate Information:

Ricky is considering dropping out of school. Before he makes this decision, help him by compiling a list of questions that will help him make the most appropriate decision.

What emotions seem to be moving Ricky toward his decision?

Is there anything missing from his thought process?

Do you see a confirmation bias?

Draw Conclusions:

Based on the facts and the questions you have presented, what conclusions can you draw?

What advice do you have for Ricky? What solutions do you propose?

Based on your suggestions, do you see any assumptions?

Finally, based on what you learned about using critical thinking to problem solve, what plan of action do you suggest for Ricky?

Priority
MANAGEMENT
3

LEARNING OUTCOMES

By the time you finish reading this material and completing its activities, you will be able to do the following:

- Develop a written schedule that provides at least two hours of study time for every hour scheduled in the classroom.

- Use and evaluate at least one priority management tool (a calendar or planner).

- Develop a weekly to-do list that ranks your tasks in order of importance.

- Identify at least three types of procrastination and a strategy to deal with each.

- Describe how applying organizational skills can help you balance your life's demands.

The Case of MARIE

Marie is a single mother with one child. She has four on-campus classes and one online class. In addition to her financial aid, she earns income by working 30 hours a week at a store in the mall.

It is now the fourth week of the term, and Marie is feeling overwhelmed by all of the projects, tests, and reading assignments she must complete for her classes. She has not had a good night's sleep in more than two weeks, and the stress of everything is beginning to show.

Marie's class averages are not impressive—one C and three Ds. One week, she spends too much time focusing on math and doesn't have time to study for other classes. The next week, she

Chapter INTRODUCTION

THE MYTH OF TIME MANAGEMENT

When you hear the word organization, what comes to mind? Perhaps you think about wasting time, spending time, finding time, stealing time, and needing more time. Or maybe you immediately think of calendars, smartphones, procrastination, and time management.

catches up in history but falls behind in everything else. She has been late to most of her classes—not by much, but she is never on time. And her homework is always late. Things constantly "slip her mind."

Marie has thought about dropping one of her classes, but she believes that will affect her eligibility for financial aid. In addition, she looks at dropping a class as being the same as failing it. "I'm not a quitter," she recently told a friend. "All I want to do is hang on for the rest of the semester. I want to earn my degree as soon as possible. Dropping classes will not get me closer to my goal. I'll just have to sleep less and work more."

CRITICALLY THINKING
about *Marie's* situation

You are Marie's mentor. What strategies would you suggest for her to follow?

A recent (December 15, 2012) Internet search for "time management" brought up approximately 1,520,000,000 results. That is more than a billion and a half possible hits for books, videos, seminars, and blogs. Considering how much attention time management receives, it is difficult to believe that the topic is a myth.

That's right. Time management is a myth. You can manage your finances. You can manage the amount of food you eat or the level of exercise you perform. You even can manage relationships. But you cannot manage time.

Consider the following:

- Everyone has the same number of hours in a week (168).
- No matter who you are—rich or poor, a college student or a college president, a mailroom worker or a corporate executive—you cannot increase the number of hours in a week. You cannot move some to next week, and you cannot borrow any from last week. You cannot manage to have more hours than the person next to you.
- Each hour is 60 minutes long. You cannot speed it up, and you cannot slow it down. You cannot manage to stretch that hour.
- Regardless of what you do (or anyone does), at midnight each day, you have the same number of hours as everyone else with which to work. You cannot manage to find an additional hour or two.

Rather than focus on something you cannot do—manage time—consider managing your priorities.

Priorities are the people, issues, and things that are important in your life—those that help you get what you need and desire. So, it makes more sense to practice priority management. When you do this, you are putting the important things first on your daily **calendar.** You are organizing your day around what moves you closer to your goals.

Priority management challenges even the best students during their first term in college. A typical college student may have only two or three hours of class on a particular day. The amount of unstructured time he or she has can be troublesome. For other students, returning to school can create a new set of challenges as they juggle family, work, and school.

In addition to time, you also need to consider space: Where will you study, how will you file your papers, and where will you keep your supplies? Regardless of where you live, you will benefit by designating a place for your out-of-class study time.

Getting organized will also allow you to feel in control of your life. This topic will explain how to organize priorities to improve efficiency and effectiveness while minimizing stress.

The clock keeps ticking no matter what you do. You cannot control time. You cannot create time. However, you can effectively use time for your benefit.

ORGANIZATION AND TIME

No one can give you a foolproof or crisis-proof system for priority management, but learning to anticipate and adapt to unforeseen or unexpected events will help to reduce pressure on you and avoid crisis.

Activity 3.1

Reflecting on Your Current Level of Organizational Skills

Before you answer the items that follow, reflect on your current level of organizational skills. Think of how well (or poorly) you have organized your priorities and your workspace.

There are no "right" answers for the questions that follow. As you do in completing all of the reflective activities with this topic, you should write from your heart. It is not meant for you to answer just like your classmates or to match what you may think your instructor wants to see. Take your time to give a respectful and responsible general accounting of your experiences with organization. Conducting a truthful self-assessment now will help you build on skills you have while developing those you lack.

For each of the following items, circle the number that best describes your typical experience with organizational skills. Here is the key for the numbers:

0 = never, 1 = almost never, 2 = occasionally, 3 = frequently, 4 = almost always, 5 = always

When considering your past successes and challenges with organization, how often:

1.	Were you able to find an item (a paper, a book, your keys) after you put it somewhere?	0	1	2	3	4	5
2.	Did you arrive on time for class or another appointment?	0	1	2	3	4	5
3.	Did you turn in assignments on time?	0	1	2	3	4	5
4.	Did you work in a study space dedicated specifically to you?	0	1	2	3	4	5
5.	Did you not overwhelm and stress yourself by limiting your workload?	0	1	2	3	4	5
6.	Were you able to handle your stress in an effective and healthy manner?	0	1	2	3	4	5
7.	Did you seek advice from a classmate, advisor, or instructor about ways to better organize your class work and to reduce stress?	0	1	2	3	4	5
8.	Did you organize your class notes and materials using an effective notebook?	0	1	2	3	4	5

Add up your scores for items 2, 3, and 5. Divide by 3. Write your answer here: _____ .

Using the key provided to explain each number (0, 1, 2, 3, 4, 5), complete this sentence: When it comes to organizing priorities, I _____ organize my priorities effectively.

Add up your scores for items 1, 4, and 8. Divide by 3. Write your answer here: _____ .

Using the key provided to explain each number (0, 1, 2, 3, 4, 5), complete this sentence: When it comes to organizing space, I _____ organize my space effectively.

Add up your scores for items 5, 6, and 7. Divide by 3. Write your answer here: _____ .

Using the key provided to explain each number (0, 1, 2, 3, 4, 5), complete this sentence: When it comes to organization in general, I _____ can organize myself so as to minimize stress.

Based on your answers, what insights have you gained about your experiences with organization?

YOU HAVE A LOT TO DO!

You have many demands on your time. A partial list of what you have to do may look like this:

- Find personal free time.
- Find time to do activities with friends.
- Find recreation time.
- Find quality family time.
- Find time to study.
- Juggle work hours, school hours, and study hours.
- Get enough good sleep.
- Juggle family responsibilities with school expectations.

The strategies discussed in this material will help you appropriately handle your daily obligations.

STUDY TIME: How Much?

If you are taking a full load of classes, then your homework and class time could very well add up to a 40-hour workweek. That is based on the long-referenced formula of spending two or three hours a week out of class for every hour you spend in class. According to that formula, if you spend 12 hours in class each week, you should devote another 24 to 36 hours for reading, writing, researching, meeting with study groups, completing assignments, and preparing for tests outside class. Doing these tasks is what is meant by **study time**.

Keep in mind that the type of work you do will also dictate how much time is necessary. A class of more complexity or difficulty may require more time than one that, for you, is easier and less involved.

HOW DO YOU ESTABLISH A STUDY SCHEDULE?

Let's ask the "How much study time?" question in a different way. How much time do you have available for homework and study purposes?

Complete Activity 3.2 on the following page, and then look at your responses for column 3. Do you have many 5s? If you find yourself with more things to do than hours to do them, perhaps it has something to do with how you look at these things. If everything is "extremely necessary," then the reality is that nothing is extremely necessary. How do you know the 5s are in fact "extremely necessary"? Recognize assumptions and separate fact from fiction here.

No magic number exists for how many hours you need to devote to your studies, but consider the formula introduced earlier. If you are taking a full load of courses (four or five a term) and the hours you have available for homework amount to only five hours per week, you will likely have a problem completing your college requirements.

Activity 3.2

Where Does Your Week Go?

In the first column of the table that follows, list all of the things you do in a week. You will find some common categories already entered for you. Add as many as apply to your week's schedule. Once you have completed that, go back and estimate the number of hours per week you devote to each category. Enter those numbers in the next column. Be as exact as you can. The third column asks you to rate how necessary the activity is to you. That is, is this something you have to do? (For more on this concept, see Hallowell [2007], pp. 148–161.)

What I Do Each Week	Number of Hours I Spend Doing It	How Necessary Is This to My Life? 1 = not very necessary 5 = extremely necessary
Sleep		
Eat meals		
Hygiene (showers, haircuts, general grooming)		
Time in class		
Time at employment		
Practice (sports, music, theater)		
Travel (time I spend on the road each week)		
Child care		
Religious or spiritual activities		
Recreation		
Chores and errands		
Other family obligations		
Club activities		
Time on social media		
Other		
Total time spent on all activities		

Table 3.1 on page 44 clearly shows that the more classes you take, the greater the demands on your time. If you have decided to take a full load and you also plan to work a 40-hour-per-week job, then you must schedule the equivalent time of having two full-time jobs. And you still must schedule sleep, family, friends, and health-related activities.

If you can do it, great! If not, stop and reevaluate before you put yourself—and those around you—through a nightmarish schedule. If you are exhausted by the end of your week, remember that you, not your instructor, established the schedule.

Consider completing this exercise before you register for next term's classes. Recognize what your time commitments are before you enroll in more classes than you will be able to handle.

Table 3.1 Determining Study Time

Number of Courses You Are Taking This Term	Course Name	Number of Credits/Hours in the Classroom for This Course	Study Time (based on 2 hours for each 1 hour in class)	Total Hours per Week for the Course (in class and out of class)	Cumulative Hours for All Courses You Are Taking This Term
1	English	3	6	9	9 (if you take only this course)
2	Math	3	6	9	18 (for two courses)
3	History	3	6	9	27 (for three courses)
4	Humanities	3	6	9	36 (for four courses)
5	Biology (and lab)	4	8	12	48 (for five courses)

Activity 3.3

Adjusting to a College Schedule

R E D

Let's apply the R.E.D. Model to examine one of your self-identified organizational challenges. Focus on your most significant challenge in priority management.

Write your challenge on a separate piece of paper.

Critical-Thinking Step	Application to Your Study Skills
Recognize assumptions	Reread the challenge you just wrote down. List the reasons you believe you have that challenge. After you have listed your reasons, identify what is fact and what is fiction. That is, how do you know this assessment of your challenge is correct?
Evaluate information	Examine your organizational challenge from more than one perspective (point of view). What information supports or refutes your assumptions? Perhaps a family member or friend can help you.
Draw conclusions	Based on your evidence, does your conclusion about your organizational challenge make sense? What is your plan to eliminate or minimize this challenge?

Table 3.2   **Types and Benefits of Calendars**

Type of Calendar	Benefits
Monthly	• See four weeks all at once • Easily spot commitments and conflicts
Weekly	• Room for more details • Schedule exact times over seven days
Daily (To-Do List)	• List all items to do for the day • Cross off what you accomplish and move other items to the next day's list.

Figure 3.1

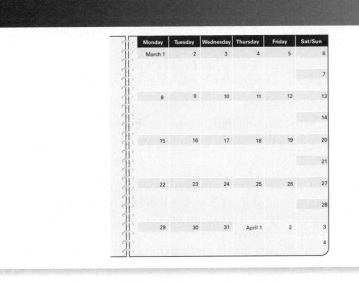

Figure 3.2

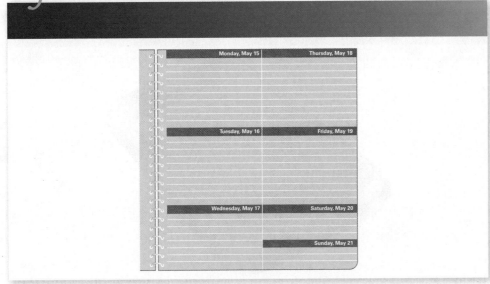

Figure 3.3

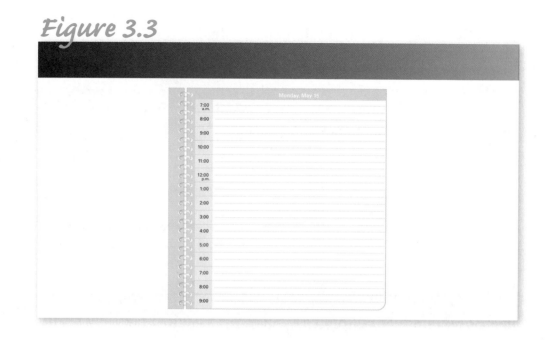

KEEPING TRACK OF TIME AND COMMITMENTS

Three common tools for keeping track of and managing priorities are the monthly calendar, the weekly calendar, and the daily to-do list. Each tool can be in a paper/book format or in the form of a digital calendar on your computer, tablet, or cell phone.

Electronic calendar. Perhaps you are more comfortable with an electronic version of one of these calendars, as shown in Figure 3.4. A cell phone or tablet, for instance, provides calendar functions along with an alarm or "Alert" option that will audibly remind you of an item on your calendar. This "Reminder" feature can be an excellent tool for people who are diligent about putting things on the calendar but then do not remember to look at the calendar.

Figure 3.4

WHAT SHOULD YOU DO FIRST?
ESTABLISHING PRIORITIES

Okay, let's recap. You have an idea of where your time goes each week. You know how many hours are available for homework and studying. You even adopted a method for keeping track of your commitments. Now you must determine what to do first, second, and so on. If you do not establish priorities (rank items by order of importance), you may end up spending time on minor tasks while ignoring the major projects that require much of your attention.

Let's consider a few basic tips. After you have your list of things to do, make the following determinations:

- Negotiable—Non-negotiable? What items on your list are **non-negotiable**? A non-negotiable item is something that, by the end of the day, you would make sure you tended to. It is so important that you would not think of letting it slide or be forgotten. A goal—if it is truly important to you—is non-negotiable. You will do whatever it takes to move closer to it. If you are a single parent, for instance, having money to feed your children is non-negotiable. This is critical and must be done. Your health is another non-negotiable item. Look at your list of activities and make decisions as to which of the items are negotiable (not priorities) and which are non-negotiable. If you think that *all* are non-negotiable, speak with a campus advisor, instructor, or mentor for clarity.
  - Something that is negotiable is not very important to you. It may or may not lead you to your goal. Something that you identify as negotiable can be postponed. There is not a sense of immediacy with it. Look at your weekly list of activities; are the negotiable items (the not very necessary items) crowding out what you identify as your extremely necessary (non-negotiable) activities?
- Which items must be addressed immediately? Studying for a quiz that will be given at 8:00 a.m. tomorrow has more immediacy than typing a research paper that is due two months from today.
- Can you plan ahead? Using your syllabi and assignment pages, map out your entire semester. Record on your calendar when each exam, quiz, and assignment is due. Then you will be able to see the "big picture"—and it will hold fewer surprises.

DOING A LOT OF STUFF ISN'T THE SAME
AS MOVING FORWARD

Have you ever looked back on a very busy day and wondered why you didn't get more accomplished? "I don't know where the day went! I did a lot of stuff, but I seem farther behind than I was at the beginning of the day!"

Do not equate "doing a lot of stuff" with making purposeful progress toward your goals. Look at your responses to Activity 3.2. Is the "stuff" you fill your life with connected to your priorities? If *everything* is a priority, it's questionable if *anything* is a priority.

SIMPLIFY

A major strategy for managing your priorities is to look at the "big picture" and then simplify that big task or project into smaller and less intimidating steps. Then take one step at a time to complete the task.

Let's assume you have an assignment to research the impact of social media on the business world. The assignment is due in three weeks. An effective way to proceed would be to break the project into smaller pieces and schedule when you would do each step. For instance, on days 1, 2 and 3, you will make sure you understand the assignment, ask the instructor any clarifying questions you might have, and begin an initial search for information.

On days 4, 5, and 6, you could go to the campus library and ask a reference librarian for assistance. Once you get your initial material, you can start reading and taking notes.

And you would continue in this manner, taking small yet steady steps toward completing the assignment. One step at a time moves you steadily (and with reduced stress) toward the conclusion.

ORGANIZATION AND PROCRASTINATION

"I'LL DO ALL OF THIS TOMORROW!"

All the tips, strategies, calendars, and campus resources in the world will do absolutely nothing if you don't take the first step toward putting them into action.

Procrastination—avoiding and postponing what should be taken care of now—can rob you of your time and derail your best intentions.

YOU CAN'T GET IT BACK—EVER!

Procrastinate enough and you will lose more than hours. Eventually those hours will stretch into days, months, and even years. To help you visualize this, here is a small challenge for you.

Find a blank copy of an annual calendar. Before you go to bed each night, place an X over that day on the calendar. Once you have done that, realize that you can do nothing to remove that X. The day is gone—forever! You cannot get back what has passed. Are you satisfied with how you used your time for the day? (Lin)

Let's relate that to your school term. Consider a project where you have 21 days to complete an assignment. If you procrastinate and do nothing toward the project for the first 14 days, you have lost those days forever. And, obviously, you have only seven days to complete what was a *21-day* project. Do you want that kind of stress and pressure?

This is a powerful reminder that today is the tomorrow you created yesterday. Procrastinate today, and your tomorrow will have more work and stress.

WHY DO PEOPLE PROCRASTINATE?

Procrastinators may have various reasons for their behavior, but regardless, the habit is usually self-defeating. Procrastination is not synonymous with laziness. In fact, one psychologist suggests that procrastinators have energy to spare (Sapadin, 1999, pp. 10–20). It is just not focused in the appropriate direction.

Thus, the first step in dealing with procrastination is to listen to associated excuses and then develop a plan to refocus one's efforts.

Table 3.3 provides an overview of six styles of procrastination, along with suggestions on how to fight these time-wasting behaviors.

Table 3.3 **Strategies to Deal with Procrastination**

Type of Procrastinator	Description	What Can You Do?
Perfectionist	Everything you do has to be "perfect." You end up postponing completion until you can get it "just right."	Know the difference between practical ("good as possible") and ideal ("perfect"). Don't settle for inferior work, yet don't put undue pressure on yourself.
Dreamer	You have big plans and big ideas, but you never put them into action.	Develop action steps for your dreams, and then do them one at a time.
Worrier	Rather than doing something different or challenging that you are unsure of, you avoid commitment and/or follow-through as long as possible.	Each week, take a little calculated risk (nothing foolish) to get used to stretching your abilities. Competence develops confidence!
Crisis maker	You wait until the last minute to do something. The more pressure involved with a project, the better. Unfortunately, as more projects stack up, you are not able to complete them satisfactorily.	Write assignment goals that include specific due dates that come before a course deadline—maybe two or three days before the due date. Use sports or some other healthy activity to satisfy your need to experience pressure.
Defier	You don't see why your time should be affected by other people's demands (like class attendance or completing a written assignment).	Refocus. Ask yourself "What can I do?" and "What do I need to do?" rather than "Why do I have to do what they want me to do?" You made the choice to come to school, and you (probably) made the choice to take the particular class.
Overdoer	You always say *yes*. You don't want to disappoint people. You eventually run out of energy and time—and crash. Ironically, you do disappoint the people you wanted to please, as well as yourself.	Learn that the healthiest word in the English language can very well be *no*. Before taking on a new project, make sure your goals are being advanced. Recognize any assumptions you have (such as "I have to do this because …"). Obviously, there is a fine line between being self-centered and willing to help others. But if you are an overdoer, you probably crossed this line long ago and have failed to take proper care of your needs.

SOURCE: Based on Sapadin, 1999.

ACTIVATION ENERGY

A **habit** is something you repeat with such frequency that it becomes an involuntary act. It seems as though you cannot help yourself from doing it.

In the book *The Happiness Advantage: The Seven Principles of Positive Psychology That Fuel Success and Performance at Work*, Shawn Achor (2010) describes the concept of **activation energy**. He states that to "kick-start a positive habit" we need an "initial spark" to get us moving. Consider this the effort you need to either begin to break a bad habit or start a positive habit (pp. 156–161).

In short, the less time or distance you put between you and a positive habit, the better chance you have of developing that habit. Reduce or minimize the obstacles, and you increase the chances of doing the task. Sometimes a little extra effort and push are needed to get by or over the obstacle. That extra effort is the activation energy that will get you closer to your goal.

Conversely, the more resistance or obstacles you put between you and a bad habit, the better the chance to break that habit.

Think about it. If you want to develop the healthy habit of doing cardio exercise every day, you have to lessen the obstacles between you and the activity. If you have to drive to a gym that is thirty minutes away, you may find excuses for why you can't get to the gym. But if you decide you will start your exercise regimen by walking thirty minutes a day around your community, maybe all you need to do is place your walking shoes by the door. It takes a moment to slip them on—and out the door you go, leaving procrastination on the couch!

THE TWO-MINUTE DRILL!

Long-term goals can be intimidating. They are generally large, and the results are not realized until the distant future. These two factors (size and lack of immediacy) can be demotivators for some people. If that is the case with one of your goals, think smaller and more short term. Think of what you could do today—right now. Think of what you could do with just two minutes!

"Two minutes!" you might say. "What can I possibly do to make any difference in just two minutes?"

Consider this example: A student has difficulty with math. She does her homework, studies for her tests, and even visits her instructor. Still, this student is barely passing the course. A classmate suggested she work with a tutor in the student success center. Today, the student took two minutes to set up an appointment.

The student still must follow through and keep the appointment. But she has taken the first step. She is now moving forward with this initial activation energy.

Activity 3.5

The Two-Minute Drill: Helping Marie Make Time for Her Priorities

For this activity, let's help Marie (from the opening scenario) by modeling behavior for her. In this case, you will show her how you can plan for the Two-Minute Drill.

Write one academic goal you have, and then write what you could do today (in two minutes) that would get you closer to that goal. Then consider a personal nonacademic goal. What could you do today in two minutes to get closer to that goal?

For each goal, what can you do tomorrow for two minutes? Do this for a week, and you will be on your way to developing a habit—and moving toward your goals!

BACKWARD PLANNING

Another planning strategy is to plan backward. Suppose you have a test scheduled in one week. Start with the end product: walking into class prepared for the exam. Then work backward: How will you get to this point? Table 3.4 provides one option.

Table 3.4 **Backward Planning to a Goal: To Receive an A on the Next Biology Exam**

Day	Task
Thursday	Successfully take the biology exam (the result).
Wednesday	Briefly review major topics—no cramming necessary.
Tuesday	Review vocabulary and potential exam questions.
Monday	Review your class notes again (reread).
Sunday	Review chapter questions in textbook; identify potential exam questions.
Saturday	Review class notes; review vocabulary and study guide sheets.
Friday	Review, reorganize, and summarize your class notes.
Thursday (the day you started)	Make sure all textbook readings have been completed.

ORGANIZATION AND SPACE

Once you set your priorities, examine your space. For the purposes of this section, space refers to those areas around you that relate to your studies outside the classroom: your home study area, your book bag or purse, and, if you have one, your car. The time that you spend searching your space for a book, notepad, or syllabus is time taken from the priorities you established on your calendar or to-do list.

PERSONAL STUDY AREA

Whether you have a separate room dedicated to studying or just a small corner of a larger room, organize your space so it works for you. Here are some tips:

Workspace. The first thing to do is to identify an area that will be yours for schoolwork—a **personal study area**. Do whatever you can to clearly "mark your private work territory." This area is for your studies—not for stacks of laundry, not for someone else's personal items, and not for trash or miscellaneous items. Do whatever you can to establish your workspace in a quiet area that will be conducive to uninterrupted study time.

Personal Storage Areas. For an organized and clutter-free workspace, you will need effective storage for your papers, books, supplies, and other items. Your personal storage area could include desk drawers, bookshelves, file boxes, plastic bins, or a file cabinet.

Whatever you use, follow these tips to help you stay organized:

- **Develop a filing method.** Avoid the urge to "toss and close" (toss an item into your desk and then close the drawer). Designate specific drawers for specific functions. One may hold supplies such as pencils, pens, tape, and staples. Another drawer—or perhaps a file box or shelf—may be home to paper, envelopes, computer disks, and ink cartridges.

- **Use file folders to organize papers.** Create a clearly labeled file folder for each class. You can keep a copy of the syllabus or assignment sheet here (as well as another copy in the notebook you carry to class each day). The folder can be a logical place to file returned papers or drafts of assignments. And then "file the file folders" in a small file cabinet, a desk drawer, or a small file-folder holder that sits on a corner of your desk.

- **Use technology when available.** Computer folders provide an efficient way to manage documents. Perhaps your computer already has a file folder labeled "My Documents." Within this folder, create a subfolder for each class you have. You may even desire to create separate folders for each major assignment or unit of material. Do the same with your e-mail, and file correspondence with your instructor and classmates, as well as any papers you submit. Whatever works for you, use it. Back up all your document files on a disk, flash drive, or the "cloud."

- **Create a message center to hold important notices.** This can be as simple as a small wall-mounted cork board on which you tack important reminders. Or you can use a chalkboard or laminated wall poster to record important dates and tasks.

Based on the above strategies, how effective and efficient is your personal study area?

AVOIDING REPETITIVE STRAIN INJURIES

In addition to being responsible for the academic integrity of your work, you must be responsible for the health and integrity of your body. Although hours sitting at a computer workstation may not appear to be demanding, they can have a debilitating effect on your body.

Repetitive strain injuries (RSIs), which are also called repetitive stress injuries, commonly occur among people who spend long hours typing at a keyboard and staring into a computer monitor. As the name implies, the injury results from repetitive (continual) motion or action. Typing at a keyboard for a prolonged period, for instance, has been cited as a cause of carpal tunnel syndrome (CTS). The repeated keystroke activity can lead to swelling of the thumbs and wrists, if care is not taken.

Perhaps your school library has information about the proper positioning of your monitor, keyboard, and chair to reduce eyestrain and muscle fatigue. The Occupational Safety and Health Administration website also provides checklists, diagrams, photos and a variety of strategies to help you "create a safe and comfortable workstation." Type the keyword "ergonomics" into the website's search box to find detailed information.

Also remember to take appropriate stretch breaks and eye breaks. Simply standing up, stretching, and walking away from the computer screen for a couple of minutes can reduce fatigue.

PERSONAL PORTABLE STORAGE AREA

Whether you use a book bag, purse, or some other item to carry your books and supplies to class, the item should be both effective and efficient for your needs. For instance, a book bag can be an effective tool for carrying your materials. But if retrieving something from the deep recesses of the bag proves time consuming and frustrating, then perhaps the manner in which you are using the bag is not efficient. Make sure that any tool, such as a calendar or book bag, serves your purposes:

- **Type of bag.** Consider using a bag that has a few compartments. With such a bag you can effectively separate books, assignments, a laptop, tablet, or cell phone as well as supplies like paper and pens.
- **Identification.** Have some form of identification attached to your bag, in case you ever forget it in a classroom or somewhere else.
- **Nightly review.** Each night, empty the book bag to make sure you have not overlooked an important piece of paper that you shoved into the bag earlier in the day. Once you complete this, pack the bag for the next day. Place it where you will not forget it in the morning when you leave for class.
- **Car.** If you use your car as a storage area, consider placing a plastic or vinyl tub (with a lid) in the trunk. The tub will protect and keep your materials in one neat location. When you place valuables in the backseat, they are easily visible to would-be thieves. The trunk, while not totally invulnerable, offers a bit more security.

ORGANIZATION AND STRESS

Disorganization—whether in the way you manage your priorities or the way you keep your work and storage areas—can create stress. Because stress is emotionally and physically draining, it makes sense to develop strategies that will help limit the stressors in your life.

TYPES OF STRESS

Stress can compromise the integrity of your body. When we refer to **stress**, we typically describe how our bodies react to external and internal pressures. Physiologically, stress represents a time of extreme arousal in the body. Blood pressure can rise, the heart and pulse beat more rapidly, the body can perspire, and clear thinking may become more difficult.

While some stressors can be beneficial, continual exposure to stress can lead to physical ailments or emotional trauma—both of which will compromise the integrity of your body.

STRESS SIGNALS

Stressors differ from person to person. Your body will give you clues when something is wrong. Some of the more common signals include the following (Smith, et. al.):*

- Cognitive symptoms, such as being anxious, having memory problems, and worrying at an unusually high level.
- Emotional symptoms, such as irritability, moodiness, and a sense of isolation.
- Physical symptoms that include headaches, rapid breathing, and chest pain.
- Behavioral symptoms that appear as anger, changes in eating habits, and abuse of alcohol or drugs.

*This list is not meant to be diagnostic. Seek professional assistance as needed.

Table 3.5 **Suggestions for Reducing Stress**

Develop a support network.	Reinterpret situations in a more positive light (reframe).
Examine your belief system.	Take a break and relax.
Exercise regularly.	Take breaks for peak performance.
Get a good night's sleep.	Engage in healthy recreation.
Learn to say "no" if saying "yes" will overwhelm you.	Concentrate on your breathing—slower, deeper, and longer.
Limit your intake of caffeine (a stimulant).	Practice guided imagery.
Maintain a sense of humor.	Meditate or pray.
Maintain realistic expectations.	Talk with a trusted friend or mentor.

Source: Based on Posen, April 1995.

SUGGESTIONS FOR REDUCING STRESS

As with stress signals, strategies for reducing stress are individualistic. What works for one person may not work for another. Table 3.5 provides a few of the most common healthful and legal suggestions. Some other strategies, while they may reduce stress in the short run, have unhealthy consequences in the long term:

- Drinking alcohol to excess
- Abusing drugs
- Promiscuous sexual activity
- Smoking
- Binge eating

Pause for a moment and consider the healthy and not-so healthy strategies you have used to deal with the stressors in your life. What is working for you, what is not working for you, and what can you do moving forward? This might be a good place to apply the Two-Minute Drill (refer back to Activity 3.5 above).

Chapter SUMMARY

Organized people respect their time. They know it is a precious resource, and they refuse to waste it.

Before leaving this topic, keep the following points in mind:

- You cannot control or create time. However, you can effectively use time for your benefit.
- What you spend your time on indicates your priorities.

- The more classes you take, the more demands you have placed on your time.
- Procrastination can rob you of your time and derail your goals.
- Organize your personal and portable spaces outside the classroom.
- Organizing time and space will help to limit the chaos and stress in your life.

CRITICALLY THINKING
What Have You Learned?

At the beginning of this topic, you read about Marie. She has taken a full load of classes—and she is not coping well.

Let's apply what you learned with this material to help Marie. However, before you dive into Marie's problem and propose your solution, take a moment to think about the main points of the topic. Review your notes from this topic and also the key terms, learning outcomes, boldface headings, and figures and tables.

TEST YOUR LEARNING

Now that you have reviewed the main points, reread Marie's story. Pretend that you are Marie's mentor. Using the R.E.D. Model for critical thinking, help Marie critically review her concerns.

**Recognize
Assumptions:**

Facts: What are the facts in Marie's situation?

Opinions: What opinions do you find in this situation?

Assumptions: Are Marie's assumptions accurate?

**Evaluate
Information:**

Help Marie compile a list of questions that will help her make the most appropriate decisions.

What emotions seem to be motivating Marie at this time?

Is anything missing from Marie's thought process?

Do you see any confirmation bias?

**Draw
Conclusions:**

Based on the facts and the questions you have presented, what conclusions can you draw?

What advice do you have for Marie? What solutions do you propose?

Based on your suggestions, do you see any assumptions?

Finally, based on what you know about using critical thinking, problem solving, and priority management, what plan of action do you suggest for Marie?

Information LITERACY

4

The Case of JAYNE

Jayne is close to graduation and has begun applying for jobs. She has diligently built a portfolio that shows examples of her talents and skills. The campus career center has helped her develop a dynamic résumé. She just completed a workshop on interviewing strategies. "I am ready to tackle the job market," she recently told her advisor. While she has a solid academic record and an impressive portfolio, she is concerned about something that is not reflected in her college transcript or résumé.

Last week, one of her instructors did a presentation on "digital tattoos." They are not the kind of tattoos that people put on their skin but the kind that mark people on the Internet.

Jayne constantly uses social media sites. She "tweets" regularly, updates her social networking site hourly, and posts photos and videos of her

Key Terms

Academic integrity
Blogs
Citation
"Digital tattoo"
Information literacy
Interlibrary loan
Keyword search
Online profile
Plagiarism
Reference librarian
Search engines
Social media
Status updates
Surfing the Web
Texting
World Wide Web

INTRODUCTION
Chapter

Have you ever considered how much information is produced worldwide in one year? One study (Lyman & Varian, 2003) discovered that the amount of information stored on disks, film, and paper doubled in less time than it would take a student to complete an undergraduate degree. In fact, according to one estimate, enough new information is produced annually to create a 30-foot-high pile of books for each person in the world.

Author Erik Qualman (2010) found that as early as 2003 the World Wide Web (WWW) already contained 17 times the volume of information found in the print collections of the Library of Congress.

outings with friends on a regular basis. She always says, "I only share this stuff with people I am 'friends' with. So, there is no harm, because they would never do anything to hurt me. Anyway, I can always delete items I don't like. And if someone 'tags' me in a photo, I can always 'untag' that photo. No big deal at all."

Now Jayne is reconsidering. Her instructor shared news stories of how employers use Internet searches to find out about applicants. He even showed the class how a few clicks on a popular search engine could turn up photos and videos—things Jayne thought were private on the Internet. While she has not done anything illegal or unethical, she is concerned that an employer will view her photos and words out of context and that that could have a negative impact on her job hunting and future career.

CRITICALLY THINKING
about *Jayne's* situation

You are Jayne's career counselor. What strategies would you suggest for her to follow?

Because there does not appear to be any slowdown in this phenomenal explosion of and access to a wealth of information, a number of challenges present themselves. For instance, just because information is increasing in volume does not mean it is increasing in quality. How can you separate the credible from the absurd? How will you know which sources have the best information? Or, more practically, what is the most effective way to trim the vast number of sources to a workable few? Do you know where to look for what you need? Do you know where you will find the information

MyStudentSuccessLab

MyStudentSuccessLab (www .mystudentsuccesslab.com) is an online solution designed to help you 'Start strong, Finish stronger' by building personal and professional development.

to support your viewpoints or intelligently challenge the views of a classmate or an instructor?

Being information literate goes beyond knowing how to ferret out the best research for a term paper. Social media and new technologies have added a new dimension to information literacy as they can let anyone communicate with hundreds, thousands, or millions of people in an instant. How do you know if the information posts you read on blogs, tweets, and status updates are factual?

This chapter will explore strategies that will help you efficiently and effectively locate, evaluate, and use the vast storehouse of information around you. It also will provide insight on how to navigate the world of social media effectively.

Activity 4.1

Reflecting on Your Current Level of Information-Literacy Skills

Before you answer the items that follow, reflect on your current level of information-literacy skills. Think of how well (or poorly) you have used these skills in the past.

There are no "right" answers for the questions that follow. As you do in completing all of the reflective activities with this topic, you should write from your heart. It is not meant for you to answer just like your classmates or to match what you may think your instructor wants to see. Take your time to give a respectful and responsible general accounting of your experiences with information literacy. Conducting a truthful self-assessment now will help you build on skills you have while developing those you lack.

For each of the following items, circle the number that best describes your typical experience with information-literacy skills. Here is the key for the numbers:

0 = never, 1 = almost never, 2 = occasionally, 3 = frequently, 4 = almost always, 5 = always

When considering your past successes and challenges with information literacy, how often . . .

1.	Did you understand what information you needed to locate to complete a project?	0	1	2	3	4	5
2.	Did you know where to look for information to complete your project?	0	1	2	3	4	5
3.	Did you evaluate information you found for accuracy?	0	1	2	3	4	5
4.	Did you find enough appropriate information to complete a project?	0	1	2	3	4	5
5.	Were you able to determine whether the information you found was well-rounded and objective?	0	1	2	3	4	5
6.	Were your projects completed responsibly and honestly, according to the standards of academic integrity?	0	1	2	3	4	5
7.	Did you protect (and not give out) your personal information on social media sites, chat rooms, or blogs?	0	1	2	3	4	5
8.	Did you maintain integrity and dignity when sharing on social media?	0	1	2	3	4	5

Add up your scores for items 1 through 8. Divide by 8. Write your answer here: ....

Using the key provided to explain each number (0, 1, 2, 3, 4, 5), complete this sentence: When it comes to information literacy, I _____ use information, technology, and social media in an effective manner.

Based on your answers, what insights have you gained about your experiences with information literacy?

FOUR STEPS TO COMPLETING AN ASSIGNMENT IN AN INFORMATION-LITERATE MANNER

Today's complex informational system creates challenges. The key is to know where to look for information and how to separate the good from the bad, the informative from the misleading. As an information-literate person, you have command of four facets of **information literacy**—knowing what information you need, where to find it, how to evaluate it, and how to use it properly. These are illustrated in Figure 4.1 (Association of College and Research Libraries, 2006).

Figure 4.1

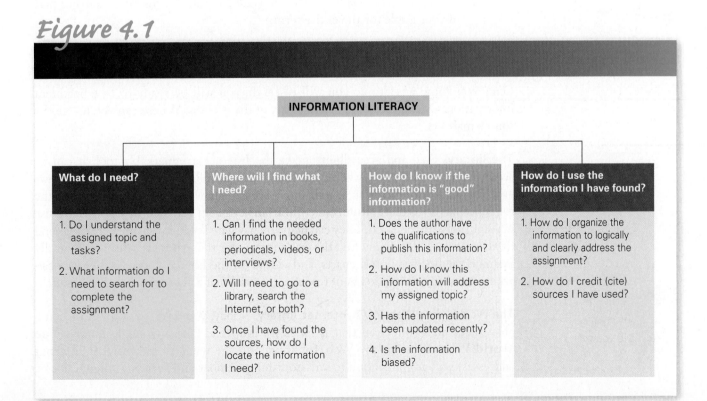

INFORMATION LITERACY

What do I need?	**Where will I find what I need?**	**How do I know if the information is "good" information?**	**How do I use the information I have found?**
1. Do I understand the assigned topic and tasks?	1. Can I find the needed information in books, periodicals, videos, or interviews?	1. Does the author have the qualifications to publish this information?	1. How do I organize the information to logically and clearly address the assignment?
2. What information do I need to search for to complete the assignment?	2. Will I need to go to a library, search the Internet, or both?	2. How do I know this information will address my assigned topic?	2. How do I credit (cite) sources I have used?
	3. Once I have found the sources, how do I locate the information I need?	3. Has the information been updated recently?	
		4. Is the information biased?	

This simple four-step process is not new for you. You have been doing this sort of thing for years. When you looked for information about a computer or a car, when you prepared a report for a class or your boss, and when you analyzed information about a political issue, you were using information-literacy skills.

Step #1. KNOW WHAT INFORMATION IS NEEDED

Knowing what information you need is a basic but often rushed step. Before digging through the library or surfing the Internet, be sure you understand what to look for.

Take, for example, the following assignment, which could be given in a history class:

Write a 10-page paper identifying and explaining five major consequences of World War II. The sources you use must include at least five books, three periodicals, and two nonprint sources. The paper is due two weeks before the final exam. The paper will be worth 25 percent of the final course grade.

By asking yourself a few simple questions, the nature of the assignment becomes clearer:

- What do I need to do?
  - *Write a 10-page paper*
- What is the topic, and what information do I need to locate?
  - *Identify and explain five consequences of World War II*
- What types of source material must be used?
  - *At least five books*
  - *At least three periodicals*
  - *At least two nonprint sources*
- When is the paper due?
  - *Two weeks before the end of the term* (You can enter this on your calendar.)
- How much is this assignment worth?
  - *Twenty-five percent of the final course grade* (In other words, this is a major part of your grade for the entire term.)

Step #2. ACCESS THE INFORMATION

Once you know what topic you will research, you will be ready to find pertinent information. One question guides this part of the process: Where can you locate the source material?

The library. Ease and accessibility make the Internet a remarkable tool. It can be accessed from virtually anywhere, and it connects to millions of sites. At times, however, you may need to or wish to walk into a library, talk with the librarians, and use the reference materials there. **Reference librarians** can help you identify keywords to use in your information search. They can help you navigate the library's online catalogs and databases as well. Once you find the call numbers for the materials, you can physically examine the books, photos, charts, and videos on the library shelves. Librarians can arrange for **interlibrary loans** of resource material that is located in another library.

The World Wide Web 24/7 Internet library. Today, you have the option of being able to search a collection that is far more immense than any single library. **The World Wide Web** (or the Web, for short and the www. found in most Internet addresses) is your connection to an astonishing number and variety of digital books, articles, nonprint sources, and personal communications. When accessed effectively, this information brings power to the hands of the users. But unfocused use of this vast resource can result in a huge waste of time.

If you were looking for information quickly and did not care about its quality, you could locate a dizzying array of information with only a few clicks of a computer mouse. However, ease does not always equal quality.

Apply the R.E.D. Model for critical thinking here, and you will have a better chance of separating the fact from the fiction—the good from the bad. That is, recognize assumptions you may make about types and locations of source material; evaluate the information you locate before using it; and draw conclusions from your research about what else you need to do to complete your assignment. The key is to know where to look for information, how to differentiate the credible from the misleading, and how to do this effectively and efficiently. The Internet can be intoxicating with its layers upon layers of texts, photos, videos, and audio recordings. One click of the mouse leads to another—and before you know it an hour has elapsed, and you have not gathered much of substance for your paper.

"Surfing the Web," as this activity is known in popular usage, has come to describe an aimless ride through cyberspace, following one link to another without much thought or direction. Therein lays a potential calamity for the uninformed or unfocused user.

Although this can be entertaining (and may uncover useful information), it does not help a college student who has multiple classes, a job, and a number of research papers to complete in a short time.

Not all information on the Internet is created equally. Some websites provide expert and scholarly analysis, while others post inflammatory personal opinions with little substance and support. Some sites promote particular products, services, or causes (Riedling, 2002, p. 72). Be aware what the sites represent. Use your critical thinking to separate the good from the bad.

Literally billions of pages of information can be found using the Internet. The use of **search engines** provides the strategy for a clearly focused information search. Use search engines for on-campus collections found in the library, or use them on the Internet to assist in gathering information related to your assignment or task. Search engines speed the search process by allowing you to find material related to the area of your research instantaneously. The Internet offers a variety of search engines like Google, Yahoo, Altavista, Bing, Dogpile, and Ask.

Once you find information through a search engine, you still have to determine its credibility. Databases tend to control for accuracy with peer reviews and the like. Libraries typically subscribe to a number of these (professional journals and newspapers are two examples). Usually, a password is required to access a library's database. Once again, the reference librarian will prove invaluable by helping you obtain the password and recommending the best databases to use based on your topic.

Search engines have unique appearances. Some open with a page full of columns, colors, and information. Others prefer a more minimalist approach, showing a few basic links on the homepage. Which is best will depend on your personal preferences. For instance, do you like a site that looks clean and neat but requires you to dig down a few "layers" by clicking through one, two, or three pages to get what you want? Or would you prefer a site that provides a lot of information with a variety of links right on the homepage?

Besides preferring a certain look of a site, you will come to prefer a site based on the good fortune you experience each time you search for information.

Whether you search for information from your campus library or conduct an Internet search from your personal computer, phone, or tablet, one of two things usually happens: Either you find very few sources, or you quickly turn up hundreds if not thousands. In the first instance, you may be frustrated by the lack of pertinent material. But in the second instance, too much information can leave you overwhelmed.

Exploring the holdings of your campus library or the Internet can be maximized with a **keyword search**, in which you use a descriptive word or phrase to help you find material on your topic. This type of search can uncover books, periodicals, and nonprint materials.

One strategy to broaden or narrow your search uses one of three words: AND, OR, or NOT. Using OR will expand your search to turn up as many hits as possible. The connector words NOT and AND will limit the number of hits received on a topic; they are valuable to use if your initial keyword search turned up more sources than you wanted. Another effective strategy is to use quotation marks (" ") to limit your search to a particular series of words and in that particular order. Surround your keywords with quotation marks and your search will uncover only sources with those words in that exact order. Your reference librarian can help with the many options available to you.

Step #3. EVALUATE THE INFORMATION

Once you locate information on the Internet, you must evaluate the information. How do you know if the information is credible? On the Internet, there is no guarantee of a "consistent and reliable" peer-review process (Riedling, 2002, p. 61). When evaluating information (the second step of the R.E.D. Model), consider these generally accepted four criteria:

1. **Accuracy and authority.** Is the site precise and expert? What experience (credentials) does the author have? Is there a sponsoring site or organization? What do you know about that organization?
2. **Objectivity.** Is the site impartial and balanced? Is the material factual, unbiased, and in-depth?
3. **Currency.** Is the site up to date and current? Is there a copyright date? (This indicates ownership; it does not indicate credibility or accuracy, however.) Has the site been recently updated, or is the information old?
4. **Scope.** Does the site provide an in-depth review of the topic, or is it a superficial overview with broad, general statements?

Activity 4.2

Evaluating a Website Article about Employer Internet Searches

The Internet provides a wealth of information. But some sites are not very accurate or credible. This short activity will help you review the Internet with a critical eye, incorporating the four criteria of accuracy, objectivity, currency, and scope.

For this activity, open a search engine of your choice and look for an article about employers using the Internet to gather information about job applicants. Once you have settled on an article, read it and complete the following items on page 65.

1. What is the common name of the site? (This is usually found on the homepage.)

2. What is the exact URL? This is the address (location) of the site. It will typically begin with http:// or http://www. (Note: When entering a URL, if only one character is incorrect, the site may not be located.)

3. What main point is the article attempting to prove? List three facts the article presents. What assumptions do you identify?

4. Accuracy and authority: Can you rely on the information you find on this site?

   a. Who is the author of the site?

   b. What evidence is provided on the site that the author is qualified to publish this material?

   c. What are the author's credentials? Include any affiliations (e.g., university professor, government agency). If none are listed, state that.

   d. Why do you or don't you trust this site?

5. Currency: Is the article current? When was it last updated?

6. Scope: Explore some of the links of this site. A link takes you immediately to another page (or another place on the same page) when you click your mouse on it. What types of links exist?

7. Objectivity: Discuss one of the links in detail. In what way is the information biased or slanted?

8. Would you recommend this site to other students? Why or why not?

9. Briefly summarize what you learned from this site.

10. What questions do you still have about this topic? Who could help you with these questions?

Step #4. USE THE INFORMATION

Contrary to popular belief, *knowing* information is not power. The responsible *use* of information is what can bring power. The information you find in your research must be conveyed in a clear and convincing manner. When you either deliver a classroom presentation, write an analysis of a current event, or describe the features of a new cell phone or tablet, what and how you communicate the information will have an impact on the power or impact it has.

Consider the history term paper described earlier in this chapter. Let's assume you had to complete that paper as an actual assignment. You put in a number of hours figuring out exactly what you were going to research; you found appropriate information in the library, on the Internet, or both; and then you determined what information was suitable for your final product. Now you have to do something credible with your research.

The presentation—how you use your information—is critical. No matter how much you may know, the impact of your knowledge will be minimal if the information is not clearly and thoroughly presented. At a minimum, do the following:

- Complete the final product in the format required by the instructor: length of the paper, cover page, illustrations, bibliography, and so forth.

- Before you turn in your final product, be sure that what you have written (the content) reflects what the instructor asked for in the assignment.

- Ask someone you respect to review your paper critically, evaluating the organization and content of the presentation as well as grammar and spelling. Ideally, this should be someone who is a better writer than you.

Activity 4.3

Post-Writing Checklist

Sometimes it is difficult for us to see our own mistakes. We either miss them or do not recognize them as errors. To us, they look right. We may spend so much time with a particular assignment that we miss errors that are readily apparent to others. These are reasons that another set of eyeballs can help notice and eliminate some common errors.

Use the following checklist to review your own paper before you submit it to your instructor:

1. Did you correctly interpret the instructions?
   ☐ Did you understand each important word in the prompt?
2. Does your paper have a clear introduction (main idea)?
   ☐ Is there a topic?
   ☐ Is an opinion (or thesis) presented about what your paper will prove?
   ☐ Did you present a brief "road map" of how you will prove your argument?
3. Is all of your support relevant to the topic and the opinion? Always ask yourself, "Why is this fact or paragraph important? How does it support the purpose of the paper?"
4. Are your conclusions based on support, or is the paper full of unsubstantiated glittering generalities? Be specific and state your case clearly.
5. Does the paper follow a logical path?
   ☐ Do subsequent paragraphs connect with the information introduced in the first paragraph?
6. Have you checked your grammar and sentence structure?
   ☐ Do subjects and verbs agree?
   ☐ Are you using the correct words to express your thoughts?
7. Are your writing style and wording appropriate for your audience? That is, is the presentation suitable for the person(s) who will read the paper?
8. Is the paper neat?
9. Have you cited all your sources?
10. Read your paper aloud. Listen to your words and sentences. This can be an effective way to hear grammatical errors. Even if you do not know all the grammatical rules, you may recognize when something sounds wrong.
    ☐ Do the sentences flow? Do they make sense? (Have a study partner read the paper to you.)
11. And in the category of "Simple things often get overlooked," make sure your name is on the paper.

THE SOCIALNOMICS REVOLUTION

Information literacy has traditionally been concerned with ensuring students can find their way around the library and Internet for research purposes. Today, those skills still remain important for a college student. But a new dynamic has presented itself: the world of social media.

Through most of the twentieth century, media was produced by "them" and consumed by "us." Clay Shirky (2010) points out in his book *Cognitive Surplus: Creativity and Generosity in a Connected Age* that media in the twentieth century was mostly a "single event" (p. 22): passive viewing. The producers of media were the "professionals" (p. 42). We sat in front of the TV (or newspaper or magazine) and consumed what they sent into our households.

Wow, how times have changed! In the *Socialnomics: How Social Media Transforms the Way We Live and Do Business*, Erik Qualman (2010) describes the **social media** revolution we have witnessed and continue to witness. No longer do we have to wait passively for the news to reach us. We—all of us—can now be the producers. In short, social media is the phenomena that allows for consumer-generated media. It has fundamentally transformed the way we live, relate with friends and family, conduct business, go to school, and get the news of the day.

TYPES OF SOCIAL MEDIA

Social networking enables millions of people to share information with friends and strangers around the world. Let's examine a few of the most popular technologies.

Table 4.1 **Brief Description of Selected Social Media Sites and Technologies**

The Social Media	What Is It?
Text Message	Brief typed message sent from cell phone to cell phone. Can include images. It has developed its own abbreviations ("text lingo"). On average, cell phones are used more for texting than placing phone calls ("USA Text Messaging Statistics," 2009).
Social Networking Services (like Facebook, Pinterest, Google Plus)	Individuals can share personal profiles (mini autobiographies) and images about themselves. Used by individuals and businesses.
Blogs	These include the opinions or observations of the writer (known as the blogger). May include images. Similar to what you might find in the editorial section of the local newspaper. A blogger can immediately post any material with or without supporting evidence. Companies can use blogs to distribute information and generate discussion.
Micro blogs (like Twitter and LinkedIn)	These allow for short updates. There may be a character limitation; that is, the user can only type so many letters and symbols per message. They are popular for sending quick ideas, updates, or suggestions.
YouTube	Users can create "channels," save their favorite YouTube videos, and upload videos they have created.

EFFECTIVE AND RESPONSIBLE WRITTEN COMMUNICATION IN THE INTERNET AGE

There is absolutely no question that social media has revolutionized our world. Social media sites, applications, and technologies allow us to communicate faster with more diverse groups of people in a shorter period of time than ever thought possible.

With these advancements, however, come considerations for responsible use. It is easy to get caught up in the speed and convenience of the technology and lose your good sense. Let's take a quick look at how to be a meaningful participant and still maintain your integrity, dignity, and privacy.

APPROPRIATE COMMUNICATION: Just Because It's Fast Doesn't Mean It's Appropriate

Probably the best advice is to communicate online just like you would in a face-to-face conversation. If you would not say something to someone in person, don't post it online.

If you post an inflammatory comment at 2:30 a.m. and think better of it at 9:00 a.m., it's too late. The post has been out there and may already have been forwarded to other people. In short, once you post something publicly, you have "lost control" of that post.

EFFECTIVE E-MAIL COMMUNICATION

Of all the technologies mentioned in this chapter, e-mail communication may well be the "oldest." Regardless, remember to observe e-mail netiquette (the rules of behavior for using the Internet). When emailing your instructors, remember they are not your buddies. Be polite, get to the point, and above all, be grammatically correct. Use a salutation ("Hi Instructor Jones" for instance) and a closing ("Thank you").

RESPONSIBLE TEXTING

While texting allows for instantaneous connection, it can have negative consequences. For instance, texting during classroom lessons and business meetings creates distractions. And texting while driving is deadly.

Be mindful of where you are. Just because a text message can reach you at any time or any place does not mean you have to answer it immediately. In class, be considerate of your classmates and your instructor. When your cell phone rings (or vibrates) and you then fumble to read or send a text, everyone around you is affected.

Call it what you want to—dependency, addiction, or self-absorption—but negative technology habits may carry into the business world. Know how to use the technology—but don't let it use you.

Table 4.3 looks at some of the technologies addressed in Table 4.1. For each, you will find a strategy or two for responsible use.

Table 4.2 **E-mail Dos and Don'ts**

E-mail Dos	E-mail Don'ts
Do follow rules of grammar, punctuation, and capitalization in all e-mails.	Don't type in all lower case letters or all capital letters (the equivalent of SHOUTING!).
Do be civil.	Don't send inflammatory notes.
Do respect the privacy of your e-mail recipients' addresses and identities. If you use a distribution list, put the names in the "blind copy" (bcc) space when composing your e-mail.	Don't abuse distribution lists. You may think the latest joke or inspirational story is great, but the 150 people in your address book may not have the same taste. Some people prefer not to have their e-mail address posted publicly.
Do choose your e-mail address wisely. "Foxylady," "spoiledrotten," "studpuppy," and "Uwannabeme" may sound creative and adorable, but they may not impart the image you want.	Don't compromise your dignity or integrity. Quick test: Would you be pleased to have your username called out by the instructor in class or by an employer's secretary at a job interview?
Do use clear language. Limit your use of emoticons (symbols used to represent emotions, such as a "smiley face").	The facial expressions behind an e-mail cannot be seen; your words must speak for themselves. Rewrite or eliminate unclear passages.

Table 4.3 **Strategies for Responsible Use of Social Media and New Technologies**

The Social Media	Strategies for Responsible Use
Text Message	Texting can create a sense of false immediacy. You can respond to a text when you want; your response does not have to occur at the time you receive the text message. You can wait until after class or a business meeting.
Social Networking Services (like Facebook, Pinterest, Google Plus)	**Status updates** are like mini-blogs. People post short messages about things they have just done or are about to do. They can convey meaningful messages, funny anecdotes, or questions. They may include images or website links. Update responsibly. Ask yourself, "Am I okay with anyone—including a future employer or graduate school—seeing this update?" People who see the update could possibly share it. If someone is taking photos at a party, that person may post the photo on his or her site and "tag" you in the photo. You might "untag" the photo, but you cannot "unsend" the photo. In short, protect your privacy and that of others.
Blogs	Be factual and be relevant. Does the universe really need one more ranting blogger?
Micro blogs (like Twitter and LinkedIn)	Share something that will positively catch attention and make a difference in the world. Don't rant and don't tweet or re-tweet inappropriate comments. Remember that your feed is public. As of March 2006, all tweets become part of the Library of Congress digital collection—even the embarrassing ones!
YouTube	Just like words—and maybe even more so—a video describes who you are. Once posted, consider it to be public. You may choose to make the video "unlisted" or "private," but others may share it.

SOCIAL MEDIA AND PRIVACY CONCERNS: Common Sense Is Not Always Common Practice

You might have heard people talk of a "digital footprint." The implication is that no matter what you do online, you leave an impression. Like footprints on the beach, you leave a trace of your visit.

That is true enough. But as we discussed earlier, your online presence leaves more than a footprint in the sand. Footprints can be washed away by an incoming tide. Removing your digital presence is not that easy, however. Instead of a digital footprint, consider the metaphor of a **"digital tattoo."** It conjures up a more permanent presence. The digital tattoo you create can be found anywhere by anyone. It consists of everything you post (video, music, poetry, updates, blogs, and tweets) about yourself and everything you write in response to someone else. Since employers can access social networking sites, avoid committing potential career suicide with your online reputation (Masnjack, 2006).

Activity 4.4

How Big Is Your Digital Tattoo?

It is becoming increasingly common for employers to do Internet searches on job applicants. Find out what an employer would find out about you by doing your own search of yourself. See what (if anything) is circulating on the Web about you. Here is a quick activity to help with that search:

1. Go to your favorite search engine. Type in your name for a Web search. What appears? Is there anything surprising?
2. Type in your name again. This time, click on "Images" or "Videos." What appears on the screen? Are there any videos or photos of you? Anything surprising?

CREATING AN APPROPRIATE ONLINE PROFILE

Online sites allow a user to post an **online profile**. Your online profile provides a short representation or introduction of you for others to see. It can include information about your likes, dislikes, education, travels, career, desires, relationships, and residence. You can also post images.

People can read your profile and think, "I would like to meet that person. I would like to get to know more about him," or they can think, "What a piece of work that guy is!"

Here are a few pointers:

- Be honest. Your profile should reflect integrity and dignity.
- Be grammatically correct when using any public forum and especially if you are posting to a professional network, such as LinkedIn.

- Be appropriate in photos. Do you really want your photo to be one that looks like you have been at an all-night party? Think digital tattoo.

- Be considerate. Remain civil in your posts.

- Be appropriate in words. This goes beyond being grammatically correct. Ask yourself, "Is this how I really talk? Would I be impressed hearing this?" Be natural, and be appropriate.

- Think of your mentor. Would he or she be proud to read your profile—and would he or she proudly say, "I know that person!"

Activity 4.5

Create an Appropriate Online Profile

As you know from the opening scenario, Jayne has concerns about her online identity. This is your chance to help Jayne by showing her what is appropriate.

Type a brief (no more than 50 words) profile of yourself. What information is important to include? What should you leave out? Remember to be honest in your representation.

SOCIAL NETWORKING: Positive Habits

If you use technology in a disciplined manner, you can access information and build networks that will help you get what you need to get closer to your goals. If you use a social networking site, evaluate how you use it. Are you using it to help you manage and advance your priorities, or have you allowed it to take control of your time? Remain disciplined, and focused on your priorities.

TRANSITIONING TO FORMAL COMMUNICATION (WITH YOUR INSTRUCTORS)

You may have heard of people being bilingual or bicultural—people who easily and effectively move from one culture to another. They understand the expectations in both worlds, and they can thrive in either one.

Table 4.4 Social Networking: Use Your Time Wisely

Positive Habit	Strategy to Build the Positive Habit
Build meaningful connections with friends.	Manage your contact/friend list.
Stay in contact with your friends anywhere in the world.	Don't let social media become a time drain. Minimize the times you "check in."
Keep undivided attention on your studies during study time.	Don't access social media until you have completed your homework or other priorities.
Protect your privacy and integrity.	Keep your updates appropriate. Consider the "digital tattoo" you create.

The same holds true for your written communication. You may be able to knock out hundreds of text messages in a short period of time. You may type in all lowercase letters, use text lingo, and not use salutations or closings in correspondence with your closest friends. In the texting world that will probably be accepted (and maybe even expected).

But when you are communicating with instructors, employers, or graduate school admission representatives, the rules are different—and you will need to make the necessary transition. As English teachers have told students for years, "You have to know your audience."

Consider these additional simple strategies:

- Use a spellchecker. Depending on what you are writing, have someone proofread it for you.
- Be respectful of the person's time. Get to the point. Consider using bullet points (•) to outline information for quick reading.
- Fully identify yourself: first and last name plus any other identifier that may help the reader know who you are and why you are communicating.
- Avoid telling the reader you need him or her to do something "as soon as possible" (ASAP!). Your emergency is not the reader's emergency or drama.
- A polite thank you is always appreciated.

RESPONSIBILITIES OF THE INFORMATION AGE

ACADEMIC INTEGRITY

When students or instructors exhibit **academic integrity**, they have completed their work (research, writing, and homework) in a respectful, responsible, and honest fashion. While violations of academic integrity are not new, technology has moved cheating into cyberspace. Whether students copy material from a website and directly paste it into their own papers (without proper citation) or buy a paper from any of the various Internet "dot.com paper mills," plagiarism has become easier.

At the very least, violations of academic integrity typically result in failure for the particular assignment. But the punishments can and do become more severe. Students can fail a course, be suspended for a term, or be expelled from school. Some schools have created a grade that reflects failure due to violation of academic integrity. (For example, see "Academic Integrity Policy," 2006.)

Locate and read your school's academic integrity policy. What are your responsibilities? What possible punishments can you receive for violating the academic integrity policy?

AVOIDING PLAGIARISM

Students—and all researchers and authors, for that matter—have an obligation to respect the sources used in their research. Whether you conduct research to write a book or complete an English class assignment, certain standards of behavior are expected. This includes providing proper credit when using the words and ideas of other authors.

Such credit is called a **citation**. It generally consists of the author's name, the title of the publication, the publisher's name, the place and date of publication, and the page numbers from which the material came. Material from the Internet will need to note the URL address (www.).

When a writer, researcher, or student takes another's words or ideas and does not give credit, a theft of intellectual property has been committed. **Plagiarism** is the dishonest representation of someone else's work as your own. When writing a paper and submitting work, it is your responsibility to provide appropriate citations. That is, you must recognize your sources for their thoughts, words, and research.

Table 4.5 provides some common strategies to avoid plagiarism. Many college and university websites have detailed information on plagiarism and consequences for such a violation of academic integrity (see Procter, 2006, for one such source). Perhaps your school does as well.

Table 4.5 Strategies to Avoid Plagiarism

Topic	Question	Strategy to Avoid Plagiarism
Citation	Since I have listed all of my sources on my references page, do I still need to include citations within the paper itself?	Yes. Give credit as soon as possible after you introduce facts, visuals, quotations, opinion, and paraphrases. Depending on what you are citing—and the length of the citation—you may also need to ask for permission from the author to use the citation.
Common knowledge	What is "common knowledge"? Do I have to cite it?	It is knowledge readily found in a variety of sources and generally known by many people. "Abraham Lincoln was the president during the Civil War" is considered common knowledge and does not have to be cited. If you were to write about secret meetings Lincoln had to push the 13th Amendment through Congress, you would need to cite that. To be safe, cite when in doubt.
Opinion	I found a great opinion in my research that solidly supports my argument. Since I have the same opinion, do I need to cite the source?	Yes. If you are using someone else's thoughts, cite them.
Paraphrase	I have substantially changed the wording. I have put the author's words into my words. And I have not changed the meaning. Since these are my words, do I need to cite the source?	If you are using someone's opinion, research, or facts, you need to give credit with a citation—whether you use their exact words or not.
Public domain	I found a great source on a government website. It is in the public domain (not privately owned). Do I need to cite it?	Yes. Unless the information is common knowledge, cite the information.
Visuals	I found a great image on the Internet. Can I just copy and paste that into my paper? After all, I am not copying anybody's words.	If the work belongs to someone else—words or visuals—you still need to cite the source. In addition, in order to use many visuals, you will need to get permission from the creator. Just citing the source may not be sufficient.

(continued)

Table 4.5 **Strategies to Avoid Plagiarism (continued)**

Topic	Question	Strategy to Avoid Plagiarism
Words	If I change a few of the words from the author, do I have to use quotation marks?	If you don't use quotation marks, you are saying that the wording is your wording. If you don't *substantially change the author's words*, you need to use quotation marks. Keep in mind, when you paraphrase you cannot substantially change the meaning of the author's words.
Words	Since I have stated who the author is in the citation, do I still have to use quotation marks?	Yes, if the words are the author's words you must use quotation marks. To do otherwise would be to indicate the words are yours. Again, you may need permission to use the words.

For more in depth information on paraphrasing, please visit **MyStudentSuccessLab** (www.mystudentsuccesslab.com).

Chapter SUMMARY

Before leaving this section, keep the following points in mind:

- The information explosion has increased the availability, types, and locations of information.

- Information literacy requires a person to know what information to look for, how to find that information, how to judge the information's credibility and quality, and how to effectively use the information once it has been found and evaluated. Academic integrity demands a strict code of conduct (moral expectations) that governs the manner in which students and professors do research and behave in class.

- Your e-mails, texts, posts, and blogs represent you in cyberspace.

- Be mindful of your online privacy and dignity. The Internet is a public gathering place.

CRITICALLY THINKING

What Have You Learned?

At the beginning of this section, you read about Jayne. She was about ready to graduate and enter the job market. She was concerned that her "digital tattoo" might affect her employment search. Let's apply what you learned in this chapter to help Jayne. However, before you dive into Jayne's problem and propose your solution, take a moment and stop and think about the main points of this topic. Review your notes and also the key terms, learning outcomes, boldface headings, and figures and tables.

TEST YOUR LEARNING

Now that you have reviewed the main steps of the information literacy process, reread Jayne's story. Pretend that you are Jayne's career advisor. Using the R.E.D. Model for critical thinking, help Jayne critically review her concerns.

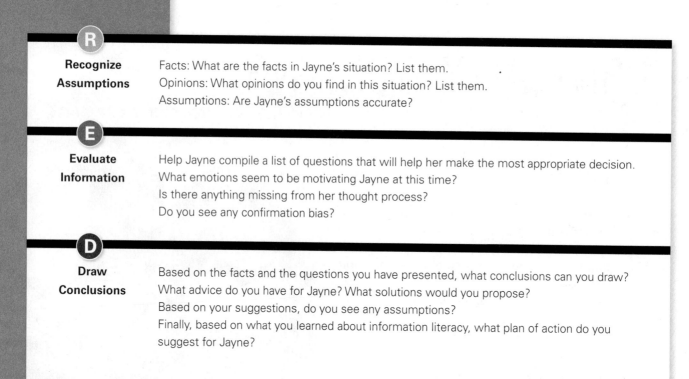

Recognize Assumptions

Facts: What are the facts in Jayne's situation? List them.

Opinions: What opinions do you find in this situation? List them.

Assumptions: Are Jayne's assumptions accurate?

Evaluate Information

Help Jayne compile a list of questions that will help her make the most appropriate decision.

What emotions seem to be motivating Jayne at this time?

Is there anything missing from her thought process?

Do you see any confirmation bias?

Draw Conclusions

Based on the facts and the questions you have presented, what conclusions can you draw?

What advice do you have for Jayne? What solutions would you propose?

Based on your suggestions, do you see any assumptions?

Finally, based on what you learned about information literacy, what plan of action do you suggest for Jayne?

Motivation 5
and ACHIEVING
Your GOALS

LEARNING OUTCOMES

By the time you finish reading this material and completing its activities, you will be able to do the following:

- List and describe the major motivating force in your life.

- Identify a motivational barrier and create at least one strategy to overcome it.

- Create a goal statement that includes what you want to do, how you will do it, why you will do it, and when you will accomplish it.

The Case of DOMINIC

Ever since Dominic could remember, he wanted to attend college. Yes, there were people—including his teachers—who had encouraged him, but something deep inside him had kept pushing him forward. He knew he needed a college education to make a good life for himself.

After the first day of classes, Dominic smiled and said to himself, "I'm here. I've achieved my dream to go to college!"

Recently, Dominic's adviser asked if he had written his long-term goals and the steps he will take to achieve those goals. Dominic had never given that much thought. Yesterday, he told a

Key Terms

Action steps
Excuse
Extrinsic motivation
Goal
Intrinsic motivation
Locus of control
H.O.G.s
Motivated learner
Motivation
Motivational barriers
Strategy
Values

INTRODUCTION
Chapter

College has been and will continue to be a series of learning experiences. You have had to find your classes, buy books, get a parking decal, locate the campus library, fight for a parking space, tackle assignments, and maybe fit in with a new roommate. At times, it might feel like you are moving in a cloud of dust. Distractions and stressors can easily become obstacles on your way to your goals.

This material will examine what motivates you to achieve your goals. When you establish a goal, you need a strategy to obtain what you desire.

friend, "If I come to class, pass my exams, and make it to the next term, isn't that good enough? I don't see the need for writing goals. It seems like a complication. After all, things change along the way."

Lately, though, Dominic has found it more difficult to remain focused on his studies. His direction seems fuzzy, and his motivation seems to be faltering. Procrastination has crept into his life, and he is falling behind in his classes. Earlier today, he confided to his advisor, "I know I have to stay motivated and remember why I am here. But staying motivated and focused on where I am going has become increasingly difficult."

CRITICALLY THINKING
about *Dominic's* situation

You are Dominic's advisor. What strategies would you suggest for Dominic to follow?

Whether you achieve the goal depends in great part on how effectively you plan and carry out your strategy.

Every successful business must have a **strategy**—a plan of action—that simply and clearly places it in an advantageous position in the marketplace. Business strategy is about making winning choices and using available resources to bring about success. The same holds true for college students. Having a well-developed plan—your strategy to reach your goals—will help you make choices that effectively use the resources you have. "Goal

MyStudentSuccessLab

MyStudentSuccessLab (www.mystudentsuccesslab.com) is an online solution designed to help you "Start strong, Finish stronger" by building personal and professional development.

setting" is the easy part of this process. The difficulty for many students lies with "goal achieving." That requires that you take appropriate action and stay motivated to reach your goals.

Motivation goes to the heart of your **values**—the things that are important to you. Your values, among other things, determine what you want to accomplish by the end of this term, end of this year—or by the end of your college experience. What do you want to gain from college? Or asked another way, why are you here (college), and what drives you to remain here?

Once you know why you are in college, it's time to focus on what you need to do. What steps do you need to take to achieve your academic and non-academic goals, and when will you take those steps? How will you stay motivated to make them become realities? The most important question to ask is this one: *What am I doing to get what I want?*

As you move toward your goals, it will be helpful to establish checkpoints to help you assess your academic choices and priorities along the way. In addition to measuring progress toward achieving each goal, you will want to reflect on the appropriateness of your goals. Ask yourself some more questions: *Is the goal I established still right for me? Is this what I want to do? Is it healthy for me?* Goals should be energizing and not betray who you are.

Activity 5.1

Reflecting on Your Current Level of Motivation and Goal-Achieving Skills

Before you answer the items that follow, reflect on your current level of motivation and goal-achieving skills. Think of how well (or poorly) you have used these skills in the past.

There are no "right" answers for the questions that follow. As you do in completing all of the reflective activities with this topic, you should write from your heart. It is not meant for you to answer just like your classmates or to match what you may think your instructor wants to see. Take your time to give a respectful and responsible general accounting of your experiences with motivation and achieving your goals. Conducting a truthful self-assessment now will help you build on skills you have while developing those you lack.

For each of the following items, circle the number that best describes your typical experience with motivation and goal-achieving skills. Here is the key for the numbers:

0 = never, 1 = almost never, 2 = occasionally, 3 = frequently, 4 = almost always, 5 = always

When considering your past successes and challenges with both motivation and goal achieving, how often:

1.	Did you establish a specific, written goal that could be easily measured?	0	1	2	3	4	5
2.	Did your goals have an established end point—a date for completion?	0	1	2	3	4	5
3.	Did your goals have specific action steps?	0	1	2	3	4	5

	0	1	2	3	4	5
4. Were you motivated to do something just because of the external reward you would receive?	0	1	2	3	4	5
5. Were you motivated to do something because of how it made you feel inside?	0	1	2	3	4	5
6. Did you expect what you did would affect what happened to you?	0	1	2	3	4	5
7. Did you establish goals that made you stretch—that were not easy to attain?	0	1	2	3	4	5
8. Were you able to identify a motivational barrier and then do something to overcome it?	0	1	2	3	4	5

Add up your scores for items 1, 2, 3, and 7. Divide by 4. Write your answer here: _____

Using the key provided to explain each number (0, 1, 2, 3, 4, 5), complete this sentence: When it comes to my goals, I _____ establish clearly stated specific goals that make me stretch and grow.

Add up your scores for items 4, 5, 6, and 8. Divide by 4. Write your answer here: _____

Using the key provided to explain each number (0, 1, 2, 3, 4, 5), complete this sentence: When it comes to motivation, I _____ am aware of what motivates me and how to take charge of my motivation.

Based on your answers, what insights have you gained about your experiences with motivation and goals?

MOTIVATION

Motivation moves you to act on or toward something. It can come from within you (this is known as intrinsic), or it can be the consequence of some outside force that drives you forward (known as extrinsic).

Before you ever set foot on your college campus, you had ambitions—and you acted on those ambitions. For instance, one of those aspirations was to attend college. You made choices and took actions to make that happen. And here you are, just as you wanted to be. Motivation provided the fuel, the energy, to move toward your goal: to go to college.

WHERE DO YOU FIND MOTIVATION?

Motivation varies from person to person depending on the opportunities, challenges, tasks, activities, and life experiences he or she faces. An athlete's love for sports may motivate her to get to practice early and remain late. A student who did not do as well on a reading quiz as he would have liked pushes himself to improve by ten points on the next quiz. Maybe you know a single parent who attends school at night, works a full-time job during the day, is the treasurer for her child's school PTA—and awakens early each day to study for her college classes.

These are motivated individuals pursuing their goals. But what creates the drive to accomplish these activities? Where does the drive come from?

EXTRINSIC AND INTRINSIC MOTIVATION

The single mother who is a student may be moved intrinsically, extrinsically, or both. Table 5.1 provides a glimpse into her motivations.

Table 5.1 **Intrinsic and Extrinsic Motivation**

	Why? Intrinsic Motivation	Why? Extrinsic Motivation
Attends school at night	She has always wanted to be the first in her family to get a college degree. She has always loved reading and learning.	The only way she can advance in her job and get a pay raise is to have a college diploma.
Works a full-time job	She loves her job and would like to become a supervisor.	She has a child to raise and rent to pay each month.
Serves as a treasurer for her child's school PTA	She is able to plan activities that will benefit the children of the school. It gratifies her to watch the children laugh and play with new playground equipment that the PTA has purchased.	She was told volunteer work would look good on her resumé.
Awakens early each morning to study	She loves the classes she is taking and thirsts for as much knowledge as she can retain.	She has to maintain a C average if she wants to keep her financial aid.

Obviously, this single mother is driven by a variety of factors. Whether they are intrinsic or extrinsic, they bring her closer to her goal of college graduation.

Let's make this a little more personal. Think about the beginning of this school term. Your instructors outlined course expectations, like class attendance, in their syllabi. Do you attend class regularly because you enjoy the lectures, discussions, and classmates (intrinsic motivation) or because you know that attendance counts toward your grade (extrinsic motivation)?

Consider that even if you do something for extrinsic reasons, it is connected to what you want intrinsically. Take the previous example. If you go to class because it counts toward your grade, the grade is extrinsic. However, the fact that you consider a grade valuable may be tied to your intrinsic motivation. Perhaps it represents the value you place on your work ethic, or maybe the grade is a reflection of how you view yourself. Something inside you moves you to want that grade.

CHARACTERISTICS OF A MOTIVATED LEARNER

Can an individual learn to be motivated? If you understand your motivation, you can more effectively evaluate your behavior—and begin to make changes, as needed. Table 5.2 breaks the behavior of motivated learners into five distinct parts (VanderStoep & Pintrich, 2003, pp. 40–41).

Table 5.2   **Characteristics of a Motivated Learner**

Behavior of a Motivated Learner	Explanation
Choice	Whatever the opportunity cost you have paid to attend college, you came here for a reason(s). You were motivated to make this choice.
Effort	As a motivated individual, you choose to make your goals happen. You take action.
Persistence	Simply put, this trait is known as "stick-to-itiveness." You can stick with a task until you complete it.
Engagement	Like people engaged to be married, as an engaged student, you choose to be committed to your work.
Achievement	Finally, if the preceding four characteristics—choice, effort, persistence, and engagement—are all present, you have increased your chances of moving closer to the goal.

Activity 5.2

Self-Monitoring Check: Are You a Motivated Learner?

Reflect on a time you were committed to something. You may have been an athlete on a team, a member of a club, an officer in student government, a musician in a band, or playing a role in some other activity on which you worked diligently. Answer the following questions.

1. Exactly why were you committed to the task? What characteristics of motivation (choice, effort, persistence, engagement, and/or achievement) were present?

2. Who helped to keep you moving toward your results? Was someone or something else driving you (extrinsic motivator), or did some force within you (intrinsic motivator) drive you forward?

3. What did you do to maintain your level of commitment over time?

OVERCOMING MOTIVATIONAL BARRIERS

At times, you cannot control the external forces that stand between you and what you would like to achieve. Whether it's an instructor's expectations, a demanding employer, or the state of the economy, we'll put those factors aside for now. Instead, your target for this section will be those things you can control. Let's examine motivational barriers that may sidetrack your progress—if you allow them to do that.

Attitude Think of something you have had difficulty staying motivated to achieve. Maybe you have not been able to get to the gym as often as you would like each week. Or perhaps you have not lost the weight you had hoped to shed this year. Listen to your words (Miller, 2005, pp. 44–47).

Consider these statements:

■ "I hope to lose weight."
■ "I will try to lose weight."
■ "I think I will be able to lose weight."

Compare them with the following statements:

■ "I will lose weight."
■ "I shall lose weight."
■ "I pledge to lose weight."

These latter statements present more forceful and more positive sentiments. Using this language of action states the point (the goal) in a very definite manner.

Suggestion: Listen to your words. They might very well reflect your attitude or commitment level. Are you using the language of commitment or the language of doubt and uncertainty? State and make the following pledge to yourself: When it comes to motivation, I will eliminate the word *try* from my vocabulary.

Get rid of those three letters. Think about the times people have told you they would try to do something. "I will try to stop by your house" or "I will try to get to the gym tomorrow" or "I will try to study more this week." Face it: Merely trying lacks commitment. Used enough, the word *try* will become an easy excuse—and a path to unachieved goals. Do you want friends who will *try* to help you or friends who will actually help you? Are you satisfied with an instructor who will *try* to be exciting in class or an instructor who is exciting in class? Would you pay a mechanic who *tried* to fix your car—but did not? How about an employer who promises to *try* and pay you? Rather than be indecisive, be decisive and move forward boldly and with purpose.

Mental paralysis Think of a ping-pong game. Two contestants paddle a small ball back and forth over a table net. One player makes an incredible shot, but the opponent makes a masterful return. Back and forth the game goes. Eventually, one player will win.

Sometimes, our minds engage in a ping-pong game of sorts. Let's call the two opponents *Yes* and *But*. Every time *Yes* presents a reason to move forward with an action, *But* skillfully returns with a reason to stay put. Back and forth the exchange goes. While *Yes* makes good attempts, the exchange can become tiring and nothing is accomplished. When *But* has been too persistent, it eventually stops the progress. Here is what such a "match" might sound like:

■ "Yes, I need to study more for my math exam."
■ "But, I really don't have any more time to devote to that class."
■ "Yes, I know that time is an issue. Still, I really must devote more time to math class."

- "But, I never have been any good at math. The extra time won't help anyway!"
- "Yes, there really is no hope. I am just a poor math student."

When used enough, *but* can be a demotivator and "erase" everything that comes before it in your sentence or thought process (Miller, 2005, p. 46).

Suggestion: Erase the word *but* from your motivational vocabulary before it erases your motivation.

Level of commitment Sometimes the initial excitement to do something fades away quickly. Maybe it is difficult to maintain motivation because you lack passion for what you want to accomplish. For instance, perhaps you committed to play intramural sports with your friends. After two weeks of practice, however, you are not excited about continuing. When you examine the issue, you recognize that you participated only because you did not want to disappoint your friends who were going to play. You also have recognized that to devote time to the sport, you have had to stay up much later each night to complete your homework and have had to give up some hours from your part-time job. After careful analysis, you decide the intramural sport is not where you need—or want—to commit your energies.

Suggestion: If you can honestly say that the cost in time, effort, or emotion to pursue a goal is more than you are willing to pay, then maybe you should look for another road to follow. Once again, pay attention to what you say—what words you use. If you continually hear yourself saying, "I *can't* do . . . ," perhaps you really are saying, "I *won't* do . . ." whatever needs to be done. The word *can't* can become another excuse—and when combined with *try* and *but*, it can be deadly to motivation and goal attainment. "I *can't* get to the tutor. I *try*—*but* just *can't!*"

That sounds like the excuse it is, even though it sounds better than "I won't go to the tutor. I did not make an appointment, so I just won't go." While that second statement sounds harsh, it may be closer to the truth. Remember, either you *do* something or you *do not*. To say you *tried* might make you feel better, but it will not get you closer to your goals.

Self-sabotage? At times, you might create your own obstacles. Sometimes, for example, two motivators might conflict with each other. For instance, perhaps you have pledged that you will earn a 3.5 *grade-point average (GPA)* this term. In addition, you have pledged to work at your part-time job as many hours as you can to save money for a car. You are motivated by the high GPA, and you are motivated by the money to buy a car. Working to get one, however, might have a negative effect on reaching the other.

Suggestion: Examine your motivators. If one seems to have a harmful effect on another, you might want to rethink what you want to do. Or perhaps look for alternatives. For instance, maybe you could work more hours on the weekends, leaving school nights for homework. Do not work at cross-purposes with yourself.

BUT, I MIGHT FAIL!

We have all heard stories of people—famous and not so famous—who failed miserably but were able to rebound from despair and achieve success. It may be hard to find the benefits in failure when it happens, but they are there.

Life is full of risks—and failed attempts. Just because you fail at something does not make you a failure. It simply means you failed at that attempt. As the story goes, Michael Jordan, arguably one of the best basketball players in the history of the National Basketball Association, did not make his high school team. If he had never rebounded from his high school failure, think of the basketball and athletic genius the world would have missed. As cliché as it sounds, the only failure in a failure is the failure to get up and do it again.

Think of what might have happened if the following individuals had not gotten up again after falling short ("Fifty Famously Successful People," 2010):

- R. H. Macy had seven businesses before his New York City store became a success.
- Actor Harrison Ford was initially told he didn't have the skills needed to be a successful actor.
- Author Stephen King's first book received more than 30 rejections.

So, the next time you do not achieve what you want and consider quitting, think of what the world might miss if you do not persevere toward your dream. Think of our ongoing question: *What are you doing to get what you want?*

UNDERSTANDING EXCUSES

To handle your excuses, you must first understand what they are and why you make them. When you use an **excuse**, you attempt to explain a particular course of action you have taken to remove or lessen responsibility or blame for a result. Generally, excuses can be traced to fears of the unknown, insecurities about the future, or a perceived inability to handle a present situation. As stated earlier, when we make excuses, we tend to fall back on *try*, *but*, and *can't* to explain why we did not take action and move forward.

LOCUS OF CONTROL

You may face one more potential obstacle—one that springs from how you see yourself in the world. Do you believe that your actions can influence the way things turn out? Do things just happen to you, or do you make things happen?

How you answer questions like these reflects your **locus of control**, a concept attributed to psychologist Julian Rotter (Mearns, 2012). It refers to how much you believe your actions can affect your future. In short, do you *expect* your actions to affect your life, or do you *wait* for someone or something to happen to you?

A simplified description of locus of control is the *focus of one's power*. Do you believe the power to control events resides within you, or do you believe events are controlled by outside forces?

A student with an *internal* locus of control, for example, explains a poor test grade by looking into the mirror and saying, "I should have studied an hour each night rather than cramming the night before the exam" or "Before the next exam, I will be sure to visit my instructor in his office." The responsibility is placed on that student's shoulders *by that* student. On the other hand, a student who is more apt to blame the instructor exhibits an *external* locus of control. Statements such as "That teacher is not fair" or "How could I possibly do well when so much material is covered each class period?" characterize a student looking to assign responsibility elsewhere.

Generally speaking, a person's locus of control can be internal *and* external. That is, there will be situations in which you exhibit an internal locus of control and other times when you are more external. As with any continuum, few people are found on either extreme. Recognize that we all face times when *other people* (external) have significant influence or control over what we will or will not do. For instance, the college or university sets the final exam schedule, and the students must adjust their own schedules to meet those dates. Most of us fall somewhere in between. But upon reflection, we notice that we tend to lean to one end or the other.

Do you generally take responsibility for your actions? Or are you someone who is more apt to blame someone else? Use this information to heighten your awareness. Pick what you can have an impact on, and then address it. You must be able to make realistic assessments of what is within your ability to change—and what is not.

ACHIEVING YOUR GOALS

WHAT IS A GOAL?

The first part of this material looked at what drives a person to a destination. Now, let's turn our attention to that result—to the goal your motivation moves you toward. Goals can be simple short-term goals, like cleaning a room, or they can be more complex long-term destinations, like becoming qualified for a particular career.

Generally, people think of a **goal** as a place they want to reach. The "place" can be academic ("I want an A in history"), it can be personal and nonacademic ("I will run and finish a five-mile race"), or it can be community oriented ("I will do volunteer work at the local animal shelter").

Activity 5.3

Critically Thinking about Your Motivation and Goal-Setting Skills

Let's apply the R.E.D. Model to your ability to stay motivated to reach your goals. Identify a best practice (something you do well) that you use to stay motivated. Then answer the questions that follow.

Critical-Thinking Step	Application to Your Motivation and Goal-Achieving Skills
Recognizing Assumptions	Examine your motivational best practice from more than one perspective (point of view). How do you know this is one of your best practices?
Evaluating Information	Explain specifically (give an example) how this best practice has helped you in the past.
Drawing Conclusions	How can your best practice help you now to reach one of your academic goals?

WHY DO YOU NEED GOALS? CONVERTING FANTASIES TO DREAMS—AND DREAMS TO REALITIES

Almost everything you have done in your life has connected directly to goal setting. For instance, have you ever done any of the following?

- Worked for a position on an athletic team?
- Decided to play a musical instrument?
- Saved your money to buy someone a gift?
- Worked with a trainer to become physically fit?
- Filled out an application for a job?
- Asked someone for a date?

If you have done any of these things or other things similar to them, you have engaged in goal setting. You have a history of goal setting and achieving. Don't forget what you have learned and remain open minded enough to examine and use some new strategies. In other words, respect your history while building your future.

Goals allow you to focus your sights on something you want to achieve, make a plan, and finally move toward that result. Effective goals, whether long term or short term, address the *why*, *when*, and *how* of our lives. If your goals lack these components, they will turn out to be daydreams or mere fantasies.

Figure 5.1

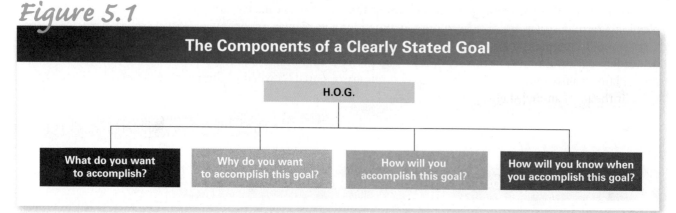

The Components of a Clearly Stated Goal

H.O.G.

| What do you want to accomplish? | Why do you want to accomplish this goal? | How will you accomplish this goal? | How will you know when you accomplish this goal? |

H.O.G.S: Huge, outrageous goals In the book *Built to Last*, Jim Collins and Jerry I. Porras (2002, pp. 93–94) describe what they refer to as "BHAGs." In their research, they found that companies that set big, hairy, audacious goals consistently outperformed their competition. In other words, these companies did not settle for making goals they could easily reach. They set goals that required effort to attain.

When setting your goals, think of the acronym **H.O.G.** (An *acronym* is an abbreviation formed by the first letters of a group of related words. You can use acronyms as memory tools.) Set a *huge, outrageous goal*. This does not mean to establish a goal that is impossible to reach. Think of it more as a reminder not to settle for something less than your best effort. If you continually set goals you can easily reach, you may never know the joy and exhilaration of stretching yourself to new heights. You may not reach the potential you are capable of fulfilling.

If you aim high and take the appropriate action steps, you may move farther than you thought possible. Yes, you may stumble. You may even fail to achieve a particular goal. Aim low (the easy way), and you will hit your mark every time—and more than likely never achieve your potential.

While it is good to have ambition and potential, without initiative, those other qualities may never be realized. Stretch! Take the initiative today to set a huge outrageous goal—and move toward the potential you have.

LONG-TERM GOALS NEED SHORT-TERM ACTIONS

Goals go beyond the classroom. In fact, goals address many issues in life. For instance, there are "personal" goals (maintaining a healthy diet), "academic" goals (completing your major), "career" goals (finding the job of your dreams), and "community" goals (making a difference in your neighborhood). These particular examples represent long-term goals. They are large goals that will be accomplished in the future. They will not be reached in a day or two. In the case of career goals, years may be required.

You may have heard a classmate say, "My long-term goal is to be rich—and my short-term goal is to get an A in my math class." While getting rich may definitely be admirable for your friend, he or she has a lot of ground to cover between getting an A in math and amassing riches for life. For our example here, let's consider an A in math as the long-term goal for this term—and one that may move you a step closer to your dream of being rich.

WHAT DOES A CLEARLY STATED GOAL LOOK LIKE?

A useful goal—as opposed to a mere fantasy—must provide the means to help you reach your desired destination (Wilson, 1994, pp. 4–9).

The first step to achieve your goal involves developing a clear *goal statement*—a concrete step to make your dreams become reality. One easy-to-remember model uses the acronym SMART (Chastain, 2012). That is, goals need to be specific, measurable, attainable/achievable, realistic/relevant, and timely.

A clearly stated written goal has the properties shown in the following table. Remember to state precisely what you want to achieve. Once it has been put in writing, it becomes an affirmation of intent. Put it where you will see it every day.

Table 5.3 Properties of Goals

Clear Goals Are	Description of the Goal Characteristic
1. **S**pecific and **M**easurable	Exactly what will be accomplished? Saying "I want to have a better English grade" is admirable, but it is incomplete. How do you define *better*? If your current grade were a D, would you be satisfied with a D+ (which, after all, is better than a D)? By *how much* do you wish to raise your grade? By *when*? How will you know when you have achieved the goal? Here is a much clearer statement: "I want to get a B in my English class by the end of the semester." There is no doubt as to what you want to accomplish and when you will achieve it.
2. **A**ttainable and **R**ealistic	It should be challenging, yet achievable. Saying you will raise your English grade from an F to an A by the end of the week is not realistic. Challenge yourself, but do not frustrate yourself.
3. **T**imely	Place a go-to point on your goals. That is, set a date by which you would like to achieve the goal. Again, be specific. Rather than say "in the next month or two," state you will reach your goal by the last day of the month. Then, move toward your goal with specific, measurable, manageable, and responsible **action steps**. For many people, taking a bite-size move forward is not as overwhelming as heading toward a more complex and long-range goal. These action steps get a person moving in the right direction. Taking specific action steps will help you mark your progress, systematically, toward your ultimate goal. If one of your academic goals is to get an A in your English class by the end of the term, action steps may include finding a study group, attending tutoring sessions, or visiting the instructor once a week with specific questions.

Goals should also be anticipatory—anticipate that there may be obstacles along the way. Don't become paranoid or obsessive about potential problems, but do consider that you may encounter some problems on your journey. If you do, obstacles will less likely surprise or demoralize you.

Finally, provide appropriate rewards for yourself as you make progress. In fact, establish a schedule of incentives (rewards) that coincide with your "bite-sized" action steps. The reward should be healthy, legal, and ethical—and provide you with a little "fuel" (motivation) to keep plugging away toward your goal.

An activity I do with my students and audiences around the nation will emphasize the importance of being specific with your goals. I pose the question "Who has a goal to have more money in life?" Most people raise their hands. Whether it is to pay for a college education, to pay off a debt, or to purchase a needed item, most people do want to have *more* money. I call a couple of people to the front of the room, and I place dimes in their hands. I tell them they have just reached one of their life goals. They now have *more* money than when they came into the room that day. The obvious point is that they were not thinking about a dime. They were thinking of hundreds or thousands of dollars. And here's the moral of the story: Be specific with your goals.

TIPS ON DEVELOPING YOUR ACTION STEPS

Once you have identified a goal, identify the most important steps you can take to move toward it.

- Make a commitment to take this important step as soon as possible. Can you do it tonight? Tomorrow? Do not let any day end without you having taken at least a small step toward the goal. After all, is this a priority for you or not? One motivational speaker refers to the "T-N-T" principle: Today-Not-Tomorrow (Winget, 2009, p. 129). Do not get sidetracked with procrastination.

- Be flexible yet focused. If your result is not what you had hoped for, it doesn't necessarily mean you lacked motivation. It may indicate that it's time to reevaluate your choices and then recommit your efforts. Flexibility is important. You can't control everything that will happen in college (or in life). Remain focused on your journey. Treat your goals and their action steps with respect, but understand that you may need to make adjustments. Sometimes not getting what you want might be positive as you will be forced to look in a new (and possibly better) direction. Remain flexibly focused.

- Be willing to ask for help. The three Fs—friends, family, and faculty—can be wonderful resources.

Here is an example of a "road map" to a goal:

Goal: To Get an A in Math by the End of the Semester	Action Steps:
	Carefully read the instructor's course description, assignment page, and any other handout. Transfer the dates to your calendar.
	Complete all assigned homework.
	Correct and rework any problems marked as incorrect on homework or tests.
	See the instructor at least once a week for extra help—for a second explanation or a chance to work additional problems.
	Find a study group and work with that group.
	Participate in class.
	Get A's on all the tests.

Activity 5.4

Establishing Action Steps to Reach Your Long-Term Goals

For this exercise, determine a long-term non-academic goal (physical, emotional, spiritual, social) *and* a long-term academic goal. Then, for each long-term goal, identify two specific action steps that will take you closer to each. As the term implies, these will be *action-oriented movements* toward your destination.

Remember to keep the goals measurable. State them in terms that will allow you to know when you have achieved them. Avoid vague terms like *better, more, harder, a lot,* and *longer.*

1. Non-academic goal. What do you want to achieve? Write two action steps to reach this personal goal. What appropriate incentive or reward will there be for you to reach this goal?

2. Academic goal. What would you like to achieve? Write two action steps to reach this academic goal. What appropriate incentive or reward will there be for you to reach this goal?

OBSTACLES, MISSTEPS, AND DETOURS

Think about your favorite movie or novel for a moment.* Can you remember the hero? That person likely started at a certain point in his or her life and ended at another at the conclusion of the story. In most novels and movies, the final scene represents some type of success or progress for the main character. However, that achievement does not occur without twists and turns of the plot. Those adventures—or misadventures— keep you turning the pages of the book or sitting in your seat watching the screen.

As the hero makes progress toward a particular goal, an obstacle presents itself and thwarts him or her from the goal. To continue requires gathering his or her thoughts, refocusing, and then moving ahead toward the goal. This continues until the final scene. The journey of the lead character has many ups, downs, and detours along the way.

Just like the hero, you, too, will probably have missteps along the way to achieving your goals. Goals are set in the *real world*. Problems, unforeseen circumstances, and "bad luck" are also part of the *real world*. Expect them, plan for them, and keep moving toward the desired result.

Here are some common obstacles as well as suggestions for addressing them (VanderStoep and Pintrich, 2003, pp. 32–35):

- **Not expecting obstacles.** If you expect to move along without any glitches and one occurs, you may become so dejected that you will give up. For instance, when planning the steps to finish a term paper, leave flexibility and time for an unexpected detour, like a computer malfunction. Being prepared for missteps or unforeseen circumstances will make you better able to handle them. They still won't be pleasant, but you will be able to remain focused in dealing with them.

- **Blaming obstacles for your lack of abilities.** It is true that bad things happen to good people. Sometimes an obstacle is beyond your control. Sometimes

*For a more in-depth discussion of this movie/novel analogy, see Beck (2001). Pay particular attention to her discussion of the change cycle.

it happens because you have never worked toward this type of goal before. You might become frustrated with a particular instructor's teaching style, or the content of a course may stretch you beyond your previous knowledge and experience. It can become too easy to say "I'm stupid" or "I don't *do* history!" Skill levels can change. Each time you enter a classroom, you bring your *old skills* to a *new situation*.

■ **Not changing your environment.** If you want to increase your biology grade by one letter grade by the end of the term, you may need to change your study environment. Or maybe the study group you work with is not right for you. Take stock of where, when, and how you are doing things, and then make a well-planned move. It may mean having to make choices about when and where to meet with your friends. Learn to say *no* if saying *yes* to a particular situation will compromise your goals. Stay committed to your goal and don't get in your own way!

W.I.N.: Do you know what's important now?   Every day, take some step toward your goal, no matter how small or seemingly insignificant. Ask yourself, What's important now for me to achieve my goal? Once you have identified the step, act on it. If you do not make progress toward your goal, no one else will.

Activity 5.5

Fix What?

R E D

Let's say you wish to lose 15 pounds. (Notice: this is a specific goal.) What's the first thing you have to do? You must understand why you are not at your optimal weight right now. That is, before you can fix the problem, you have to know what the problem is. You must recognize assumptions and evaluate information. This is a basic step for critical thinking and problem solving.

For this activity, focus on one dimension of your life (physical, emotional, intellectual, social, occupational, spiritual) that needs fixing/changing. Complete this sentence: I need to fix/change ....

....

Assumptions: Now, briefly explain how you know this change is needed. What specific facts tell you that you need to change or fix something?

Evaluating information: From the following list, choose the items that may be connected to your problem. Check as many as apply and then briefly explain your selections.

☐ Boss   ☐ Classmate   ☐ Economy   ☐ Friend   ☐ Government   ☐ Parent

☐ School   ☐ Society   ☐ Partner   ☐ Instructor   ☐ Something   ☐ Some
   administration   else   combination

Drawing conclusions: Finally, look at what items you checked. What is your connection to each one? Can you, in fact, make an immediate impact on each item you checked? Or are some more long-term and therefore not of help right now? For instance, you may believe you have gained weight because your school does not require physical education classes. Well, that may be the case. Nevertheless, you probably aren't going to change the school's requirements by the time the semester ends.

Goal: Based on the critical thinking you did in the previous item, write a goal that establishes a plan of action for what you need to fix or change.

Chapter SUMMARY

This college term will pass quickly—and another will approach just as quickly. The weeks ahead will require you to complete academic work, focus on planning, have a strong knowledge of yourself, and apply strategies to take responsibility for your time and behavior (an internal locus of control). In the end, it will be up to you to set goals, stay motivated, and achieve success. You control your fate.

Keep the following points in mind as you move with determination through your semester:

- Motivation is the driving force moving you toward your goals.
- Your locus of control influences whether you believe life will just happen to you or that you will be able to influence what happens.
- Goals provide purpose and energy to life.
- Effective goals are written, specific, measurable, realistic, and have an end point—a date for which to strive.
- Action steps need to be taken each day.
- Goals are set in the real world—and problems, unforeseen circumstances, and bad luck are also part of the real world. Expect them and plan for them.

CRITICALLY THINKING

What Have You Learned?

Let's apply what you learned in this topic to help Dominic from the opening scenario. However, before you address Dominic's problem and propose a solution, take a moment to think about the main points you have examined thus far.

Review your notes from this material as well as the key terms, learning outcomes, boldface headings, and figures and tables.

TEST YOUR LEARNING

Now that you have reviewed the main points of this topic, reread Dominic's story. Pretend that you are Dominic's advisor. Using the R.E.D. Model for critical thinking, help Dominic critically review his concerns.

R

Recognize Assumptions

Facts: What are the facts in Dominic's situation? List them.

Opinions: What opinions do you find in this situation? List them.

Assumptions: Are Dominic's assumptions accurate?

E

Evaluate Information

Help Dominic compile a list of questions that will help him make the most appropriate decision.

What emotions seem to be motivating Dominic?

Is there anything missing from his thought process?

Do you see any confirmation bias?

D

Draw Conclusions

Based on the facts and the questions you have presented, what conclusions can you draw?

What advice do you have for Dominic? What solutions would you propose?

Based on your suggestions, do you see any assumptions?

Finally, based on what you learned about motivation and goals, what plan of action do you suggest for Dominic?

Learning 6 STYLES

LEARNING OUTCOMES

By the time you finish reading this material and completing the activities, you will be able to do the following:

- Identify the preferences of your particular learning style.

- Develop practical strategies to use your learning style in class.

- Develop practical strategies to use your learning style in your life outside class.

- Apply your knowledge of multiple intelligences to develop strategies for academic success.

The Case of ALLEN

Allen is a happy and well-adjusted first-year college student. He reads his assignments, attends class, participates in all discussions, and studies for all of his exams. Unfortunately, his grades are not what he would like them to be.

On the suggestion from an adviser, Allen recently took a learning-styles assessment. Although the assessment did not reveal anything new, it reinforced that Allen was a visual learner and that he preferred a quiet and well-lit study area.

Key Terms

Attention
Auditory learning
Environmental factors
  (affecting learning)
Intelligence
Kinesthetic learning
Learning preference
Learning style
Multiple intelligences
Visual learning

Chapter INTRODUCTION

Imagine this: You walk into a doctor's office and announce, "Doc, I don't feel well. Can you give me a prescription?" Any reasonable doctor would first need to know some specifics: What are your symptoms? What medications are you taking? To what drugs are you allergic? In other words, the doctor would have to recognize you as an individual patient with characteristics that make you distinct and separate from other patients in the waiting room.

The same applies to your academic skills and strategies. While your instructor and textbook will introduce you to a variety of success strategies,

Allen knows that one of his current challenges is that all of his instructors lecture with very few visual aids. Some do not even use PowerPoint or videos. He is having difficulty staying focused in class. After about 10 minutes of a lecture, his mind wanders, and he misses notes and important points.

Allen's grades are beginning to suffer, and he is becoming discouraged. He is considering switching to all online classes to fix the situation.

CRITICALLY THINKING
about *Allen's* situation

You are Allen's advisor. What strategies would you suggest he follow?

you will want to be mindful of how you learn and be willing to examine what you have done in the past and make necessary adjustments. Just because you have developed the habit of studying this way or that does not mean that method produces the best result for you.

At times, many of our habits are not productive in terms of accomplishing tasks. We do things a certain way, well, because that is how we have always done them.

MyStudentSuccessLab

MyStudentSuccessLab (www.mystudentsuccesslab.com) is an online solution designed to help you "Start strong, Finish stronger" by building skills for ongoing personal and professional development.

The main goal of this topic is to help you become a more mindful learner. Rather than do things because that is how you "have always done them," you will be asked to examine strategies that will help you efficiently and effectively process the information you receive each day. Question old habits, build on what works, and embrace new strategies.

Activity 6.1

Reflecting on Your Learning Style

As you do in completing all reflective activities, complete Activity 6.1 from your heart. This exercise is not meant for you to answer just like your classmates—or to match what you may think the instructor wants to see. Take the time to give a respectful and responsible general accounting of your experiences with your study environment and how you prefer to learn (verbally, visually, or with movement). Conducting a truthful self-assessment now will help you build on the insights you already have while developing those you lack.

For each of the following items, circle the number that best describes your *typical* experience. Here is the key for the numbers:

0 = never, 1 = almost never, 2 = occasionally, 3 = frequently, 4 = almost always, 5 = always

When considering your past successes and challenges with learning, how often:

1.	Did you notice that a classroom lecture—when it was accompanied with photos, video, or a PowerPoint presentation—either positively or negatively affected your ability to understand the material?	0	1	2	3	4	5
2.	Did you notice that directions—when they were given verbally, without any visuals—affected your ability to understand the message?	0	1	2	3	4	5
3.	Did you notice that being allowed to do something physically with material, like create a picture or model of it, had an impact on your learning?	0	1	2	3	4	5
4.	Did you notice that the amount of lighting in a room either positively or negatively affected your ability to study or pay attention?	0	1	2	3	4	5
5.	Were you aware of how the temperature of a classroom or study space had an impact on how well you focused on the topic at hand?	0	1	2	3	4	5
6.	Did you perform better when the instructor clearly mapped out the exact steps you had to follow to complete a task?	0	1	2	3	4	5
7.	Did you notice the effect that eating or not eating a meal before an exam had on your performance?	0	1	2	3	4	5
8.	Did you notice how background noise helped or hindered your concentration?	0	1	2	3	4	5

Add up your scores for items 1, 2, 3, and 6. Divide by 4. Write your answer here: ....

Using the key provided to explain each number (0, 1, 2, 3, 4, 5), complete this sentence: When it comes to how I receive and understand information, I _____ am aware of my learning preference (for taking in or giving out information).

Add up your scores for items 4, 5, 7, and 8. Divide by 4. Write your answer here: ....

Using the key provided to explain each number (0, 1, 2, 3, 4, 5), complete this sentence: When it comes to how environmental factors affect my learning, I _____ am aware of these factors.

Based on your answers, what insights have you gained about your experiences with identifying and using your learning style?

PROCESSING INFORMATION

Brain researchers have found that the more closely we pay **attention** to something, the better chance we have of learning it. While that sounds obvious, remember that when we pay attention, we tend to concentrate on the topic, issue, or event that is before us. Studies suggest that it is common for people to mentally "check out" somewhere between 10 and 15 minutes from the start of a lecture.

Think of the implications for you. When you are attentive and engaged—that is, when you pay attention and take an active part in your course work—the chances for success increase significantly. John Medina, author of *Brain Rules: 12 Principles for Surviving and Thriving at Work, Home, and School*, reminds us that brain research proves that the more attention we give to a situation, the better the chance that learning will occur (2008, p. 74).

So, in simple terms, pay attention to the instructor, and you will have a better chance of remembering the material. However, what is simple is not always easy. You could make a great argument that "It is up to the instructor to make the class interesting enough to pay attention to." But there are things you can do to help yourself concentrate in class and beyond.

LEARNING STYLES

One way to become an engaged student is to know as much as possible about the way you learn—and then apply that knowledge to your academic tasks. When you take time to examine your **learning style**, you attempt to understand the characteristics or traits of *how* you learn. In other words, you look at what factors affect your learning. These factors may provide clues as to how you prefer to learn. For instance, students typically have a particular preference that helps them best understand the material being presented. They prefer to take in stimuli in a certain manner; and they prefer to present information in a particular way.

You may have heard someone say that she is a *visual learner* (learns by seeing photos or pictures, for instance). Another might claim to be an *auditory learner* (he has to hear something to understand it). Or some of your friends may have mentioned how **environmental factors** affect them. For instance, the following environmental factors can affect learning:

- Lighting (how the room is illuminated)
- Sound (how much silence or noise surrounds us)
- Temperature (how cool or hot the room is)
- Comfort of furniture (how soft, hard, or firm the chair is)
- Structure of time and/or task (how much time you have to sit in the classroom or in a group)
- Ability to move about (how much movement you can have while in the classroom)
- Peer interaction (who you work with during the class)

Although the material in this section just scratches the surface of a large body of research, it will provide an opportunity for you to think critically about how you best process your course materials.* Generally, you will hear about three particular preferences: auditory, visual, and kinesthetic.

Auditory learning Some individuals can listen to a verbal explanation of a task and then carry out the assignment successfully. These students receive auditory (oral) directions and translate them into a product. They prefer taking in information by using their sense of hearing. Many times, these are verbal individuals. They may find group discussions enjoyable, and they probably have a talent for explaining (or at least attempting to explain) things to others.

Visual learning Other students must see something before processing it effectively. For example, if these students had to set up a new high-definition, flat-screen television, they would find it very helpful to have diagrammed instructions (and even colorful lines and arrows) about what to do. The use of such visual aids enhances their ability to learn. If they receive only oral instructions, the process will be more difficult for them to complete. Students who gravitate to this type of learning tend to respond well to videos, photos, PowerPoint slides, and graphic illustrations.

Kinesthetic learning Other people work best by moving, handling, or manipulating objects. A student who, for instance, is better able to understand a biological principle

*A great deal has been written about learning styles and preferences. The intent here is to provide a brief overview. This chapter uses the VAK instrument to help you examine your learning style. You may also wish to examine the following sources: Nancy Lightfoot Matte and Susan Hillary Henderson, *Success, Your Style: Right- and Left-Brain Techniques for Learning* (Belmont, CA: Wadsworth, 1995); Rita Dunn and Kenneth Dunn, *Teaching Students Through Their Individual Learning Styles: A Practical Approach* (Reston, VA: Reston, 1978); Roger G. Swartz, *Accelerated Learning: How You Learn Determines What You Learn* (Durant, OK: EMIS, 1991); James Keefe, *Learning Style Handbook: II. Accommodating Perceptual, Study and Instructional Preferences* (Reston, VA: National Association of Secondary School Principals, n.d.); and Neil Fleming, "Is VARK a learning style?" *VARK: A Guide to Learning Styles.* Retrieved from http://www.vark-learn.com/english/page.asp?p=faq).

by physically *doing* a laboratory experiment learns in a kinesthetic (or body movement) manner.

This student might get more out of a lesson if he or she were able to go on a field trip to see and touch rock formations rather than simply read about them from a geology textbook. Similarly, for this student, a role-play activity may hold more interest than a lecture. Athletic competition is another example of a kinesthetic activity. Active physical engagement may tend to keep this type of learner focused and on task.

HOW DO *YOU* LEARN?

The activity that follows gives you the chance to use The VAK Learning Styles Survey. As the designer of the VAK Survey has stated,

> This survey is designed to help you gain an understanding of learning styles so that you can incorporate the various learning styles in your daily learning activities . . . it is a tool for learning-to-learn in order to increase self-awareness about your strengths and weaknesses as a learner so that you will try the various means of learning in order to choose the best one, rather than sticking with your preferred methods (Clark, 2013).

There is no right or wrong preference. There is *your* style and your preferences.

Activity 6.2

VAK Learning Styles Survey

VAK SURVEY

Read each statement carefully. To the left of each statement, write the number that best describes how each statement applies to you by using the following guide:

1	2	3	4	5
Almost Never Applies	Applies Once in a While	Sometimes Applies	Often Applies	Almost Always Applies

Answer honestly, as there are no correct or incorrect answers. It is best if you do not think about each question too long, as this could lead you to the wrong conclusion.

Once you have completed all 36 statements (12 statements in three sections), total your score in the spaces provided below.

SECTION ONE — VISUAL

_____ **1.** I take written notes and/or draw mind maps.

_____ **2.** When talking to someone else, I have a difficult time understanding those who do not maintain good eye contact with me.

_____ **3.** I make lists and notes because I remember things better if I write them down.

_____ **4.** When reading a novel, I pay a lot of attention to passages that help me to picture the clothing, description, scenery, setting, etc.

_____ **5.** I need to write down directions so that I can remember them.

_____ **6.** I need to see the person I am talking to in order to keep my attention focused on the subject.

_____ **7.** When meeting a person for the first time, I notice the style of dress, visual characteristics, and neatness first.

_____ **8.** When I am at a party, one of the things I love to do is stand back and observe the people.

_____ **9.** When recalling information, I can see it in my mind and remember where I saw it.

_____ **10.** If I had to explain a new procedure or technique, I would prefer to write it out.

_____ **11.** In my free time I am most likely to watch television or read.

_____ **12.** If my boss has a message for me, I am most comfortable when she sends a memo.

Total For Visual _____ (note: the minimum is 12 and maximum is 60)

SECTION TWO — AUDITORY

_____ **1.** I read out loud or move my lips to hear the words in my head.

_____ **2.** When talking to someone, I have a difficult time understanding those who do not talk or respond with me.

_____ **3.** I do not take a lot of notes, but I still remember what was said. Taking notes often distracts me from the speaker.

_____ **4.** When reading a novel, I pay a lot of attention to passages involving conversations, talking, speaking, dialogues, etc.

_____ **5.** I like to talk to myself when solving a problem or writing.

_____ **6.** I can understand what a speaker says, even if I am not focused on the speaker.

_____ **7.** I remember things easier by repeating them over and over.

_____ **8.** When I am at a party, one of the things I love to do is talk in-depth about a subject that is important to me with a good conversationalist.

_____ **9.** I would rather receive information from the radio, rather than read a newspaper.

_____ **10.** If I had to explain a new procedure or technique, I would prefer talking about it.

_____ **11.** With my free time I am most likely to listen to music.

_____ **12.** If my boss has a message for me, I am most comfortable when he or she calls me on the phone.

Total For Auditory _____ (note: the minimum is 12 and maximum is 60)

SECTION THREE — KINESTHETIC

_____ **1.** I am not good at reading or listening to directions. I would rather just start working on the task or project at hand.

_____ **2.** When talking to someone, I have a difficult time understanding those who do not show any kind of emotional or physical support.

_____ **3.** I take notes, doodle, and/or make mind-maps, but I rarely go back and look at them.

_____ **4.** When reading a novel, I pay a lot of attention to passages revealing feelings, moods, action, drama, etc.

_____ **5.** When I am reading, I move my lips.

_____ **6.** I often exchange words, such as places or things, and use my hands a lot when I can't remember the right thing to say.

_____ **7.** My desk appears disorganized.

_____ **8.** When I am at a party, one of the things I love to do is enjoy the activities such as dancing, games, and totally losing myself in the action.

_____ **9.** I like to move around. I feel trapped when seated at a meeting or a desk.

_____ **10.** If I had to explain a new procedure or technique, I would prefer actually demonstrating it.

_____ **11.** With my free time I am most likely to exercise.

_____ **12.** If my boss has a message for me, I am most comfortable when she talks to me in person.

Total For Kinesthetic _____ (note: the minimum is 12 and maximum is 60)

SCORING PROCEDURES. Total each section and place the sum in the blocks below:

While you prefer to learn by using the method with the highest score, you will normally learn best by using **all** three styles, rather than just your preferred learning style.

Visual	Auditory	Kinesthetic
number of points:	number of points:	number of points:
_____	_____	_____

RELIABILITY AND VALIDITY. This survey was designed as a learning tool for use in training programs, such as leadership development and learning-to-learn (metalearning), rather than as a research tool, thus it has not been formally checked for reliability or validity. However, in order to be of any use to the learners, it has to be fairly accurate. Source: Donald Clark. *VAK Learning Styles Survey.* May 13, 2013. Retrieved June 29, 2013, from http://www.nwlink .com/~donclark/hrd/styles/vak.html.

PRACTICAL APPLICATIONS

Instruments such as the VAK can provide important insights that allow you to use your critical-thinking skills. For instance, if you have difficulty in the classroom (say, paying attention), apply what you have learned from your VAK survey results. Have you been handling information in the most effective manner *for you*. If you are a visual learner but never play to that strength, you might be making things harder for yourself.

Let's assume, for example, you have to study for a quiz on the branches and functions of the nervous system. If your preferred method for learning is auditory, you could recite the information aloud to yourself in an attempt to hear and "burn" the concepts into your memory. You could also record the information into a digital recorder and then play it back.

You could just as well draw a diagram of the nervous system and physically label it as a warm-up activity for your in-class quiz. Such a study approach would encourage you to use various preferences. Drawing a diagram and then labeling the particular parts engages more of the brain than just staring at a piece of notebook paper with terms written on it. It also allows you to work kinesthetically (drawing and physically labeling the diagram) and visually (looking at the diagram and the labels).

For the remainder of this material (as well as this school term), refer to your VAK results. Use them to help you process, organize, and understand the vast amounts of information you will receive. Moreover, do not forget to use your problem-solving skills when you encounter academic challenges. If, for example, you end up with a professor whose teaching style is at odds with your learning style, first acknowledge that the difference exists, and then come up with a plan that draws on your strengths.

MAKING LEARNING-STYLES INFORMATION WORK FOR YOU

It is one thing to *know* how you learn best, but it is quite another to use that knowledge. When we actively learn, we listen, view, or manipulate information, *and then* we process that information. That is, we *use* it in some way.

Critically Thinking about Your Learning Styles

R E D For this activity, concentrate on how you can use the preference information you identified for yourself in the VAK Survey (Activity 6.2). Apply the R.E.D. Model to your learning style. After you read each step and its application to you, write your reaction.

Critical-Thinking Step	Application to Your Learning
Recognizing Assumptions	Based on your experiences, how do you know the VAK Survey has (or has not) accurately identified your preference?
Evaluating Information	Clearly state what your particular learning style is, according to the VAK. Explain specifically (give an example) how this style has shown itself in your school experiences.
Drawing Conclusions	Based on the evidence before you, does your conclusion about your learning style make sense? How do you believe the VAK Survey connects to your academic progress? That is, how can this assessment help in school and in your world outside school? What insights have you gained about your learning style?

Table 6.1 (see the next page) provides questions and suggestions to apply learning style information to your academic success. As you read these suggestions, think back to the opening situation about Allen. Would any of these suggestions help him solve his problem?

MULTIPLE INTELLIGENCES

Whereas *learning style* looks at (among other things) environmental factors affecting learning as well as our preference for taking in and putting out information, **intelligence** refers to our ability to use information to solve problems—to use the information for practical purposes. *Learning style* looks at ways we feel comfortable using information. *Intelligence* examines what we do with that information.

Think of it this way: Intelligence is the *what*, and learning style is the *how*. When we use our intelligence, we reason, solve problems, and use a set of skills to interact with our environment. That is *what* we do. We do those things with our hearing, sight, and touch—our learning style. That is *how* we do it.

Harvard professor Howard Gardner did pioneering research in the area of **multiple intelligences**. He maintains that the traditional manner of measuring

Table 6.1   Make Learning Styles Work for You

If You Show a Preference for...	Then Ask Yourself...	A Few Suggestions Include...
Auditory learning	How can I use verbal cues to help me understand my class work?	• Sit as close to the instructor as possible to make sure you hear all that is said. • Record lessons (with instructor knowledge). • Record yourself as you describe your notes. Then play back and listen. • Join a study group. • If available, use the audio e-version of your textbook located online. • Find and download a podcast that relates to the material the instructor presented in class.
Visual learning	How can I use visual aids to help me understand my class work?	• If available, use the visual aids on the textbook's online website. • Perhaps your instructors have posted PowerPoint presentations or outlines on their websites; if so, print them out. • Supplement your note-taking strategy by drawing more diagrams and flowcharts. • Find online videos that relate to the class lesson for the day. • Read textbook introductions, key terms, chapter learning outcomes, and summaries to help focus your attention on the key points.
Kinesthetic learning	How can I use movement to help me understand my class work?	• If possible, construct a model of your class material. • Perform a skit, role-play, or debate that uses the main ideas from the lesson. • If it helps, move, walk, or pace while you learn new concepts. • If there are activities in the chapter, write answers and review them.
Structure and clear explanation	How can I more formally structure my assignments?	• If your instructor's instructions sound vague, stop by his or her office and ask for clarification. • Join a study group to help you organize your thoughts. • Ask a classmate for his or her interpretation of the assignment instructions. • Use textbook organizers, like key terms, learning outcomes, and summary sections.
A quiet study environment	How can I minimize noise so that I can concentrate more on my studies?	• If you do not have a quiet space at your residence, block regular time on your calendar to work in the campus library. • Consider using noise-cancelling headphones.
A brightly lit study area	How can I have the best lighting for my studies?	• Buy a small desk light for your study area. • Be mindful of eyestrain, which can be caused by certain types of lighting. • When possible, read outdoors in sunlight.

intelligence (IQ) with a single number is misleading. It leads us to believe that there is only one intelligence. According to Gardner in his breakthrough book *Frames of Mind: The Theory of Multiple Intelligences* (1983), we have eight different intelligences to pick from when solving problems. Many of us, though, use only two or three of them. Just think of what you will be able to do once you tap into as many of the eight intelligences as possible.

Researchers have investigated a ninth intelligence: spiritual or existential. It refers to the ability to connect with nonphysical or metaphysical stimuli. But for our purposes, we will look at the first eight intelligences.

THE EIGHT INTELLIGENCES

Gardner maintains we all have at least a trace of each intelligence. Some of the intelligences may be highly developed, and some a little less developed. Here is Gardner's list, with a brief explanation of each category and possible connections to life choices (Armstrong, 1994):

- **Linguistic intelligence ("word smart"):** You are good with the written word. You can express yourself with language. Occupations that might rely on this intelligence include writer, speaker, lawyer, and teacher.

- **Logical-mathematical intelligence ("number smart"):** You can think abstractly and solve problems. Logic and order are strengths for you. You understand cause and effect. You can analyze material. Numbers do not scare you. Occupations include scientist and mathematician.

- **Spatial intelligence ("art smart"):** You can visually re-create your world. A clear sense of direction is involved, too. Occupations include sculptor, painter, and anatomy teacher.

- **Bodily-kinesthetic intelligence ("body smart"):** You have coordinated control of your own body. You have a strong sense of learning by movement or action. You can effectively use your hands, fingers, and arms to make something. Occupations include athlete, actor, and dancer.

- **Musical intelligence ("music smart"):** You have the ability to use the major components of music (rhythm and pitch). You can recognize patterns and use them effectively. Occupations include musician and dancer.

- **Interpersonal intelligence ("people smart"):** You understand the moods and motives of the people with whom you associate. If you are to deal effectively with other people, you must be skilled in this intelligence. Occupations include teacher, politician, and salesperson.

- **Intrapersonal intelligence ("me smart"):** You draw strength and energy from within yourself. You understand yourself and can apply that knowledge in real-life situations to produce the best results. You understand what is good for you. You know who you are and what you can do. You know what to get involved with and what to avoid. Occupations include independent-type positions, such as researcher and entrepreneur.

- **Naturalistic intelligence ("nature smart"):** You can understand, explain, and relate to things in the natural world around you. You have a unique ability to classify and separate items based on their characteristics. Occupations include botanist, zoologist, archaeologist, and environmentalist.

Figure 6.1 provides a visual view of the multiple intelligences.

Figure 6.1

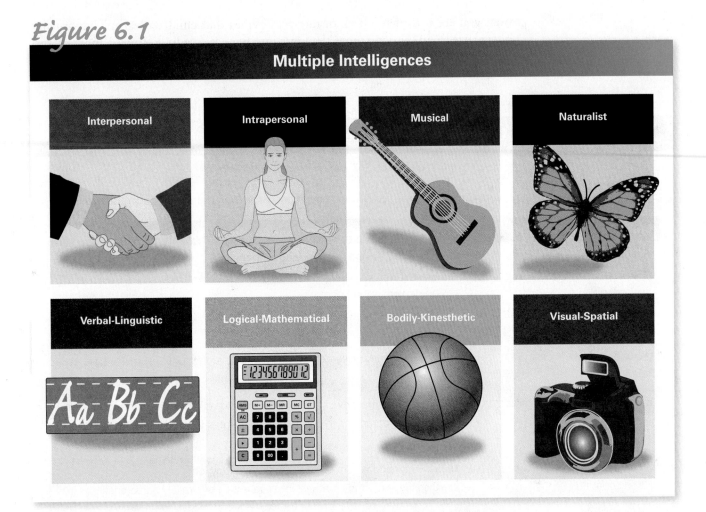

HOW CAN YOU USE THIS INFORMATION TO ORGANIZE YOUR STUDIES?

There are critics of Gardner's theory. For one critical review, see Ferguson (2009) who maintains that some of the indentified intelligences are examples of "personal interests and personality traits." Gardner's response to one critic can be found in an article he co-authored with Seana Moran (2006).

At times, you will learn well by visual means, and other times auditory techniques will be more productive. There will be times when you're "word smart" intelligence stands out above all the others, and other times when you will exhibit great spatial capabilities ("art smart"). Or perhaps individual work might be your normal routine, but a study group can be appropriate when working with a troubling concept.

The point is to understand what works best *most of the time*. Then, use that knowledge to adapt to the situation in which you find yourself.

You may benefit from tapping into multiple intelligences when learning class material. That means if you have a tendency to understand your textbook readings or class lecture notes primarily through your linguistic intelligence, you may benefit by reprocessing the same information with your interpersonal (study group) or spatial intelligence (model). Doing so will help your brain to develop a stronger connection with the information. And you will have a better chance to remember what you are learning. Think of nursery rhymes that children learn. They usually internalize them by using more than one intelligence: reading, singing, moving, and interacting with others.

Activity 6.4

Using Multiple Intelligences to Help Allen

The following table suggests two study strategies to use with each intelligence. Add a third strategy that might work (or has worked) for you. Again, consider what strategies might be appropriate for Allen (from the opening scenario).

Multiple Intelligence	Practical Suggestions for Your Academic Success
Linguistic intelligence ("word smart")	1. Use a note-taking summarizing strategy. 2. Text message, establish a Facebook poll, or tweet a friend about your homework assignment. 3. ....
Logical-mathematical intelligence ("number smart")	1. Construct a chart or pie graph to help you analyze the material. 2. Apply your newly learned information to a situation or problem you have. 3. ....
Spatial intelligence ("art smart")	1. Use an informal flowchart format with colored highlighters for note taking. 2. Create infographics to summarize your notes with pictures. 3. ....
Bodily-kinesthetic intelligence ("body smart")	1. Move around when you study. Change study locations. 2. Classify your study material into categories of similar characteristics. 3. ....
Musical intelligence ("music smart")	1. Listen to background music while studying (as long as you can still concentrate on the study material). 2. Perhaps you can put the class notes into a rhyme or rhythm. 3. ....
Interpersonal intelligence ("people smart")	1. Find a study group that will help you master the class material. Maybe you can develop a virtual study group using Facebook, or some other type of social networking service. 2. Tutor a classmate. 3. ....
Intrapersonal intelligence ("me smart")	1. Before you start to work, meditate, pray, or quietly reflect about the assignment you have to complete. Perhaps you could write a brief journal entry for yourself. 2. Find a quiet place to study. 3. ....
Naturalistic intelligence ("nature smart")	1. Study or read outside. 2. Classify your study material into categories of similar characteristics. 3. ....

Chapter SUMMARY

In this material, you thought about *how* you learn and *what* you can do with your learning style. You have examined the importance of taking control of your learning process. As you continue with your coursework this term, you will begin to notice what is working for you and what is *not*. You will know where your challenges lie and what strengths you can draw on to meet them.

Before leaving this topic, keep the following points in mind:

- Learning style examines the factors that influence how you process information.
- Learning preference addresses processes like how you take in and produce information.
- Various factors—from the classroom setting to the manner of presentation by the teacher—will affect different people differently.
- Your style and preferences will not necessarily reflect the style of the person sitting next to you in class.
- The theory of multiple intelligences looks at what skills you will use to reason and solve problems in your environment.

CRITICALLY THINKING

What Have You Learned?

Let's apply what you learned in this topic to help Allen from the opening scenario. However, before you look into Allen's problem and propose your solution, take a moment to think about the main points of this topic.

Review your notes, the key terms, learning outcomes, boldface headings, and figures and tables.

TEST YOUR LEARNING

Now that you have reviewed the main points, reread Allen's story. Pretend that you are Allen's advisor. Using the R.E.D. Model for critical thinking, help Allen critically review his concerns.

R

Recognize Assumptions

Facts: What are the facts in Allen's situation? List them.

Opinions: What opinions do you find in this situation? List them.

Assumptions: Are Allen's assumptions accurate?

E

Evaluate Information

Help Allen compile a list of questions that will help him make the most appropriate decision.

What emotions seem to be motivating Allen?

What, if anything, is missing from his thought process?

Do you see any confirmation bias?

D

Draw Conclusions

Based on the facts and the questions you have presented, what conclusions can you draw?

What advice do you have for Allen? What solutions would you propose?

Based on your suggestions, do you see any assumptions?

Finally, based on what you learned about using learning styles, what plan of action do you suggest for Allen?

Class-Time Listening and NOTE TAKING

7

LEARNING OUTCOMES

By the time you finish reading this material and completing the activities, you will be able to do the following:

- Identify three expectations each of your instructors has for you this term—and explain what you are doing to fulfill those expectations.

- Identify and use three strategies that will help you pay attention in class.

- Describe a strategy to help develop respectful working relationships with your instructors.

- Use and evaluate one note-taking style for at least one week.

The Case of CONSUELA

Consuela enjoys college life. She likes her instructors, her courses, and her classmates. She is positive and excited about participating in her classes. However, she just received the grades from her first round of exams for the term. They were not what she had hoped for. Each grade was a full letter grade lower than she expected to receive.

"I don't understand," she said to herself. "I write everything that comes out of the instructor's mouth. How come I am not doing well on the exams?" Consuela knew she had difficulty identifying the important things from the lessons. And that is why she diligently worked to

Key Terms

Active learning
Attention
Civility
Classroom success
Distractions
Instructor styles
Note-taking styles
Online classes

INTRODUCTION
Chapter

Students are expected to listen, remember, comprehend, and apply a great deal of information. In some cases, the information is quite complex. Each class brings new concepts, skills, and strategies. This can be both energizing and overwhelming: energizing because of the new insights gained but overwhelming because of the sheer volume of material.

This topic describes strategies for **active learning** that will help you manage and learn course information while becoming an active

get every word in her notes that she needed to remember.

Consuela had found that although she liked the course material, she was having a difficult time paying attention in class. When she pulled her crumpled notes from the bottom of her book bag (where she had placed them after class last week), she noticed large gaps in what she had written—and there was a good bit of doodling in the margins. "Perhaps there is a problem with my notes," she said to herself. "I thought I knew how to take notes, but obviously not!"

Consuela has come to you for assistance.

CRITICALLY THINKING
about *Consuela's* situation

How would you advise Consuela?

participant in class. Although it is the responsibility of the instructor to plan well-thought-out lessons, active learning places responsibility on the students to do what they can to be engaged—involved—in their lessons.

Being a successful student results from what you do in and out of class. This material will examine what you can do to get the most from the hours spent in class, and it will propose strategies to help you focus your attention, find the main points of a lesson, and then record those ideas in

MyStudentSuccessLab

MyStudentSuccessLab (www .mystudentsuccesslab.com) is an online solution designed to help you "Start strong, Finish stronger" by building skills for ongoing personal and professional development.

an organized and usable format. You will read about and practice ways to develop mastery (competence) in what you do in your classes. This will help you gain confidence. And that will help you remain calm and in control of your life.

Activity 7.1

Reflecting on Your Current Level of Classroom Performance Skills

Before you answer the items that follow, reflect on the current level of your performance skills in the classroom. Think of how well (or poorly) you have performed in past classes—and classes so far this term.

As you do in completing all reflective activities, you should write from your heart. This exercise is not meant for you to answer just like your classmates or to match what you may think the instructor wants to see. Take your time and give a respectful, responsible general accounting of your experiences with classroom success. Making a truthful self-assessment now will help you build on skills you have while developing those you lack.

For each of the following items, circle the number that best describes your typical experience with that skill. Here is the key for the numbers:

0 = never, 1 = almost never, 2 = occasionally, 3 = frequently, 4 = almost always, 5 = always

When considering your past successes and challenges in the class, how often:

1.	Were you able to figure out what most of your instructors expected you to do to achieve at the highest levels possible?	0	1	2	3	4	5
2.	Did you adjust successfully to your instructors' teaching styles?	0	1	2	3	4	5
3.	Did you develop respectful and civil relationships with your instructors?	0	1	2	3	4	5
4.	Were you able to remain focused and pay attention to the instructor?	0	1	2	3	4	5
5.	Did you take notes of lessons during class time?	0	1	2	3	4	5
6.	Were you able to pick out the most important ideas from your instructor's lectures?	0	1	2	3	4	5
7.	Did you use a consistent note-taking format during class?	0	1	2	3	4	5
8.	Did you maintain an organized notebook of your classroom notes and papers?	0	1	2	3	4	5

Add up your scores for items 1, 2, 3, and 4. Divide by 4. Write your answer here: _____

Using the key provided to explain each number (0, 1, 2, 3, 4, 5), complete this sentence: When it comes to class, I _____ am able to develop positive and focused working relationships with my instructors.

Add up your scores for items 5, 6, 7, and 8. Divide by 4. Write your answer here: _____

Using the key provided to explain each number (0, 1, 2, 3, 4, 5), complete this sentence: When it comes to note-taking skills, I _____ take and organize my notes effectively.

Based on your answers, what insights have you gained about your experiences with successful classroom strategies?

DO YOU KNOW WHAT THE INSTRUCTOR IS DOING IN THE FRONT OF THE ROOM?

Just as you have a particular learning style to process information, so, too, do instructors have their own teaching styles. These **instructor styles** may range from lecture, to question and answer, to group work, to lab work, to discussion, to seatwork.

Regardless of the method of presentation, each instructor also has a set of expectations for student performance. Some emphasize minute details; others seek broad generalizations for application to new situations. One may require you to be actively involved, while another wants you to sit and diligently copy his or her words of wisdom.

You will be able to determine instructor style and emphasis from class attendance and the course syllabus. If you are aware of your instructors' styles, expectations, and emphases, your preparation for each class can be more focused, and any anxiety you might have will lessen.

Furthermore, knowledge of teacher methodology can be very useful in determining what courses you want to take next term. If you learn best from lecturing instructors, then you might want to avoid instructors who rely heavily on interactive work. Obviously, the reverse also holds true. Activity 7.2 will help you to identify what expectations your instructors have. You may wish to make a copy of the chart provided in the activity and complete it for each instructor you have this term. Check all the items that apply. Then place the completed chart where you will see it to remind yourself of these expectations.

Activity 7.2

Do You Know Your Instructors' Expectations for Success?

This activity consists of two parts. Part I asks you to consider all of your instructors this term. Part II gives you an opportunity to focus specifically on one instructor.

PART I: Write your instructors' names across the top-right part of the chart. Down the left side of the chart, you will find descriptions of styles and methods. Check the ones that apply to each instructor.

Write Your Instructors' Names on Each Line →					
Instructor Style ↓					
Primarily lectures the entire class					
Uses lots of question-and-answer discussions					
Uses lots of group activities					
Uses lots of in-class seatwork					
Concentrates on details such as dates, formulas, and classifications					

Write Your Instructors' Names on Each Line →					
Pays close attention to grammar and writing skills					
Seldom assigns a writing assignment					
Is very serious and does not allow for any joking in class					
Is very serious but allows some lighthearted moments					
Never accepts an assignment late					
Accepts assignments late but with a penalty					
Accepts assignments late with no penalty					
Takes attendance each class					
Expects punctual attendance in class					
Goes off on tangents (strays from the topic)					
Stays on target, seldom straying from the topic at hand					

How can you use this information to help you be successful in each of your classes?

PART II: Focus on *only one* of your instructors for this part of the activity. It may be helpful to do this for a class in which you are having some challenges. Refer to this form often.

Course title: _____ Instructor's name: _____

My instructor requires me to:
- ○ Maintain a notebook
- ○ Complete mostly reading homework
- ○ Complete mostly writing homework
- ○ Complete reading and writing homework
- ○ Participate in class
- ○ Do group work
- ○ Attend class
- ○ Other

My instructor grades me with:
- ○ Reading quizzes
- ○ Homework assignments
- ○ Class participation
- ○ Exams
- ○ Projects and/or research papers
- ○ Group work
- ○ Service-learning activities
- ○ Other

My instructor uses a lot of:
- ○ Group work
- ○ Lecture
- ○ Class discussion
- ○ Worksheets
- ○ In-class problems or writing assignments
- ○ Material from the textbook
- ○ Field trips/real-world experiences
- ○ Other

My instructor's tests are:
- ○ Multiple choice
- ○ Matching
- ○ Completion/Fill in the blank
- ○ True/False
- ○ Short answer
- ○ Essay
- ○ Some combination of the above
- ○ Other

In this class, my biggest challenges will be/are:	Steps I can take to do well in this class:
○ Taking notes	○ Seek tutoring from the teacher
○ Understanding the teacher	○ Seek tutoring from a classmate
○ Dealing with distractions	○ Follow through on my assignments
○ Staying focused	○ Reevaluate how I prioritize my time
○ Completing my homework on time	○ Ask for a seat change
○ Following instructions	○ Review my notes regularly
○ Answering questions orally	○ Prepare earlier for exams
○ Working with groups	○ Break big projects into small easy-to-manage steps
○ Getting ready for tests	○ Be on time for class
○ Dealing with the volume of homework	○ Come to class each day
○ Being a procrastinator	○ Ask the teacher for assistance
○ Managing my priorities	○ Seek online help where available
○ Getting to class on time	○ Read the textbook more carefully
○ Having excessive absences	○ Review class notes regularly
○ Having a negative attitude	○ Devote more time to high-quality studying
○ Feeling sleepy	○ Find/Form a study group
○ Other	○ Other

Based on what you know about this instructor, what is your biggest asset *and* challenge in this course?

DO YOU KNOW WHAT YOU ARE DOING IN THE BACK OF THE ROOM?

Classroom success is directly connected to active learning (see above) and attention (see below). If you can discuss a concept, you will have a much better chance of understanding it. You also can be actively involved by anticipating the content of a lecture (based on reading assignments outside the classroom and past class sessions), asking questions of yourself, and writing notes of classmates' observations.

If you understand your instructor's style and expectations (Activity 7.2), you will be better able to identify the important class material and maintain focus. Understanding the major points of a lesson will make note taking easier.

YOU REALLY WANT TO PAY ATTENTION IN CLASS—BUT IT'S NOT EASY

The class has just started. You're in your seat, the teacher starts the lesson, and you start to "drift away." You really want to pay attention, but you find it difficult. And if you are representative of students in research studies, you may very well start "drifting" within 10 to 15 minutes of the beginning of class (Medina, 2008, p. 74).

Distractions—all the things or people that interrupt your thoughts and actions—are all around us. We live in a 24/7 world that is littered with short-term distractions that hinder concentration and affect our long-term goals.

HOW DOES ONE "PAY ATTENTION"?

Before you can remember a name, a process, a date, or a telephone number, you must first notice it. This requires attention. But how does one "pay attention"?

Attention requires listening to and observing your surroundings. More specifically, it requires you to sort through the vast amount of information that comes your way in class, through homework, or even on a job. You have to make sense of what is before you.

When you pay attention, you focus on smaller pieces of information from a larger amount of available information. You begin to extract particular data (Zadina, 2007). In other words, when you pay attention, you have to sift through all the stimuli bombarding you—and then decide to focus on a particular pertinent piece of that information.

Consider the tips in Table 7.1 to improve your ability to pay attention (Hallowell, 2007, pp. 178–185):

You can also allow yourself the luxury of "accepting" a distraction, jotting it on a piece of paper ("Call Joe tonight")—and then letting it go. You have mentally told yourself that you will address the issue later.

Recognize that your attention has to be renewed from time to time. Just like motivation, it is not an unending resource.

Table 7.1   Tips for Paying Attention In and Out of Class

In Class	Outside Class
Listen for verbal clues from the instructor.	Get appropriate sleep each night.
Stay involved in the class discussion.	Eat well, and avoid foods that make you sleepy.
Move your seat away from distractions.	Exercise regularly (and appropriately for your health).
Listen to what classmates say and ask.	Eliminate distractions as best you can.
Take notes and review them.	Enjoy what you do.
Come to class prepared; do all homework.	Avoid substance abuse.
Find connections to what you enjoy.	Find humor in what you are doing.
Turn off your cell phone and focus.	Turn off your cell phone and focus.

CLASS-TIME LISTENING AND NOTE TAKING

A FRIENDLY REMINDER OF WHAT YOU ALREADY KNOW

You probably have heard instructors explain the importance of attendance. "You need to be here," they will say, "to learn and understand the material." The reality is that your physical presence, while important, is only part of the success equation.

Not only do you need to have your body in class, you need to have your head there as well. Your attention and your thoughts need to be focused on the class lesson. Your physical presence is important, as it allows you to hear explanations, ask questions, and add to the class discussions.

The following table provides reminders of basic lessons and tips.*

Table 7.2 **Seven Steps to Classroom Success**

Friendly Reminder	Reason for the Reminder
Do you come to class?	Effective instructors have well-thought-out lessons and objectives for each class. You might miss these if you are sitting in the student lounge or asleep in your bed during class time.
Do you bring everything you need for class?	This is not the time to be without paper, pen, textbook, calculator, laptop, spare battery, or some other tool.
Do you arrive on time?	A review of the last class might be provided at the beginning of the current class. Or the instructor might announce test information.
Do you sit where you will benefit the most?	Distance yourself from distractions (both in the classroom and at your computer).
Do you carry your passion with you?	Practice your active-listening skills. Listen intently. Ask questions. Online students: read and respond to classmate posts.
Do you remain actively engaged?	Think of a movie. If you come late or leave early, you will miss critical scenes that will hinder your understanding of the entire film. Class sessions have recognized starting and ending times. Plan to participate for the entire session.
Do you review class notes immediately?	Review your notes as soon as possible after class (at least within 24 hours). Write any questions you have. Ask for clarification the next class session. Or visit your instructor during office hours to ask questions.

*I would like to thank Professor Emeritus Joe Cuseo for helping me focus these thoughts. He facilitated a session at the 2004 Conference on the First Year Experience (Dallas, Texas) that addressed many of these issues.

DEVELOPING RESPECTFUL RELATIONSHIPS WITH YOUR INSTRUCTORS

Perhaps you have heard the expression "Do unto others as you would have them do unto you." When dealing with your professors, treat them as you want to be treated yourself.

Paying tuition does not entitle a student to treat *any* college employee or classmate in a rude, disrespectful, or demanding manner. If you are in the classroom, visiting your instructor during office hours, or corresponding by e-mail, remember that you are interacting with a fellow human being. Be courteous and respectful. You can expect top-notch teaching and appropriate feedback. However, your instructors are not there to respond to your every demand whenever you want.

CIVILITY IN THE CLASSROOM

Civility—acting appropriately and with respect—should be a basic component of any working relationship. Let's review a couple basic rules of behavior that will go far in developing a respectful relationship with your professor and classmates:

- **Class participation.** Students who respectfully respond to instructors with on-task comments and questions help create a positive classroom atmosphere. When a student responds to an instructor's request with a grunt, shrug of the shoulders, or rude and inappropriate comment, he or she is being disrespectful to the instructor and the classmates (whether that is the intention or not).

- **Entering and leaving the room.** At times (and they need to be very few), you may enter class after it starts or leave before it is over. Basic courtesy dictates that you make your way to a seat quietly and with limited distraction to other students and the instructor. Remember, any disturbance you create (such as a slamming door) is not only being rude to the instructor, but it also shows a lack of respect for your classmates—who are attending to the instructor.

- **Communicating with other students.** Unless talking with classmates is part of the lesson, once class has started, do not hold conversations (written or verbal).

- **Texting.** One area of increasing concern in the classroom is the use of cell phones for texting. Estimates indicate that upwards of 91 percent of students regularly send and/or receive text messages during class (Harris, 2013; Shamoon, 2009). While nearly two-thirds of students surveyed believe texting should be allowed during class, the practice does create a number of dilemmas:

  - It takes your attention away from the class.
  - It is distracting to those around you.
  - It is rude to the person speaking.
  - It is a bad habit that can have negative implications in the world beyond school.

On a related note, review your e-mails to professors for appropriateness. Do not treat a professor like your best friend or a personal assistant, expecting him or her to be available at every moment to serve your every need. Be grammatically correct and be civil. (See Glater [2006] for a look at how e-mail has affected the professor/student relationship.)

If you disrupt the class with inappropriate behavior, you will have a difficult time building a positive relationship with the key person who is in the classroom to assist you and evaluate your performance.

WHEN PROBLEMS OCCUR

Rarely does a problem fall totally in the lap of one person. For example, if you have a personality clash with a particular instructor, sit back and evaluate the situation. Have you contributed to the problem? What can you do to change the predicament? Is the instructor a difficult grader, or is it simply that you lack some basic process skills?

Use your critical-thinking skills to examine all assumptions. Some students assume that because they received high grades in previous classes, they will (or should) get high grades in subsequent classes. Please question that assumption. While getting good grades last term may establish a great foundation for this term, it does not guarantee anything. Just because you got an A in a previous course does not mean you are destined to get A's in all succeeding classes.

Activity 7.3

Critically Thinking about Classroom Challenges

R E D

Let's apply the R.E.D. Model to examine one of the challenges you identified for yourself in Activity 7.2. Write one of those challenges on a piece of paper. Then answer the clarifying questions in the table below.

Critical-Thinking Step	Application to Your Classroom Skills
Recognize Assumptions	How do you know the challenge you listed is actually a problem? Be specific (give examples) in explaining this classroom challenge. What assumptions do you make about why you have this challenge?
Evaluate Information	What evidence supports your assessment that this is a problem area for you? Examine the challenge from different perspectives. Where can you get more information about this personal challenge?
Draw Conclusions	Based on your evidence, how does your conclusion about your challenge make sense (or not)? What insights have you gained? What is the next step you will take to eliminate this challenge?

As you move through your program of study, each course will (generally speaking) provide a little more challenge. If you are prepared and apply good study and learning strategies, you will have an excellent chance of meeting the challenges effectively.

NOTE TAKING AS AN ACTIVE LEARNING STRATEGY

Note taking is a personal activity. Do not feel that you must copy any of the following **note taking styles** exactly as shown. If the style you currently use works for you, great! If what you currently do is not working or if you do not have a consistent note-taking style, find one that works for you and use it consistently. The purpose of your notes is to reconstruct the main points of a lesson. Taking notes will help in three ways:

1. Practicing note taking will help make the habit permanent.
2. Writing notes helps you stay focused on the class and the material.
3. Writing helps you translate oral information to visual information (words and graphics on your paper), thereby using multiple learning preferences to help you remember the material.

The styles described in this section are very basic approaches. You might also consider using different pieces of each style to develop your own. However you decide to take class notes, keep the following points in mind about your style:

- Be consistent.
- Periodically review your style to make sure it is working for you.

- Practice daily. Strategies will do little good if you do not use them. Practice may not make perfect, but it can help to make a skill permanent.

If you learn best by using a highly structured and orderly model, then the format in Figure 7.1 may be for you. Note that this outline is organized with Roman numerals, letters, and Arabic numerals. Each indentation represents a subcategory, or information of less importance. Examples may be included to support the topics.

Perhaps you cannot easily use this note-taking strategy. You are not too sure where the instructor is moving with the lecture, and it is extremely difficult to determine the subcategory of a larger category. In other words, you need a model that allows more flexibility.

If visuals help you learn, why not record your notes in a picturelike or chartlike structure? The model in Figure 7.2 has the same basic information as the traditional outline. It is also very easy to add information when using this model by using a simple arrow or line.

The format in Figure 7.3 is an adaptation of the Cornell note-taking system (Pauk, 1993, pp. 110–114). The expanded margin on the left side of the page is for student questions and other organizing comments to use as a study guide. This model is more linear in fashion than the flowchart model (Figure 7.2) but not quite as structured as the traditional outline (Figure 7.1).

Figure 7.1

Traditional Outline Note-Taking Style

NOTE TAKING: THE TRADITIONAL OUTLINE

I. Main topic 1
    A. Subtopic
        1. important detail
        2. important detail
    B. Subtopic
        1. important detail
        2. important detail
II. Main topic 2
    A. Subtopic
        1. important detail
        2. important detail
    B. Subtopic
        1. important detail
        2. important detail
III. Main topic 3
    A. Subtopic
        1. important detail
        2. important detail
    B. Subtopic
        1. important detail
        2. important detail

Figure 7.2

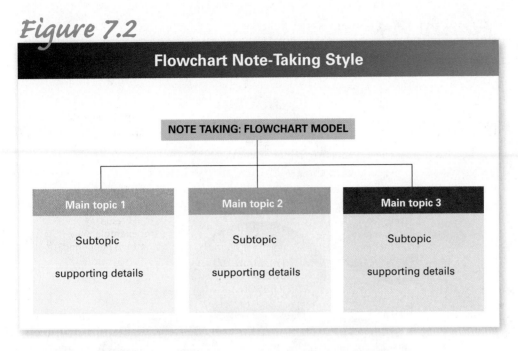

Flowchart Note-Taking Style

NOTE TAKING: FLOWCHART MODEL

Main topic 1	Main topic 2	Main topic 3
Subtopic	Subtopic	Subtopic
supporting details	supporting details	supporting details

Figure 7.3

Notes with a Study Guide (Modified Cornell Note-Taking Style)

Personal	Date

Study Guide	Class Notes
Write a question you might have about topic 1 or any of its subtopics.	I. Main topic 1
	A. Subtopic
Comment on an important detail the instructor emphasized.	1. important detail
	2. important detail
	B. Subtopic
	1. important detail
	2. important detail
Write a question you might have about topic 2 or any of its subtopics.	II. Main topic 2
	A. Subtopic
Comment on an important detail the instructor emphasized.	1. important detail
	2. important detail
	B. Subtopic
	1. important detail
	2. important detail
Write a question you might have about topic 3 or any of its subtopics.	III. Main topic 3
	A. Subtopic
Comment on an important detail the instructor emphasized.	1. important detail
	2. important detail
	B. Subtopic
	1. important detail
	2. important detail

Figure 7.4

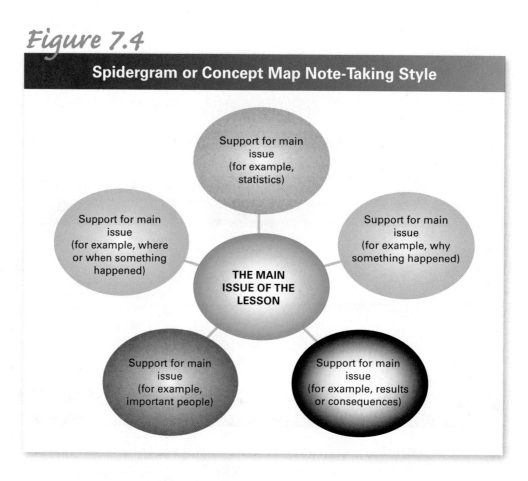

Spidergram or Concept Map Note-Taking Style

Figure 7.4 offers one more model for you to consider. This format allows you to arrange details around the body of an issue. Some people refer to this type of overview as a spidergram, while others call it clustering (Matte & Henderson, 1995, p. 84). You even may hear "mind mapping" used. Using this format allows quick organization. It can be helpful in reorganizing your notes prior to a test, as well as in putting your thoughts together for an essay.

COMPARING AND CONTRASTING NOTE-TAKING STYLES

Table 7.3 provides a quick comparison and contrast of potential benefits and drawbacks of all the note-taking styles explained.

Examine the notes you take in class now. Do they resemble one of the styles discussed? Is there *any* organization to your notes? If not, make some adjustments; maybe a study partner, instructor, or a tutor can help.

USING SIMPLE ABBREVIATIONS TO INCREASE NOTE-TAKING SPEED

Regardless of your note-taking technique, avoid taking notes word for word. That is, do not write every word the instructor says or every word that is on a PowerPoint slide. Look for key terms—words that have been emphasized and repeated by the instructor or those that are underlined or written in italic or boldface type. If you are not sure what the main point is, ask.

Table 7.3 **Comparing and Contrasting Note-Taking Styles**

Note-Taking Style	Potential Benefit(s)	Potential Drawback(s)
Traditional Outline	Very organized and structured; items follow directly from one to another	Instructors jump around in lessons
	Provides a neat presentation of main points and supporting points	May be difficult to distinguish main versus minor points *during* the lecture
Flowchart/Spidergram/Clustering/Mind map	Easy to insert information if the instructor skips around in the lecture	As the notes move to a second or third page, it may be difficult to see connections to previous pages.
	The chartlike/picturelike structure may help visual learners	The loose structure may appear chaotic and hinder organization
Notes with a study guide (modified Cornell)	The note-taking section can be in any style	More paper is required as the note-taking section is reduced in size
	Provides space for an ongoing study guide, review, and questions	Requires a little extra time to complete the review questions

Once you have determined what to write, abbreviate words to increase your speed. If you are not sure how to abbreviate, you can find examples online. Table 7.4 provides a few basic ideas. If you know how to text message, you already use this strategy and can add to the list.

Table 7.4 **Abbreviations to Use in Your Notes**

If the Word(s) Is (Are):	Consider Using:	If the Word(s) Is (Are):	Consider Using:
as a consequence	→	less than	<
because	b/c	number	#
decrease	↓	percentage	%
equals	=	plus	+
Florida	FL	question	Q or ?
greater than	>	therefore	∴
important	*	United States of America	US
increase	↑	with	w/
information	info	without	w/o

MANAGING YOUR STUDIES WITH A NOTEBOOK

Having well-organized notes will help you prepare for final course tests, national certification exams, and future courses. Having great notes is useless, however, if you cannot find them once you get *outside* the classroom or finish an online session.

Table 7.5 **Follow-Up Strategies for When You Miss the Basics**

The Basics	Oops! I Missed the Basics. What Can I Do Now?
Take notes diligently each class session.	If you miss class, leave space in your notebook as a reminder to get notes for that class from a classmate or to visit the instructor as soon as possible.
Be punctual for each class.	Car trouble, a cantankerous alarm, a family emergency, or a late night out can make even the best student tardy. If you arrive late to class, enter the room quietly. Have your cell phone in the "Off" position.
Come to class each day with your notebook and a fresh supply of writing paper (or a fully charged laptop battery).	Maybe you dashed out to class and left your class notes behind. As soon as you discover this, borrow some paper, quickly and quietly. You can transfer these notes to your class notebook later in the day. You might tuck an extra pad of paper and a few extra pens into one of the pockets of your book bag for such emergencies. If you are using a laptop, it may be beneficial to arrive early to get a seat next to a wall outlet, in case your laptop requires recharging.
Focus on important points in each class. Write them down in your notebook.	Sometimes, you may not know what is important. Maybe a study partner can help by comparing notes. You may wish to visit your instructor during office hours and ask if your notes are capturing the main points of the lessons—and if he or she has any suggestions for you.
"Keep your head in the class" for the entire class period. Do not stop listening and participating before the class has ended. You enrolled in the section knowing the starting and ending times.	The classroom clock may seem to move backward, and the last 10 minutes of each class may seem like a week. Fight the urge to pack up. Shoving your books and papers into your backpack early is distracting.
Review your day's notes immediately after class—before you leave the classroom, if possible.	Sometimes, you need to get to another class or an appointment immediately and thus have to leave the classroom hurriedly at the conclusion of the lesson. In that case, make a commitment to review your notes as soon as possible later that day. Contact your study partner, if you have one. Working with someone else is a great way to review notes.

Consider using a class notebook to organize and store your notes. A notebook will allow you to find past notes and handouts that may prove helpful during a class discussion or group activity. Students have found the notebook hints in Figure 7.5 helpful.

STAYING ACTIVELY ENGAGED AS AN ONLINE STUDENT

The availability of **online classes** has increased tremendously within the last few years. Technology has extended the classroom beyond the campus. Students today can complete coursework from locations beyond campus grounds and classroom walls.

Figure 7.5

Notebook Hints

HINT: Nothing can be more frustrating than finding English class notes buried in the middle of information on the lives of the Roman emperors or tips on how to solve a quadratic equation. Avoid this by having a separate three-ring binder for each class. Also, think twice about using those "stuff-it-in-the-pocket" folders.

HINT: Place the course name, professor's name, and your name on the front cover of each notebook.

HINT: Keep all general yet important handouts in the first section of the notebook. They may include the syllabus, a listing of term assignments, and the instructor's office hours.

HINT: File all papers appropriately. Do not simply stick them in your notebook or textbook. Always follow an established order.

HINT: Have a separate section for each unit of the class. It may be helpful to identify the units with tab dividers, so it will be easy to find material. Each unit may include the following items:

- A summary outline or study guide for the entire unit
- Daily notes, with the date of each class noted clearly at the top of the page
- Handouts that pertain specifically to that unit
- Quizzes and other graded assignments
- The unit exam

HINT: Keep a grade sheet. Create one following this simple three-column format:

Assignment	Points Earned	Points Possible

Using this grade sheet, you will always know your grade. This is important for two reasons:

1. There will be no surprises about your final grade. You know all along how well (or poorly) you are doing. Just because you turn in all the assignments does not mean you will pass the course. Understand your instructor's grading scale, your grades, and what your average is throughout the entire term.

2. Sometimes, an instructor may make an error in grade calculation. If you have retained all your graded assignments and have kept an ongoing record, you will have a credible way to politely challenge an error. (This is similar to holding on to the receipt from a store purchase, on the chance you need to return or exchange it later.)

The obvious advantage is flexibility: You can complete a course from (virtually) anyplace in the world that has Internet access. Even so, online education is not for all students. It requires a great deal of responsibility and self-discipline. The following list provides a few tips to help you successfully complete an online class.

- **Technology tips for online classes**
  - You need a computer (or maybe a tablet) and Internet access. Having your own computer—with unlimited access to it—will make life as an

online student much easier. If you use a computer in a campus lab or library, you may not be able to download required files or programs for your course. Computer availability in a public setting can be problematic.

- Know how to use a computer and its programs for creating content. Know how to create, save, and send different kinds of files.

- **Collaboration and communication tips for online classes**
  - Practice good "netiquette" (online etiquette). Keep your communication civil. Once you post a message on a discussion board, it is out there for the class to see.
  - Ask a current online student for advice. If you have already completed an online class, you can be a mentor for a new online student.

- **Course expectations**
  - If there is an orientation for the class, find a way to participate. Practice navigating the course site. Click on buttons and links, and know where everything is on the site. Be proactive and learn as much about the site as you can—as soon as you can.
  - As you would for an on-campus class, turn in assignments for an online class according to the class schedule. Stay current with all work.
  - Online courses may be flexible, but they still require a large quantity of time.
  - Don't confuse flexibility with lack of rigor. An effective online course will require as much—if not more—time to complete as an on-campus course. You may wish to talk with (or e-mail or text) the instructor prior to registering for the course. Make sure you understand the time commitment the course will require.
  - Ask for help as soon as you recognize you may have a problem with content, timing, or technological glitches.

- **Back up work**
  - Back up all computer work—and back it up regularly. (This tip will be helpful for students taking traditional in-the-classroom courses, as well.)

Chapter SUMMARY

To be successful, students need to engage in active learning inside the classroom. Before leaving this topic, keep the following points in mind:

- Improve your class performance by being aware of your instructors' styles and expectations.

- Paying attention requires listening and observing, eliminating or controlling distractions, and sorting through the vast amount of information presented to you.

- Being present in class allows you to hear explanations, ask questions, and add to class discussions.
- Choose a note-taking style you feel comfortable with and use it consistently.
- Make your notebook work for you. Keep it current, and review it every night.

CRITICALLY THINKING

What Have You Learned?

R
E
D
Let's apply what you have learned to help Consuela, from the opening situation. However, before you examine Consuela's problem and propose a solution, take a moment to think about the main points covered in this topic. Review your notes, the key terms, learning outcomes, boldface headings, and figures and tables.

TEST YOUR LEARNING

Now that you have reviewed the main points of this topic and reread Consuela's story, what advice do you have for her? Using the R.E.D. Model for critical thinking, help Consuela review her concerns:

130

Recognize Assumptions

Facts: What are the facts in Consuela's situation?

Opinions: What opinions do you find in this situation?

Assumptions: Are Consuela's assumptions accurate?

Evaluate Information

Help Consuela compile a list of questions that will help her make the most appropriate decision.

What emotions seem to be motivating Consuela?

What, if anything, is missing from her thought process?

Do you see any confirmation bias?

Draw Conclusions

Based on the facts and the questions you have presented, what conclusions can you draw?

What advice do you have for Consuela? What solutions do you propose?

Based on your suggestions, do you see any assumptions?

Finally, based on what you learned about using critical thinking and class success strategies, what plan of action do you suggest for Consuela?

Memory and STUDYING

8

LEARNING OUTCOMES

By the time you finish reading this material and completing its activities, you will be able to do the following:

- Establish a schedule for immediate review of each day's class notes.

- Develop and write at least one T.S.D. for your class notes from the past week.

- Visit each of your professors at least once to discuss material from class.

- Understand why you should (or should not) consider working with a study partner.

- Identify and use at least two strategies to improve your skills of noticing, storing, and reclaiming what you need to remember.

- Create a mnemonic to recall information from assigned reading.

The Case of MYRON

Myron is a quiet student. Although he seldom misses a class, he rarely participates from his seat in the last row of the classroom. He is doing mostly "C" work in his classes—except biology, which he is not passing. Science has never been his strongest subject area, but in the past, he has been able to read his textbook and do well. He has found that his biology instructor's exams rely heavily on classroom lectures, group discussions, and demonstrations.

Myron listens to everything his professor says. He copies all of the PowerPoint presentations word for word. His notebook is complete with classroom notes and handouts—all filed in precise order. The professor actually posts class notes on her websites. Myron prints them out and then puts them in his notebook. This gives him a record of virtually every word the professor has used.

Myron recently told a study group member, "My thought has always been if the professor believes it's important enough to put on the screen, a website, or on the board, then it should go into my notebook." His classmates are in awe about how thick his class notebook has become.

Key Terms

- Acronym
- Active listening
- Connections
- Data retrieval chart (D.R.C.)
- Forgetting
- Long-term memory
- Memory
- Memory block
- Notice
- Office hours
- R.O.I.
- Reclaiming
- Review-Relate-Reorganize strategy
- Short-term memory
- Storing information
- Study partner
- T.S.D. strategy
- Working memory

Chapter INTRODUCTION

While building relationships with classmates and instructors will help you persist and succeed in your studies, another type of relationship building is every bit as vital to your school success.

Research has shown that learning is more likely to occur when students establish **connections**—build relationships—between what they know

Myron reads his textbook, although it is not easy. The book is filled with a lot of terms and complicated explanations. Moreover, Myron is not particularly interested in the subject. He wants to major in business and does not see the connection between that and his science and math courses.

He studies for each exam by setting aside three hours the night before to review notes and textbook readings and to quiz himself on the major concepts. Since he does not really understand the material, Myron does his best to memorize everything he can. The night before each test, he sits at his desk elbow deep in papers, notes, and PowerPoint copies, doing the best he can to understand it all. With all of these notes and handouts, he has so much material to study that he ends up getting lost in the details. He is tired of pulling all-night cram sessions prior to exams—and he is tired of getting less-than-satisfactory grades. By the time he gets to class, he is exhausted—and he remembers very little of what he studied.

Myron knows he can do better. He told his professor that his biggest problem is with memory. "I take notes. I study the notes. But I still do poorly on the exams. I have a terrible memory. I can't remember a thing!"

CRITICALLY THINKING
about *Myron's* situation

As a member of Myron's study group, what suggestions do you have for him?

from their experiences and what they read in textbooks and hear from their instructors and classmates. Note taking provides the chance to build these connections. In fact, opportunities for learning will occur at two levels: while writing or typing notes and while reviewing notes (Armbruster, 2000, p. 176).

MyStudentSuccessLab

MyStudentSuccessLab (www .mystudentsuccesslab.com) is an online solution designed to help you "Start strong, Finish stronger" by building skills for ongoing personal and professional development.

LEARNING WHILE TAKING NOTES

You can learn while taking notes in class, attending a guest lecture in the campus auditorium, or reading your textbook. At this point in note taking, however, you will not have much time to build connections. You will more than likely be concentrating on following the speaker and writing or typing the main points in your notebook or on your laptop. Even if you have a well-honed note-taking style, the chance of creating a lasting connection with this new information *while* recording it will be difficult. You will need to focus on determining what is important and what you need to write, not on how the new information supports or refutes what you already know.

Just having the notes is not enough. The next step is knowing what to do with the notes—and when to do it. Your learning will deepen when you take the time to review your notes (Armbruster, 2000, p. 178).

LEARNING AFTER YOU HAVE TAKEN NOTES: R.O.I.

Businesspeople invest their money and time when presented with an opportunity to earn a profit. The concept of **return on investment (R.O.I.)** many times drives business decisions. Why invest resources if no return, or benefit, seems likely?

The same concept can be applied to your investment in class. Beyond tuition and the cost of books, every day that you enter class, you invest your time and attention in what is being taught. Let's assume you take picture-perfect notes. You have recorded every piece of important information in an organized, legible form—much like Myron in the opening scenario. So far, so good.

But at this point, what is your R.O.I.? Perhaps you were able to see connections between the classroom discussions and your textbook. Possibly, as you wrote the instructor's remarks, you had an insight about the material.

The second part of note taking—reviewing and storing—allows you to make deeper connections between what you know and what you are learning. This chapter will focus on these strategies.

Activity 8.1

Reflecting on How Your Notes Help You Understand and Remember Class Material

Before you answer the items that follow, reflect on your current skill level of using your notes to help you study and remember information. Think of how well (or poorly) you have been able to remember information and use your notes from past classes.

As you do in completing all reflective activities, you should write from your heart. This exercise is not meant for you to answer just like your classmates—or to match what you may think the instructor wants to see. Take the time to give a respectful and responsible general accounting of your experiences with your notes. Making a truthful self-assessment now will help you build on skills you have while developing those you lack.

For each of the following items, circle the number that best describes your typical experience when it comes to using your notes to study. Here is the key for the numbers:

0 = never, 1 = almost never, 2 = occasionally, 3 = frequently, 4 = almost always, 5 = always

When considering your past successes, challenges when using your notes, and remembering information, how often:

1.	Did you review your notes within the first 24 hours of taking them in class?	0	1	2	3	4	5
2.	Did the notes (the words, sentences, phrases) you wrote during class make sense to you when you reviewed them after class?	0	1	2	3	4	5
3.	Did your notes put the instructor's words into your words, rather than copy the instructor's PowerPoint slides or lecture notes almost word for word?	0	1	2	3	4	5
4.	Did you review your notes and relate them to your textbook reading or the previous lesson's notes?	0	1	2	3	4	5
5.	Did you attempt to make connections between what you read in a textbook assignment and what you heard in class from the instructor?	0	1	2	3	4	5
6.	Did you participate in class by asking questions (or answering questions) about the day's lesson?	0	1	2	3	4	5
7.	Did you visit the instructor's office to seek clarification or ask a question to make sure you understood the class material?	0	1	2	3	4	5
8.	Did you use memory aids (such as charts, acronyms, and sayings) to help you remember the information for a test?	0	1	2	3	4	5

Add up your scores for items 1, 2, 3, and 4. Divide by 4. Write your answer here: _____

Using the key provided to explain each number (0, 1, 2, 3, 4, 5), complete this sentence: when it comes to my notes, I _____ review and use my notes to understand class material.

Add up your scores for items 5, 6, 7, and 8 divide by 4. Write your answer here: _____

Using the key provided to explain each number (0, 1, 2, 3, 4, 5), complete this sentence: when it comes to memory, I _____ use strategies to make connections between class discussion, reading assignments, and my notes.

Based on your answers, what insights have you gained about your experiences with note taking and memory strategies?

USING YOUR NOTES TO UNDERSTAND THE "BIG PICTURE"

NOW THAT YOU HAVE YOUR NOTES, IT'S TIME FOR REFLECTION

Taking clear notes in class moves you another step closer to mastering your course content. But more needs to be done. In fact, your studying begins the next time you look at those notes.

A common study skill recommendation is to review your notes as soon as possible after class. One study found that years of research support the conclusion that when students use note-taking strategies to "rehearse and review" class material, they improve their chances for learning the information (Pardini et al., 2005, p. 39).

For this review to be meaningful, however, you need to do more than passively read the notes. A simple three-step strategy—Review-Relate-Reorganize—will help you understand the class material, cut down on last-minute test preparation (cramming), and be ready for your next test-day performance.

Review As soon as possible after class, look at the day's notes. Read them and highlight what you consider important information. Make sure you have written all the words legibly, and neatly correct any words that are difficult to read. Is anything unclear? Do you understand all the principles, generalizations, and theories?

If you have a question about an item, put an asterisk or question mark next to it in the margin of your notes. This can be the first question you ask at the beginning of the next class meeting or when you visit the instructor during office hours. If you wait to clarify the question until the night before the unit exam, it probably will be difficult to get clarification from the instructor.

In addition, by asking the question in the next class, you are actively participating—which is, coincidentally, another success strategy. Doing a nightly review of your class notes will help focus your attention on what you know and what you need to clarify.

Relate Avoid the temptation to memorize isolated pieces of information. Memorizing long and isolated lists of dates, names, spellings, and formulas can be a daunting and boring task. As an alternative, look at the previous day's notes and reading assignments and ask yourself these questions:

- What connections exist between my new notes and the previous material?
- What patterns, or repetitions, are developing? Can I use these to help me remember?
- Does the new material help me, or am I confused and in need of clarification?
- What textbook information could help me fill in my notes?

Once you start seeing this big picture, the material will make more sense and be easier to remember.

Activity 8.2

Helping Myron to Review, Relate, and Reorganize

The topic-opening story revealed that Myron writes many notes and that using this study method alone is not helping him. As a member of his study group, demonstrate how he can translate the instructor's words into his.

For this activity, choose the notes from one of your classes this term. They could come from this class or your history class, psychology class, math class, science class, computer class, or foreign language class. It might be best to pick the class in which you are having the most difficulty. In your notebook (or in a computer document file), practice the **Review-Relate-Reorganize strategy** for notes review.

- **Review.** Read your notes. Highlight important words. Make sure everything is written legibly. Mark any areas of question or concern about the material.

- **Relate.** As best you can, make connections between the class notes and what you talked about in earlier classes. Use the textbook to help you clarify your notes.

- **Reorganize.** Do you need to reorganize your notes in any way? This can be as simple as writing some clarifying comments in the margins or as involved as rewriting or typing your notes. One last time, ask yourself whether any part of the notes is confusing to you. Perhaps you need to ask the instructor about this for further clarification.

Reorganize Perhaps all you need to do is reorder your notes. Organize your notes so they make sense to you. You may wish to write a brief outline in the margin of the notes. Highlighting important concepts and facts with different-colored pens can help you focus on key points.

TALK TO YOURSELF—AND THEN TO SOMEONE ELSE

"I've tried all this stuff, but I still don't understand the new math formula," you say. In this case, "talk" your math problem through, step by step. Fully explain each step as best you can. Go as far in the process as possible. You may make it through four or five steps—or you might not be able to get past the first step.

Once you have done this, ask a classmate to listen to your explanation. Perhaps he or she can help you get past the spot where you stumble.

If you are still confused, it might be a good time to visit your professor. You will be able to explain exactly what you know and exactly where you get stuck. Doing so will help the professor understand where he or she needs to start working with you.

WHAT SHOULD YOU DO IF YOU STILL DON'T GET THE BIG PICTURE?

Even the best note-taker can be overwhelmed by a mountain of information and miss the overall meaning of a lesson. One complementary strategy you can use in conjunction with the Review-Relate-Reorganize strategy is the T.S.D. strategy.

Title/Summary/Details (T.S.D.) You will have a better chance of understanding class notes if you record the material in your own words. Copying your instructor's lesson word for word (or nearly word for word) will not be useful if you cannot explain the material in language that makes sense to you. The **T.S.D. strategy** is an active review strategy that consists of three simple steps:

- **T**: Start by giving the notes a *title*. What is the big picture? Come up with your own brief title that effectively captures the day's notes.
- **S**: Write a brief *summary*. In a sentence or two, summarize the notes in your words. What was the main point? Again, do not quote the instructor's words. *Use your own words.*
- **D**: List three *details* that support your summary. What do you see as the major details in the lecture? What questions might the instructor pose on the exam?

When you have written your review (or typed and saved it in a computer file), it may be no longer than one-quarter of a page in length. Thus, the T.S.D. strategy is quick, easy, and efficient.

Continue to review, relate, and reorganize each night in this manner. Add to them each day. By test time, you will have a full set of concise notes to serve as a practical study guide. You will have developed an ongoing study guide based on your class notes.

T.S.D. in reverse The T.S.D. strategy asks you first to see the big picture (topic and summary) and then to look at the details that support that larger view.

Activity 8.3

Critically Thinking about How to Use Your Notes

Let's apply the R.E.D. Model for critical thinking to examine one of the challenges you identified for yourself in Activity 8.1. Write one of those challenges on a piece of paper. Then answer the clarifying questions posed in the table below.

Critical-Thinking Step	Application to Your Note-Taking Skills
Recognize Assumptions	Clearly state this particular note-taking challenge. How do you know this assessment of your challenge is correct?
Evaluate Information	Provide a specific explanation (give examples) of this note-taking challenge. How is your assessment of your note-taking challenge connected to your academic progress? Examine your note-taking challenge from more than one perspective (point of view).
Draw Conclusions	Based on your evidence, how does your conclusion about your note-taking challenge make sense?

Based on your answers, what insights have you gained about your note-taking challenge?

What is the next step you will take to eliminate this challenge?

Perhaps you are the type of student who has to focus on the details first before you can see the big picture. If so, you can still use the T.S.D. strategy, but do it in reverse. Work backward.

First, list the main details. Then, based on the details you have listed, write a summary that shows the connections among the details. Finally, write the title that captures the idea of the entire class or reading assignment.

ADDITIONAL OUT-OF-CLASS STRATEGIES TO IMPROVE YOUR NOTES

HAVE YOU CREATED WORKING RELATIONSHIPS WITH YOUR INSTRUCTORS?

If you are still confused after a careful review of your notes and use of the strategies provided, consider a visit to your instructor's office.

Instructors typically post the **office hours** they are available to students. You can usually find this information in the syllabus, on the instructor's office door or website, and in the department office. If you still cannot locate an instructor's office hours, send him or her a quick e-mail or leave a voicemail.

Make it a goal to visit each of your instructors this term. These visits allow students to:

- Obtain clarification on class notes.
- Obtain clarification on future assignments.
- Seek assistance on a particularly troubling lesson.
- Ask to review the last exam or quiz to learn from any mistakes you may have made.
- Develop a face-name relationship, as your instructor will likely remember you as a student who has taken the time to seek help and get clarification of course material.
- Discuss challenges you are experiencing in the class.
- Seek advice about future courses, majors, or a career field.

DO YOU NEED A STUDY PARTNER OR GROUP?

The importance of having a strong support network to help you develop your intellectual and collaborative skills cannot be overemphasized. Students who feel connected to their classes and their campus have a better chance to experience success. This support system can be as simple as a compatible roommate, as effective as a good mentor, or as socially dynamic as a study group.

A **study partner** (or a study group) can help you do all these things:

- Make sense of your class notes.
- Understand lengthy and confusing reading assignments.
- See different perspectives (interpretations) of the course material.
- Choose a topic for a class project.
- Prepare for an upcoming exam.
- Understand a difficult concept.
- Cope with classroom failures.
- Celebrate classroom successes.

A major reason students leave college (especially within their first year) is because they do not feel part of the college community (Cuseo, 2013; Tinto, 2002). Getting a study partner is a small step toward building a much larger network of support.

Sometimes, however, working with a study partner or study group can present challenges. Differences in schedules, personalities, and work ethics require understanding and compromise. This is where knowing your learning style will be helpful. Take time to know who you will work with in a group *before* you decide to work with those people.

Your campus may have peer tutors or other types of academic support services that can provide you with the resources you need if a study group does not work for your learning style.

MEMORY

In the late 1800s, psychologist Hermann Ebbinghaus described the "forgetting curve." He found that if you do not immediately use what you have learned during, for instance, a class lecture or demonstration, you will lose it—forget it. According to Ebbinghaus's findings, most of what you will forget will happen within a few hours of your leaving the classroom or lecture hall. And if you don't work with the material within 30 days of receiving it, you will forget 90 percent of it (Medina, 2008, p. 100).

Besides reviewing and working with the information, other factors affect what you will remember, such as your interest in the topic and the complexity of the material. Nonetheless, spending time with the material is still the critical component. Figure 8.1 provides a visual approximation of the rapid loss of material that is not reviewed soon after receiving it.

Now, apply this information to the context of a school term. You listen to and take notes on a class lecture during a 9:00 a.m. psychology class on Monday. You leave class and do not review your notes. Four weeks later, it's test time. Unless you have a remarkable and rare type of memory, you will have lost most of that information.

Think about Ebbinghaus's finding. You can put in "seat time" (actually sit through each class), take notes, and still fail to remember or understand the information if you do not *do* something with it. That is what the material below will focus on: how you can *do* something effective to retain information.

Figure 8.1

Ebbinghaus's Forgetting Curve

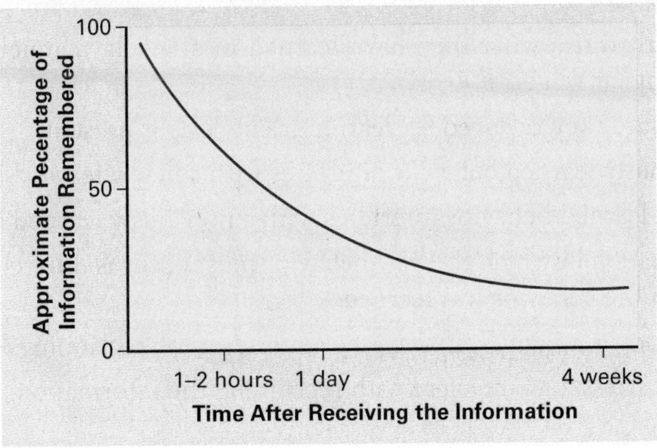
100
50
0
Approximate Pecentage of Information Remembered
1–2 hours
1 day
4 weeks
Time After Receiving the Information

Rather than simply memorize information and spit it back on a test, college requires students to read a lot of material, absorb a great deal of detail, and truly understand the readings and lectures.

Like Myron in the opening scenario, you may have heard someone say (or you may even have said it yourself), "I have a terrible memory. I can't remember a thing!"

Typically, this is an overstatement. You can remember things. If you didn't, how would you have found your way to class today? When someone complains of having a poor memory, he or she needs to dig deeper and critically examine assumptions and broad generalities. Below you will examine three basic components of memory and strategies to help you improve each one.

THREE SIMPLE STEPS TO IMPROVED MEMORY

The concept of **memory** simply refers to your ability to grab, hold, and recall information. If you want to improve your memory, you will need to do three things (Minninger & Dugan, 1994, pp. 27–41):

1. **Notice** the material. Before anyone can learn anything, he or she must notice the material. If you want to remember the date and time of a study group meeting, you must make note of it. Do you want to remember the formulas for the math test? You have to notice them. So, step 1 in improving your memory requires you to take note of what is around you. In short, you must pay attention.
2. **Storing information** is the second step in improving your memory. When we want to protect a cell phone or a tablet, we keep it in a safe and secure spot. Then, we want to remember where we put it so we can retrieve it for later use. The same holds true for information that we want to remember. If we store the information in a secure place in our minds, we will be able to access it easily when we need it.
3. **Reclaiming** (or retrieving) the information you have stored is the third step. When you reclaim information, you are finding it and using it.

IMPROVING YOUR MEMORY: Noticing the Information

Why do you forget? **Forgetting** is the failure of a previously learned behavior to re-appear. If you do not notice and effectively store information, it becomes much more difficult to recall it (as on a test, for example). People forget for a variety of reasons:

- They fail to use what they have learned in a timely manner. (Refer to the forgetting curve above.)
- The reward they received for learning is no longer present.
- A previously learned behavior interferes with a newly learned behavior.
- A newly learned behavior interferes with a previously learned behavior.
- The situation in which the new behavior must occur is different from the one in which the behavior was learned.
- An emotion (fear, anger, anxiety) may interfere with reclaiming the information.
- Physical stress may interfere with reclaiming the information.

Choosing to notice Each of us encounters a dizzying amount of stimulation within a day. Most of it, we hold on to for a very brief period (milliseconds) and then let go. In other words, we do not pay attention to this information, and we do not store the information.

The information that we do give attention to moves into **short-term memory**, which is also known as **working memory**. Our short-term or working memory will allow us to work with (manipulate) anywhere from five to nine items for a short time. The average is seven and is sometimes referred to as "Miller's magic number"—named after George Miller, who studied short-term memory.

Think of remembering a phone number without writing it down or punching it into your cell phone. You may repeat the seven-digit number over and over until you can physically touch each number on the keypad. The information may or may not eventually be transferred to long-term memory. If it is not, we typically say it has been "forgotten" (Miller, 1956).

Sometimes, we forget because we *choose not to remember*—or at the very least, we choose not to *notice*. If we can train ourselves to notice—to use our senses—we will have a better chance of remembering those things we come into contact with. When we learn to heighten our senses of seeing, listening, touching, tasting, and smelling, we will find it easier to recall a particular situation or reading or physical experience.

Listening, for instance, is an activity that requires focus. It goes beyond hearing; you will do better if you choose to *listen*. That is, when you want to understand the words you are hearing, you will have a better chance of remembering the information by paying attention to the material.

IMPROVING YOUR MEMORY: Storing the Information You Have Noticed

Once you notice the information, you need to file it away for future use. Remember, just because you have *heard* or *seen* or *touched* or *tasted* or *smelled* something does not mean you have paid attention to it.

To move information (a textbook reading, lecture, song lyrics, or statistics about a sports team) from your working memory to long-term memory, you have to learn how to encode it into something meaningful to you. This section will suggest strategies that, if practiced (rehearsed), can decrease the times you freeze or go blank when you want to recall something important.

Active listening improves memory Following the tips below will help you become a more active listener—and effectively store more information:

- **Focus.** Practice basic courtesy, and you will retain more. Pay attention to the speaker's words and meanings. Put aside other distractions. Take notes, if need be.

- **Find relevance.** Not every speaker, instructor, or reading assignment will be exciting and engaging. Find something you connect with in the presentation, and then focus on it. Perhaps you can find a relationship to something you already know or an explanation you have never heard of before.

- **Listen rather than hear.** Do this with your ears—not your mouth. If you mentally begin phrasing your response while the speaker is still talking, you may very well miss an important point. It can be difficult to understand the speaker if you are just waiting to jump in and give your opinion. If you "listen" in this manner, you are creating your own distraction.

- **Participate.** Once the speaker has finished, rephrase what he or she said. If you can explain, in your own words, what has just been presented, you will have a better chance of retention. By paraphrasing, you rehearse the new material, which leads to understanding.

- **Ask questions.** This is also part of the participation strategy. Ask for clarification, relationships, or the significance of the topic at hand. This will help you see the "big picture" and develop so-called memory hooks (discussed later).

- **Offer another explanation or application.** This is a particularly effective strategy to use in classes that follow a discussion or seminar format. As you process the instructor's information, offer another side of the issue in a tactful, noncombative manner. This allows for analysis and, consequently, better understanding.

Using charts to make connections Another helpful technique to organize information is the **data retrieval chart (D.R.C.)**. This model allows for easy categorization, comparison, and contrast of information.

As shown in Figure 8.2, a D.R.C. can be used to show how one event leads to another. In this case, it allows students to see the connection between the actions and responses of two groups. This simplified view of cause and effect demonstrates how England found itself in a war with its colonies.

Figure 8.2

D.R.C. Showing Cause and Effect in American War for Independence

Prime Minister	Example of British Action	Example of Colonial Response
Grenville	Stamp Act passed to collect taxes	Colonists upset with Stamp Act; Congress convened
Townshend (Pitt)	More taxes placed on the colonists	Colonists upset; boycott English goods
North	Tea Act passed	Colonists REALLY upset; Boston Tea Party dumps tea into Boston Harbor

A D.R.C. can be used to compare authors, scientific findings, historical developments, artistic relationships, and the like. Each cell can be easily compared with another cell. Relationships and connections, which are vital to improving memory, can be easily established.

Create your own D.R.C. when reviewing and reorganizing your notes. It will provide a great (and brief) study guide—efficient, effective, and practical.

Activity 8.4

Practice: Creating Your Own D.R.C.

Myron, from the opening scenario, has been attempting to memorize lists of terms and definitions. Demonstrate for him how a D.R.C. can make the course material more memorable with connections and visualizations. To do this, complete the following D.R.C. using five strategies introduced in the material you previously read on this topic.

Chapter Concept	Brief Description of the Strategy	Specific Example of How to Use the Strategy
1.		
2.		
3.		
4.		
5.		

Use your imagination: Create mental pictures Albert Einstein reportedly said, "If I can't picture it, I can't understand it." This leads us to another suggested way to improve memory: think in pictures.

For instance, refer to the D.R.C. on the American War for Independence in Figure 8.2. Visualize the British in their red coats. See the Boston Tea Party in your mind. Imagine the first shots fired at Lexington and Concord. This sort of creativity uses much more of the brain (think: multiple intelligences) than if you just attempt to memorize facts, dates, and so on without having a clear conception of what actually transpired. By bringing together the creative brain and the orderly brain, you use the whole brain to help you make connections—and increase your chances of being able to recall information.

IMPROVING YOUR MEMORY: Reclaiming the Information You Have Stored

The third step of memory, reclaiming (retrieving, recalling) the information you have stored, typically refers to what we have remembered or forgotten. In the storage process (described above), you placed the information in "files." To reclaim it, you have to flip through the "file cabinet" and locate the "folder." In this step, you reach back into your brain's file drawers and pull out the information you need to use.

Whether it is a phone number, directions to a party, or information for a test, this step requires that you effectively noticed and stored the material.

Retrieval: Start with what you already know Before we examine some new strategies, pause for a moment and reflect on what you have read about so far in this topic. Think about how you can use other study-skill strategies to improve your memory. For instance, if your retrieval problem (failure to remember something when you need to know it) stems from poor labeling, review the SQ4R reading strategies (surveying, questioning, read, recite, record, and review). Scanning, questioning, outlining, and anticipating make information processing more efficient.

The more you review (study), the more likely you will be able to retain and retrieve. And the more timely your review is (soon after being exposed to the material), the more dramatic the increase in the chance for storing and reclaiming.

"What about my class notes?" you may ask. "I can't seem to make any lasting sense of these scribbles." You can practice a couple of strategies here. First, think of the links you can make with other academic skills you have. You could ask yourself, "What are the connections between my homework readings and the instructor's presentations?"

For instance, perhaps your economics instructor has been describing how the economic concepts of supply and demand set the price of a product. Later that day in your textbook assignment, you read about gas prices in the United States. Looking at your notes from class, draw a connection (a relationship) between your instructor's lecture and what you just read: How do the concepts of supply and demand affect the price you pay to fill your car at the gas pump?

With a little practice, you will be able to determine these relationships easily. Once you establish them, you will have an increased ability to retain, understand, and retrieve. This moves beyond sheer memorization. The material starts to take on a life of its own. It makes sense—you understand it.

Memory blocks It has happened to most students at one time or another. They have prepared for an exam, they know the material, but they "freeze" on test day because of a **memory block**—something that impedes their ability to notice, store, or reclaim information. There are different types of memory blocks:

- **Emotional memory blocks.** Perhaps you have struggled in your math class. No matter what you seem to do, your grades are less than satisfactory. As you prepare for the next math exam, you do not expect to do any better. Whether it is a fear of failure, the memory of a distressing prior experience, or some other traumatic issue, some students fear the challenges that await them inside the classroom door. The emotion effectively blocks any attempt to reclaim the information.

- **Physical memory blocks.** Our physical well-being can affect how clearly we think and remember. For instance, you stay up late studying for tomorrow's psychology exam. You gulp caffeine drinks and snack on donuts while you review all your readings, notes, and study guides. When you awaken the next morning, you are so tired you cannot think clearly—and what you studied just a few hours earlier is a jumbled mess. A physical memory block can result from lack of sleep, an inappropriate diet, or a lack of exercise. This is a reminder to keep all dimensions of your life balanced.

- **Mechanical blocks.** You put a lot of time into your studies, but you can't seem to recall the data during the exam. You feel at ease, and you are well rested. But you still can't pull the information you studied "out of your brain." This can be an indication of some retrieval difficulty. It is typically due to a problem with the second step of the memory process: You did not store the information in a clear and recognizable location in your brain's "filing cabinet." If you just throw the information into the "drawers" without "labeling" it, so to speak, you will have difficulty retrieving it.

Retrieval failure: What can you do about it? Failure to retrieve is another way of saying "I forgot it!" For whatever reason, you cannot access—find—the information that you tucked away in your mind. It is still there—you just can't locate it (Cherry, 2013).

Remember that the short-term (working) memory can last anywhere from 30 seconds to a couple of days. If you do not use the information, though, it will be lost to you.

Long-term memory consists of those items that have not been "lost." For whatever reason—practice, concentration, or desire—you have retained this information. "But," you reasonably may ask, "Why do I still forget things when it comes to test time? I've practiced. I have desire. But my test grades sure don't reflect that!" Let's examine a few reasons this may be. After each point in the following list, you will find a strategy or two to combat the retrieval challenge:

- **Disuse (or decay).** Your memory is like your muscles, in a sense. If you don't use information you have filed away, you will more than likely lose it.

  - **Strategy.** Once you have stored the material, find ways to practice (rehearse) it as soon and as often as possible. For instance, once you learn a vocabulary word in class, use it soon after. Doing so will increase your chances of remembering the word.

  - **Strategy.** Research tells us the best way to remember is to review information at "fixed, spaced intervals." That is, if you have seven days to review for an exam and you know you want to review at least five times before test day, the best strategy is to space out the five study times. Do not squeeze all your study time into the hours before the test. The more repetitions, the better (Medina, 2008, p. 133). Daily review of your notes provides this type of repetition.

  - **Strategy.** If you find practicing information tedious and boring, reframe the way you view the information (or course) that does not hold interest for you. Make a short-term commitment to yourself to find in the instructor's lesson at least two items of interest each day you go to class. Perhaps you can go a step further and search for a connection between the course and your passion (or eventual major). If that proves difficult or impossible to do, use that as a reason to visit your instructor's office. For instance, "I love science and do very well in those courses. Could you help me find a connection between your U.S. history course and science? Do they have anything in common?" Such questions let the instructor know of your passion and your interest to do well in the course.

- **Extinction.** School is based, in part, on providing a series of rewards. These incentives vary, ranging from grades to awards for having a high grade point average (GPA)—like making the dean's list. Many students have been conditioned by these extrinsic rewards—that is, awards given by someone else. Getting a good grade, for instance, becomes the overriding reason for performance. Once the reward (grade) is removed, the incentive to continue to work with the material is removed. It has been extinguished, or at the very least, it has been greatly diminished. No reward, less effort, minimal retention.

  - **Strategy.** Can you find an intrinsic (internal) reward to help motivate you? If the reading is related to your major, you might be motivated because you have a passion for the content. However, the reality remains that your required courses may hold little interest for you. Someone with a deep passion for literature may find it difficult to stay focused in a science course. Perhaps the best advice is to remember that these prerequisites serve as "gatekeepers." You must pass through them to move into the course work that really interests you. Once you navigate these early courses, you will be able to concentrate on the subject areas that hold intrinsic motivation for you. Perhaps networking with a study partner will help, too.

■ **Response competition (*interference*).** Visualize this scenario: You have studied for a science unit exam. Your science class, however, comes right after your math class, in which the instructor has introduced a new process complete with formulas and equations. Or perhaps earlier that morning, you had an argument with a friend. In your mind, you are still running through what he or she said. By the time you get to science class, your mind is moving in three or four directions—and none of them seems related to the exam in front of you. The new information interferes (competes) with what you studied for the exam.

   ■ **Strategy.** An efficient filing system in your brain really will pay off. If you develop connections, rehearse (practice) the material, and develop a feeling of confidence, you have a better chance of the material becoming second nature (almost automatic) to you. While you may not be able to stop the competing signals, you will have a better chance of finding and recalling the information needed.

   ■ **Strategy.** When scheduling classes for your next term, leave an hour or two between classes so that you will have time to sit somewhere quiet and refocus before going into a test situation. The same goes for work schedules. Leave yourself some breathing room, rather than rushing from work to the parking lot to the classroom.

■ **Situational variation.** Let's call this *stage fright*. Consider these scenarios: You practiced a guitar lead for months. You never missed a lick. But the first time you perform it in public, your fingers fumble with the strings. Or you are in a play. You never flubbed a line during rehearsals. But it is opening night, and you can't remember your name! Why? The situation—the setting—has changed. You practiced in one environment but had to perform in quite another environment.

   ■ **Strategy.** Practice the material in various situations to help eliminate this distraction. Perhaps you can sit in the classroom where you will take the real exam. If you can, complete practice exercises within the same time frame as you will have on test day. If your instructor will allow only 50 minutes for the test, practice in 50-minute blocks of time. Prepare for the content as well as for the timed situation. Does your textbook have an online lab (like MyStudentSuccessLab) that provides practice questions? If it does, use it regularly. Maybe the instructor has an old exam for you to practice with. Do as many practice tests as you can in a test-like environment. Depending on how much of a concern this is for you, you might think about actually doing a practice test in the classroom for the specified time.

Mnemonics This strange-looking word (pronounced "nih-MON-icks") refers to memory tricks that help you recall information. Mnemonics allow you to get creative. Let's look at three examples:

■ **Acronyms.** An acronym is a word formed from the letters (usually the first letters) of other words. Do you wish to remember the names of the Great Lakes? Just remember HOMES: Huron, Ontario, Michigan, Erie, and Superior.

- **Acrostics.** An *acrostic* uses the first letter of each word in a sequence to create a message. Do you want to remember the notes (EGBDF) assigned to the lines of a musical staff? (*Every Good Boy Does Fine*). How about the taxonomic levels in biology? *King Philip Came Over For Green Spaghetti* (*Kingdom, Phylum, Class, Order, Family, Genus, Species*).

- **The hook, number, linking, location, or peg system.** A peg is something you can hang an item on. Using a mental peg (or mental hook) allows you to attach a concept, word, or item to one or more known objects. You "locate" what you want to remember by calling up the object. For instance, you may tend to forget where you put your keys after using them. The next time you toss them onto the table, think of the table spinning or maybe even lighting up. By creating a vivid and outrageous picture of the peg (movement, light), you engage your brain with this concept. Doing so makes it more likely you will be able to reclaim what you want to remember—where you put your keys.

Here's another example: If you have to remember the steps of a mathematical formula, visualize the rooms in your house. Have each room of the house hold one of the steps of the formula. As you move from one room to another, you find the next step until you finally complete the formula. The associations do not have to be logical. All you are doing is creating a picture of the item or items you need to remember. This system works well with lists, such as vocabulary words, bones of the body, and parts of speech.

Practice, practice, and more practice When learning new material, it helps to do three things: practice, practice, and practice some more. To learn a new skill, perform activities that stretch your mind. Just like an athlete does stretches, calisthenics, and wind sprints to get in shape, you will improve your ability to learn if you do "mental gymnastics." Consider your mental warm-ups as mind exercises. Use them and you will expand your capabilities. Rehearse the material as often as possible.

Memory does not mean understanding Having an effective memory may seem impressive, and it may even help you get by on tests. But it does not indicate that you understand the material. In fact, a good memory might end up being one of your (unknown) weaknesses.

For instance, some students spend many hours in school *memorizing* lists of vocabulary words and spelling words. Their exams and quizzes reflect high scores. But in reality, these students could be missing out on understanding the important rules that guide spelling exceptions.

True learning usually causes some frustration. After all, learning indicates a change in behavior. Learning anything new can be challenging to some of us. The same thing is true of memory strategies.

As you look back on the ideas included in this material, keep two points in mind:

1. If you are not accustomed to using memory strategies, they may seem awkward. Please don't give up on them for that reason alone.
2. Not every technique is for everyone. Pick and choose, but find something that works for you—and then use it regularly. Remember, consistent practice makes permanent.

Chapter SUMMARY

To be successful, students need to become active learners outside the classroom. Before leaving this topic, keep the following points in mind:

- You will have a better chance of understanding class notes if you record material in your own words.

- As soon as possible after class, review your class notes.

- Learning is more likely to occur when you establish connections between class material and what you already know.

- Once you start seeing the "big picture" (that is, how the little pieces fit together), the material should make sense and be easier to remember.

- Whatever it takes, find your instructors' offices, know their office hours, and make it a goal to visit all of them this term.

- Remembering information involves three steps: noticing, storing, and reclaiming. You must see something, put it someplace, and be able to find it.

- Practice active listening every day.

- Whatever you learn, use the new knowledge as soon and as often as possible.

CRITICALLY THINKING

What Have You Learned?

Let's apply what you learned to help Myron from the opening scenario. However, before you consider Myron's problem and propose your solution, take a moment to review your notes, key terms, learning outcomes, boldface headings, and figures and tables.

TEST YOUR LEARNING

Now that you have reviewed the main points and reread Myron's story, what advice do you have for him? Using the R.E.D. Model for critical thinking, help Myron critically review his concerns:

R

Recognize Assumptions

Facts: What are the facts in Myron's situation? List them.

Opinions: What opinions do you find in this situation? List them.

Assumptions: Are Myron's assumptions accurate?

E

Evaluate Information

Help Myron compile a list of questions that will help him make the most appropriate decision.

What emotions seem to be motivating Myron?

What, if anything, is missing from his thought process?

Do you see any confirmation bias?

D

Draw Conclusions

Based on the facts and the questions you have presented, what conclusions can you draw?

What advice do you have for Myron? What solutions do you propose?

Based on your suggestions, do you see any assumptions?

Finally, based on what you learned about using critical thinking, memory, and study skills, what plan of action do you suggest for Myron?

9 READING

LEARNING OUTCOMES

By the time you finish reading this material and completing the activities, you will know how to do the following:

- Identify the purpose of a reading assignment.

- Demonstrate how and why to use the SQ4R reading process.

- Use highlighting to identify key information and improve understanding.

- Determine the meanings of vocabulary words by using the context of the reading assignment.

- Use graphics to help understand a reading assignment.

The Case of LENA

Lena is a second-semester college student. She works hard, completes all of her assignments, and comes to class punctually every day. Her biggest challenge has been her history reading quizzes.

Actually, using the word *challenge* is putting things mildly. Although she uses the instructor-provided study guides, Lena has not passed one reading quiz this term. Lena says she has always been a poor reader.

Recently, Lena told her instructor, "I don't have a lot of free time, so any spare moment I have, I open the book and begin reading." She proudly showed her textbook, pointing to the pages as she flipped through the assigned chapter. "See, I highlight a lot. You can tell I read this stuff. I don't have time to

Key Terms

Active reading
Brain-based learning
Comprehension
Context
Graphics
Highlighting
Main idea
Purpose (for reading)
Scan
SQ4R
Strategic reading
Vocabulary

Chapter INTRODUCTION

In today's society of instant Internet, on-demand videos, and music downloading, one may wonder whether reading has become a lost art. Some people wonder, "Why read a book when I can *listen* to a book or *see* a movie on my smartphone or tablet?"

While the medium has changed—becoming more digitized—reading remains a crucial skill. In fact, being able to read well is perhaps even more important today than in the past.

As you progress through your college program of study, the required reading will increase in volume, difficulty, and complexity. Besides traditional

take notes, so I make sure to mark all the important things. And I was very lucky to have bought a used book, where all of the important words were already marked." Sure enough, anywhere from 50 percent to 75 percent of every page had been highlighted with a yellow marker.

Lena also told her instructor how she has prioritized her reading time extremely well by skipping over the chapter introductions and summaries. "I get right to the business of reading the meat of the chapter," she said.

Tomorrow is the last day to withdraw from classes—an option Lena has strongly considered. In one last effort to save her history class, Lena has come to you for advice.

CRITICALLY THINKING
about *Lena's* situation

Identify three strategies you would suggest to Lena. Tell her how using each strategy will help improve her reading quiz scores.

textbooks, you will use library databases, indexes, and e-books for research purposes. Whether you read electronic material (Internet articles and blogs), a novel for English class, or your chemistry textbook, you will want to find effective and efficient ways to complete the reading and prepare for discussions, applications, quizzes, and exams.

To do these things, you need to take an active part in the reading process. Reading involves more than your eyes seeing words on a page. Effective and skilled readers know that reading is a strategic process. That is, if you follow a few basic steps, you can tackle your assignments more effectively

MyStudentSuccessLab

MyStudentSuccessLab (www .mystudentsuccesslab.com) is an online solution designed to help you "Start strong, Finish stronger" by building skills for ongoing personal and professional development.

and effortlessly. **Active reading** requires you to *do* something, not just passively look at the words on the page.

Regardless of your current comprehension level, you and your fellow students have at least one thing in common: You have read books before. This is not new territory for you.

Respect the reading skills you currently have and build on them. Activity 9.1 will give you the chance to reflect on your reading skills—and think about how you can make immediate improvements.

Activity 9.1

Reflecting on Your Current Level of Reading Skills

Before you answer the items that follow, reflect on your current level of reading skills. Think of how well (or poorly) you have performed on past reading assignments.

As you complete this activity, write from your heart. This exercise is not meant for you to answer just like your classmates—or to match what you may think the instructor wants to see. Take the time to give a respectful, responsible general accounting of your experiences with reading. Conducting a truthful self-assessment now will help you build on skills you have while developing those you lack.

For each of the following items, circle the number that best describes your typical experience with reading skills. Here is the key for the numbers:

0 = never, 1 = almost never, 2 = occasionally, 3 = frequently, 4 = almost always, 5 = always

When considering your past successes and challenges with reading, how often:

1.	Did you scan your reading assignment for main points before jumping right into reading?	0	1	2	3	4	5
2.	Did you take effective notes from your reading?	0	1	2	3	4	5
3.	Did you use your reading notes to help you with class discussions?	0	1	2	3	4	5
4.	Were you able to read an assignment and understand its main idea?	0	1	2	3	4	5
5.	Could you figure out the meaning of a word from the words surrounding it?	0	1	2	3	4	5
6.	Were you able to remember what you read?	0	1	2	3	4	5
7.	Did you review your reading notes immediately after completing your reading assignment?	0	1	2	3	4	5
8.	Was your vocabulary strong enough so that you could understand the meaning of the textbook?	0	1	2	3	4	5

Add up your scores for items 1, 4, and 6. Divide by 3. Write your answer here: _____

Using the key provided to explain each number (0, 1, 2, 3, 4, 5), complete this sentence: When it comes to identifying the main points of a reading, I _____ do this effectively.

Add up your scores for items 2, 3, and 7. Divide by 3. Write your answer here: _____

Using the key provided to explain each number (0, 1, 2, 3, 4, 5), complete this sentence: When it comes to reading notes, I _____ take and use reading notes effectively.

Add up your scores for items 5 and 8. Divide by 2. Write your answer here: _____

Using the key provided to explain each number (0, 1, 2, 3, 4, 5), complete this sentence: When it comes to vocabulary, I _____ understand the vocabulary in my reading assignments.

Based on your answers, what insights have you gained about your reading skills?

DO YOU KNOW WHY YOU READ AN ASSIGNMENT?

At first glance, the question "Do you know why you read an assignment?" appears simplistic and obvious. You would likely reply, "Of course I know why I read my assignment—because the instructor said it would be on the test."

Okay. That might identify the motivation that gets you to open the book. But once you have the assignment in front of you, why do you read it? Or even more to the point, *do you know what you are looking for in the reading?*

If you were asked to clean the garage (or the student government office, or your room, or the athletic workout room), would you start working just anywhere, moving anything? Probably not. You would likely want to know exactly what should be moved, thrown away, put away, or cleaned. In other words, you would want to know the intended *purpose* or *result* of your work. Knowing that would help you avoid wasting time. You would be able to finish the job as effectively and efficiently as possible.

IDENTIFYING THE PURPOSE

The same holds true for reading. A key to increased reading **comprehension** is to know what the result should be. When you comprehend material, you can describe it in your own words. You understand it.

There are various **purposes**, or reasons, for reading (Fry, 1991, p. 18; Sholes, 2013). Common purposes for reading include the following:

- To answer specific questions (like those at the end of a chapter)
- To apply (use in new situations) the reading material (to solve a problem)
- To find details (to support an argument or to answer questions)
- To get a message (such as from a political candidate's statement)
- To evaluate (judge) the reading material (to help you make a decision)
- To entertain (as when you read a novel, a blog, or song lyrics)

If you can identify the purpose of a reading assignment before you start reading, you will have less chance of slamming the book closed in frustration.

The following list provides some quick tips to help you determine what to look for in your reading material:

- Pay attention for in-class instructor clues about purpose.
- Review your class notes. Perhaps you will find a clue as to what has been emphasized over the past few lessons.
- Ask a classmate or study group partner for advice.
- Ask your instructor for advice.
- Use the features of the textbook that give clues as to what is important. Look for key terms, graphics, an introduction, and a summary.

BRAIN-BASED LEARNING: Making Sense of What May Seem to Be Chaos

Research indicates that the brain seeks out meaning. It looks for connections as it establishes patterns that help it make sense of the world. These **brain-based learning** studies suggest we can take raw facts and make them mean something. And after all, isn't that what you want to do with all of the details thrown at you during the course of a college term? You want to make sense out of what, at times, can seem like chaos.

For learning to take place, you have to take three steps (Shapiro, 2006):

1. Sense or notice the material.
2. Integrate or combine it with what you already know.
3. Act on or use the information.

The same steps are involved in reading. If you want to understand and remember more of what you read, you have to do these three things:

1. *Notice* what you read—the words, the headings, the boldface type, the graphics, the questions, and the key terms.
2. *Connect* what you already know to the topic you are reading about.
3. *Use* the information as soon as possible to strengthen your learning and retention.

HOW TO COMPLETE A TEXTBOOK READING ASSIGNMENT

A PROVEN PROCESS FOR EFFECTIVE READING: SQ4R

Probably the most common approach to tackling a reading assignment is the **SQ4R** method. It is based on the now-famous method developed by Franklin Pleasant Robinson during World War II. The SQ4R method has extended Robinson's pioneering work. Today, numerous sources reference the SQ4R method (see, for example,

"SQ4R: A Classic Method for Studying Texts," 2007), and variations of the model have been developed (see "SQ4R Reading Method," n.d.).

Activity 9.2 provides a quick overview of this strategy. It also gives you the chance to identify how often you do each step.

Activity 9.2

SQ4R: What You Need to Know Right Now to Improve Your Reading

This introduction to SQ4R will allow you to rate how you currently use each of the six steps. A more detailed description of this process follows later in this material.

1. **Survey.** Quickly look over (**scan**) the reading assignment for clues as to what you will be reading. Look at the headings, captions, boldface terms, and any other features the assigned pages might include. Engage your curiosity.

   ■ Circle the number that best corresponds to your answer to this question: *How often do you survey a reading assignment?*

   0 = never, 1 = almost never, 2 = occasionally, 3 = frequently, 4 = almost always, 5 = always

2. **Question.** Ask yourself questions about what you think the assignment will address. Also, while reading, continue to ask yourself questions about what you have just read.

   ■ Circle the number that best corresponds to your answer to this question: *How often do you ask yourself questions about a reading assignment?*

   0 = never, 1 = almost never, 2 = occasionally, 3 = frequently, 4 = almost always, 5 = always

3. **Read.** In this step, you actually read your assignment.

   ■ Circle the number that best corresponds to your answer to this question: *How often do you actually read an entire reading assignment?*

   0 = never, 1 = almost never, 2 = occasionally, 3 = frequently, 4 = almost always, 5 = always

4. **Recite.** Periodically stop reading and put what you have just read into your own words. Consider this a self-quiz on your comprehension of the material.

   ■ Circle the number that best corresponds to your answer to this question: *While you are reading an assignment, how often do you pause and summarize in your own words what you have read?*

   0 = never, 1 = almost never, 2 = occasionally, 3 = frequently, 4 = almost always, 5 = always

5. **Record.** Physically mark your book or write/type notes about the important words you are reading. You could highlight, underline, write in the book, type on a laptop or tablet, or jot down notes on a separate piece of paper.

   ■ Circle the number that best corresponds to your answer to this question: *How often do you highlight or take notes on a reading assignment?*

   0 = never, 1 = almost never, 2 = occasionally, 3 = frequently, 4 = almost always, 5 = always

6. **Review.** Once you have completed your assignment but before closing the book, review what you have read to make sure you understand the material. If you find the material confusing, make a note of the troubling passages and ask a classmate or the instructor for assistance.

   ■ Circle the number that best corresponds to your answer to this question: *How often do you review a reading assignment as soon as you complete the assignment?*

   0 = never, 1 = almost never, 2 = occasionally, 3 = frequently, 4 = almost always, 5 = always

Based on your answers, what insights have you gained about how you approach a reading assignment?

The SQ4R method is graphically portrayed in Figure 9.1.

Call it what you will, but the plan has three broad stages, essentially: preread, read, and postread.

Preread   This part of the process involves the survey and question steps introduced earlier. Consider it the warm-up phase of reading. Athletes perform stretching exercises to limber up their muscles. Reading should be no different, in terms of preparation. If you just open your book to the assigned page and start reading, you will have started "running" without warming up.

Two simple questions will help you focus during this warm-up stage: "What do I already know about this material?" and "What would I like to know about this material?"

Figure 9.1

- **Warm up your intellectual muscles and establish a purpose.** Actively prepare to read. If you don't know what to look for, your reading may seem like torture. Refer to the purposes for reading listed earlier. Ask these basic questions:

  - What is this instructor concentrating on in class?
  - What kinds of test questions might come from this reading?
  - What past knowledge do I have about the reading assignment?

- **Scan the material.** If you were asked to find the phone number for Dominic Jones, would you look at the phone listings and start reading from the A's? Probably not. That would be a waste of your time. You would search for the J's and then scan for the last name and finally for the full name until you found it.

Make your reading as efficient as possible. While still warming up, quickly flip through the pages of the assignment. When you scan your reading assignment, you get a quick feel for what the "big picture" is. What you want is to get a general sense of the assignment. Read the introduction and the summary of the chapter. If you have to accomplish a certain outcome by the end of your reading—say, answer teacher-provided questions—then scan the material with that particular purpose in mind.

Although using this strategy adds a little time to the front end of your reading, it will aid your comprehension, and you will have a better idea of what you need to read.

Activity 9.3

Helping Lena: Practice Scanning

In the topic-opening situation, Lena mentioned that she typically jumped right in to complete her reading assignment. Let's demonstrate for Lena how a little thought can help improve her reading interest and comprehension.

Before you move to the next section of this material, practice your scanning skill. Complete this activity using the textbook you are reading right now. Do the following:

- Read the topic introduction and the summary.
- Based on the introduction and the summary, write a sentence or two that explains what you will learn with this information. Hint: Be more specific than "This material will teach me how to read better."
- Look at the key terms listed at the beginning of the material. As you scan, ask yourself, "Why have these words been labeled key terms?"
- Read the headings/subheadings, and form questions based on them. These questions will give you a purpose for reading. As you read, you will be actively looking for information (answers to your questions). For instance, one section is titled *Identifying the Purpose*. The question you form might be "Why do I need to identify the purpose?" or "Can there be more than one purpose?"
- Write a couple of the questions you formed.
- Look at all pictures, graphics, and captions in the material. They have a purpose for being in the text. What types of graphics have been included? Why do you think they have been chosen?
- Look at the boldface, italicized, and underlined words and phrases. Why do you think these particular words and phrases have been highlighted?

Read Once you have warmed up, you are ready to read, recite, and record.

- This is the time to satisfy your curiosity and look for answers to the questions you posed in the activity above. As you read, ask more questions. Look for the **main idea** of the reading selection. What is the main reason the author wrote the paragraph, chapter, or book you are reading? In short, what is the main opinion, view, or objective of what you are reading? Understand this and you are well on your way to comprehending your reading assignment (Henry, 2004, p. 108). Remember your English training. Whether you find paragraphs in a textbook or on a website, they (usually) have a topic sentence—a sentence that explains the main idea of the paragraph. Many times, the topic sentence is the first sentence, but sometimes it appears later in the paragraph. As you develop stronger reading skills, you will find the topic more easily and have a better understanding of the passages you read.

- Textbooks of different disciplines require different approaches (Adler & Van Doren, 1972, chapters 13 and 19). Recognize the differences and make adjustments:

    - When reading a *history* text, look for cause and effect, names of important people, impacts of events on people, turning points, and hints of bias or prejudice by the author.
    - When reading a *science* book, focus on classifications, experimental steps, hypotheses, and unexplained phenomena.
    - When reading a novel for *English*, look for symbolism, plot, a hero, tragic flaws, and a developing message.
    - Even when reading a *math* book, look for its particular characteristics. Determine which variables, functions, theorems, and axioms are the "building blocks" of the material you are reading.

Strategic Reading

Highlighting is a **strategic reading** behavior. That is, when used properly, it is part of a planned and thoughtful action to achieve a desired result. In this case, reading comprehension is the goal. If highlighting is done without thought—that is, just "painting the page yellow" by marking everything—then it is neither strategic nor effective. Apply your skills of surveying, questioning, and using context clues in highlighting. Consider highlighting just one more form of active learning. As one study found, students will perform more effectively if they actively participate with the material they are reading (Gier et al., 2011, p. 40).

Record The importance of this step is to make the words you read your own. The better able you are to put the author's words into your own words, the more likely it is you will remember the material.

There are a couple of ways to handle the recording part of SQ4R:

- **Highlighting.** Use a pen, pencil, or brightly colored marker to underline, circle, or box important information. But remember this word of caution about **highlighting:** Identify only the *major* points. Again, avoid highlighting almost every word. If everything is highlighted then nothing stands out. Look for key words and phrases.

- **Making margin notes.** As you read, make notes in the margins of your book. Maybe you have a question about the paragraph you just completed reading. If so, jot it down in the margin. Or as you highlight part of a sentence or passage, write the main point—in your words—in the margin. Learn to use your book: Read it, write in it, and consume it! And consider keeping your textbooks for future reference—especially those in your major area of study.

- **Note taking.** Using the strategies you have already practiced, actually record notes in your notebook. You may find note taking more effective than highlighting, because it forces you to encode the material—putting it into your own words. If you can do this, you *understand* the material. Concentrate on main points, themes, and questions you might have.

Used Books, Highlighting, and Effective Reading

Buying used textbooks gives students an opportunity to save money. However, as with buying anything that has been previously owned, the buyer has to be a wise consumer. Carefully review any used book to see how it was used by the previous owner(s). One group of researchers advises used-book buyers to examine the highlighting, in particular. Consider these findings: "Students who buy used textbooks may find that the previous owner(s) highlighted the passages in the textbook inappropriately . . . [and that] relevant material was not highlighted, and non-relevant material was highlighted" (Gier et al., 2011, p. 39). Assuming the previous owner has already "done all the work" by picking out the important material could be costly for the student who buys a used book. Because unfortunately, "all the work" may be totally wrong.

Review Once you have completed your reading assignment, do not immediately close the book. It's time to review! Even if your review is brief, the repetition will help you strengthen connections and deepen your learning. Use an effective memory strategy here: Repeat to remember. The more you practice, the better your chances of remembering the information. Once you remember, make sure you understand (Medina, 2008; Jensen, 2000, p. 78). The question to ask yourself at this point is "What did I just read?"

Immediately after reading, take five or ten minutes to study the notes you just wrote or the words you highlighted. Organize and reorganize your notes according to categories, theories, trends, or other qualities. It may help to ask yourself these questions:

- What is the "big picture"?
- How can I connect this new knowledge to previously learned material?
- What relationships do I see emerging?

Performing this step keeps you focused while preparing for the next class and the upcoming exam. If you are confused about the reading, bring your question(s) to the next class.

Well, there you have it. SQ4R provides an achievable plan with many benefits. The notes you develop while reading, for instance, will serve as an excellent complement for your classroom notes. With your reading complete and organized, you will be ready for the instructor's presentation. You can participate, actively learn, and get better grades, and you will be able to use your precious time more effectively.

Activity 9.4

Critically Thinking about How You Read Your Assignments

R E D

Let's apply the R.E.D. Model for critical thinking to examine one of the reading challenges you identified for yourself in Activity 9.2.

Write one of those challenges in your notebook.

Critical-Thinking Step	Application to Your Reading Skills	Your Explanation (Here or on a Separate Piece of Paper)
Recognize Assumptions	Clearly state this particular reading challenge. How do you know your assessment of your reading challenge is correct?	
Evaluate Information	Provide a specific explanation (give examples) of this reading challenge. Examine your identified reading challenge beyond a superficial (simplistic) explanation, and look at all of the complexities involved. Examine your reading challenge from more than one perspective (point of view).	
Draw Conclusions	Based on your evidence, does your conclusion about your reading challenge make sense?	

Based on your answers, what insights have you gained about your reading challenge? What is the next step you will take to eliminate this challenge?

ADDITIONAL STRATEGIES FOR READING SUCCESS

VOCABULARY

Your **vocabulary** is your "bank" of words, the words you know and can use appropriately. It contains the words that allow you to communicate your feelings and views. Moreover, the richness of your vocabulary will have an impact on how well you understand the people—and the world—around you.

The broader your vocabulary, the better you will read. Here are two strategies to help you continue to add to your word bank:

1. Use a dictionary to clarify meanings of words you don't understand. Look up new words, correct misspellings on exams and homework, and learn synonyms and antonyms. You can buy a small (pocket) dictionary and thesaurus, or you can use online tools.

2. Play word games, such as Scrabble, or work with crossword puzzles. (You may even be able to download apps for these and similar games to your cell phone.) This strategy has two benefits: it builds your vocabulary, and it limbers up your "mental muscles" for the coming academic day.

USING CONTEXT CLUES TO BUILD YOUR VOCABULARY

The reality is that few of us stop, reach for a dictionary, leaf through the pages (or, if online, type and search for a word), and read the definition of a troublesome word. In addition, in some situations, such as taking an exam, using a dictionary may not be practical or permissible.

In such instances, you will want to rely on context clues. In this usage, **context** refers to the words that surround the word you want to understand. Using the words you do understand, you make an educated guess about the meaning of the unknown word.

Activity 9.5

Practice Using Context Clues

For each sentence, write the meaning of the underlined word and briefly explain how the context (surrounding words) helps define it.

- *Rather than <u>rant</u>, Jeremy stopped talking and counted to ten before calmly responding to the offensive remark.*
    - The meaning of <u>rant</u>: ....
    - How does the context help you understand the underlined word?

- *Successful leaders know when to <u>delegate</u>, or assign, work to other people.*
    - The meaning of <u>delegate</u>: ....
    - How does the context help you understand the underlined word?

- *The customer showed his <u>integrity</u> when he came back to the store to return the extra money the cashier had given him in error.*
    - The meaning of <u>integrity</u>: ....
    - How does the context help you understand the underlined word?

- *In order to avoid using <u>clichés</u>, Joe always looked for new and novel ways to write and speak.*
    - The meaning of <u>clichés</u>: ....
    - How does the context help you understand the underlined word?

HAVING TROUBLE FINDING THE MAIN IDEA? USE MINI-SQ4RS

If you have difficulty determining the main idea, then break your reading task into smaller pieces. Read one paragraph at a time, and use the SQ4R strategy: Scan the paragraph, ask yourself a question or two about it, jot down a few notes, and then review what you have read.

Once you find that you can understand a single paragraph, expand your reading to two, three, or more paragraphs at a time. If you get to a point where you do not comprehend the main idea, back up and read fewer paragraphs. While using this approach will take more time at first, think of the time you will have wasted if you read an entire chapter and do not understand most or all of the content.

UNDERSTANDING AND USING GRAPHICS

Authors use **graphics** to simplify and energize their messages. Using fewer words than sentences or paragraphs (and sometimes using colors, shapes, and images), they can help readers make the connection between concepts, understand the main point of a paragraph, and show support for a particular opinion. Graphics also are important guides to help you survey your reading—the first step of SQ4R. (For a review, see Smith, Brenda [2008], pp. 534–547.) Some of the most common kinds are shown in Figure 9.2.

"NOW, WHAT DO I DO WITH MY READING NOTES?"

Completing your reading assignment is important, but as you study, you also need to review, reorganize, and find relationships in the information you read. Once you have mastered the reading assignment, bring your reading notes to class. Using reading notes in class serves a variety of purposes. These notes can serve as a guide for discussion, help you answer teacher-posed questions, remind you to ask clarifying questions, and/or allow you to focus on the important points the teacher is making.

As a reflective self-assessment, ask yourself whether you can intelligently discuss the reading material in a class discussion. If you can, congratulate yourself. If you can't, review the assignment briefly before you get to class. Remember that practice makes permanent.

"MY INSTRUCTOR ALWAYS FALLS BEHIND SCHEDULE"

Instructors have great intentions. They meticulously plan a unit of study, neatly matching and spacing reading assignments to complement well-thought-out lectures and activities as they move toward the unit exam.

Unfortunately, great plans sometimes get lost in the realities of day-to-day classroom activities. Have you ever had an instructor who painstakingly covered one chapter in three *weeks*, only to finish the unit with a "big push"—covering four chapters in three *days*? Picking up the pace like this can be stressful for everyone concerned, but you have to deal with it.

It's best to do homework reading that corresponds with classroom topics—for example, preparing for the lesson prior to coming to class. But don't wait to digest 90 pages of new material in a couple of nights. Put yourself on a schedule, read, and keep your notes handy for when the teacher finally reviews that material in class.

Figure 9.2

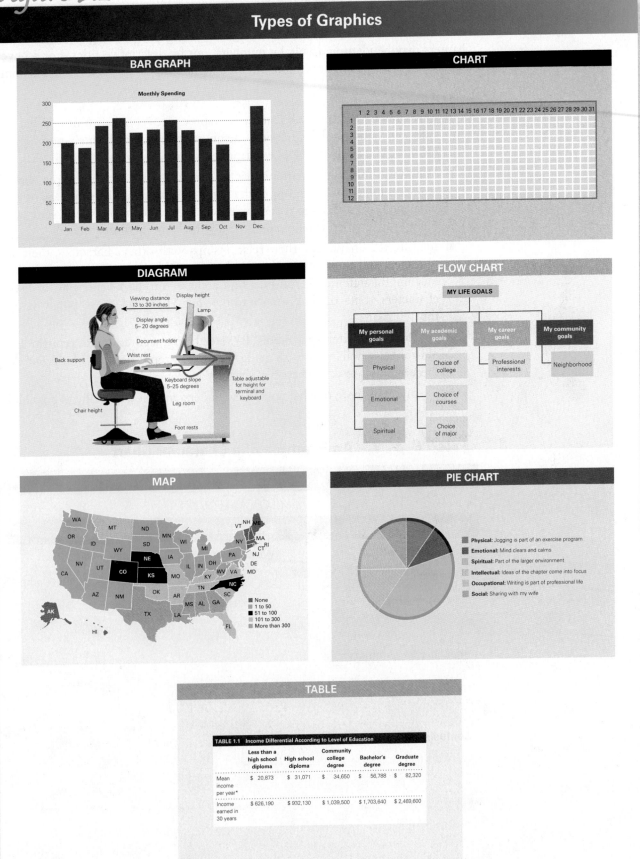

Types of Graphics

BAR GRAPH — Monthly Spending

CHART

DIAGRAM — Viewing distance 13 to 30 inches, Display height, Display angle 5–20 degrees, Lamp, Document holder, Wrist rest, Back support, Keyboard slope 5–25 degrees, Table adjustable for height for terminal and keyboard, Chair height, Leg room, Foot rests

FLOW CHART — MY LIFE GOALS; My personal goals (Physical, Emotional, Spiritual); My academic goals (Choice of college, Choice of courses, Choice of major); My career goals (Professional interests); My community goals (Neighborhood)

MAP — None, 1 to 50, 51 to 100, 101 to 300, More than 300

PIE CHART — Physical: Jogging is part of an exercise program; Emotional: Mind clears and calms; Spiritual: Part of the larger environment; Intellectual: Ideas of the chapter come into focus; Occupational: Writing is part of professional life; Social: Sharing with my wife

TABLE

TABLE 1.1 Income Differential According to Level of Education					
	Less than a high school diploma	High school diploma	Community college degree	Bachelor's degree	Graduate degree
Mean income per year*	$ 20,873	$ 31,071	$ 34,650	$ 56,788	$ 82,320
Income earned in 30 years	$ 626,190	$ 932,130	$ 1,039,500	$ 1,703,640	$ 2,469,600

"THE READING PLAN IS FINE FOR TEXTBOOKS, BUT WHAT ABOUT NOVELS?"

Most novels do not provide readers with neat headings, subheadings, and key terms. Chapters may be identified only by numbers, not by descriptive titles. For a novel, your reading strategy might be more difficult but not impossible. It will just take some creativity. For instance:

- Once you have completed reading a chapter, give it your own title. Whatever title you choose, it should answer the question "What is the main point of this chapter?" Be as creative and descriptive as you can.

- Why was the chapter written? Briefly summarize the purpose of the chapter and its connection to the rest of the book. Also write a brief summary of what happened and why. Even if you can't identify the plot at this point, summarizing what happened will help point you in the general direction.

- Identify the characters, their relationships with other characters, their significance, and their connection to the plot. Did anyone utter a particularly meaningful statement? You may find a character chart beneficial for listing characters' traits and importance to the story. Table 9.1 shows one way to do this.

- Be sensitive to literary symbols. Is water being used to depict rebirth? Is an old animal synonymous with dying? Is autumn representative of old age? Add these symbols to your character chart, as appropriate.

- Finally, make note of what you do *not* understand. Be as specific as possible.

Table 9.1 An Example of a Character Chart

Chapter 1		
"MY CREATIVE TITLE"		
Character 1	**Character 2**	**Character 3**
When introduced:	When introduced:	When introduced:
Connection to another:	Connection to another:	Connection to another:
Significant quote:	Significant quote:	Significant quote:
Symbolism:	Symbolism:	Symbolism:
Brief chapter summary:		
Confusing points:		

Chapter SUMMARY

This topic examined efficient reading strategies to improve comprehension. Before leaving this topic, keep the following points in mind:

- Always know your purpose for reading.

- Use the SQ4R method to organize your reading.

- Make connections between what you read and what you already know.

- Use context clues to help you understand unknown vocabulary.

- Immediately after finishing your reading assignment, evaluate your reading comprehension.

CRITICALLY THINKING
What Have You Learned?

Let's apply what you learned in this material to help Lena from the opening scenario. However, before you address Lena's problem and propose your solution, take a moment to review your notes, key terms, learning outcomes, boldface headings, and figures and tables.

TEST YOUR LEARNING

Now that you have reviewed the main points and reread Lena's story, what advice do you have for her? Using the R.E.D. Model for critical thinking, help Lena critically review her concerns:

R

**Recognize
Assumptions**

Facts: What are the facts in Lena's situation? List them.

Opinions: What opinions do you find in this situation? List them.

Assumptions: Are Lena's assumptions accurate?

E

**Evaluate
Information**

Help Lena compile a list of questions that will help her make the most appropriate decision.

What emotions seem to be motivating Lena?

What, if anything, is missing from her thought process?

Do you see any confirmation bias?

D

**Draw
Conclusions**

Based on the facts and the questions you have presented, what conclusions can you draw?

What advice do you have for Lena? What solutions do you propose?

Based on your suggestions, do you see any assumptions?

Finally, based on what you learned about using critical thinking and reading strategies, what plan of action do you suggest for Lena?

Test Preparation *10* and TEST TAKING

LEARNING OUTCOMES

By the time you finish reading this material and completing its activities, you will be able to do the following:

- Identify at least two successful test-preparation strategies you have used in the past, and evaluate their benefit to you now.

- Apply one strategy to address an unsuccessful test-preparation practice.

- Identify and use at least one strategy to combat test anxiety.

- Apply at least one study-skill strategy to improve your test-performance skills.

- Use the post-exam analysis strategy to review at least one of your most recent exams.

The Case of AMANI

It seems to be the same tired story. Even though Amani has taken hundreds of tests over the years, she still gets nervous every time an exam is placed in front of her. There have been times when she has gone into a test situation unprepared, but usually Amani has at least done a little studying to get ready. Still, whether she is prepared or not, as soon as the test starts, she gets jittery, her mind goes blank, and, eventually, she runs out of time.

A couple of weeks ago, the campus testing center offered a workshop on test-taking skills, so

Key Terms

Academic integrity
Anxiety
Distracter
Emergency studying
Post-exam analysis
Reframe
Test anxiety
Test-preparation skills
Test-taking skills
Trigger words
Types of exams

Chapter INTRODUCTION

Tests may strike fear into the hearts of many students, but they are nothing new. Whether you are a student right out of high school or one returning after a 20-year break, you have confronted—and mastered—tests all your life.

Tests provide opportunities for you to demonstrate that you understand course materials and can perform required skills. Because your academic success depends in part on the grades you receive on tests, begin to prepare for tests the day you enter a class. That preparation includes participating in class discussions, completing course assignments,

Amani went. When she was asked about her testing strategies, she told the workshop leader that she does all of the following:

- Attends class regularly.
- Studies everything from class two days prior to the exam to keep it fresh for the test.
- Depends on her study group for additional information, since she did not buy the Internet access code that came with her textbook. (She said she didn't see the need to have this code.)
- Is using the same study methods that have brought her some success in the past.
- Feels like she is about to faint every time she walks into a testing situation.

CRITICALLY THINKING about *Amani's* situation

Pretend you are the workshop leader. What advice would you give Amani?

and reviewing course materials on a regular basis. In other words, if you apply basic study-skill strategies long before test day, you will improve your chances for success.

You probably visualize walking into class on test day, taking the test, and earning the highest grade possible. All students want that result. However, before you can *perform*, first you must *prepare*.

Too often, "test prep" is seen as an ending activity: how to successfully complete (or take or perform on) an exam. This topic will separate the two very distinct parts of testing: preparation and performance.

MyStudentSuccessLab

MyStudentSuccessLab (www .mystudentsuccesslab.com) is an online solution designed to help you "Start strong, Finish stronger" by building skills for ongoing personal and professional development.

First, you will examine effective strategies to prepare for a test. You will examine how to organize and prioritize your efforts from the beginning of a unit of material, so that you will be preparing long before the actual performance is required. If you use simple organizational tools early, both in class and outside class, you will not need to cram for tests. Moreover, you will be able to reduce your anxiety about tests, and you can enjoy successful test results.

Once you have mastered how to prepare for exams, you will turn your attention to the second part of testing: strategies for effective test performance. Just like test preparation, test performance is influenced by many factors. Those factors affect how successful you will be when you step into a testing situation. Draw on your past successes. Ask yourself, "What strategies have worked for me in the past—and how can I use them today?"

Activity 10.1

Reflection on Your Current Level of Test-Preparation and Test-Taking Skills

Before you answer the items that follow, reflect on your current level of test-preparation and test-taking skills. Think of how well (or poorly) you have performed on tests in past classes.

This exercise is not meant for you to answer just like your classmates—or to match what you may think the instructor wants to see. Write from your heart. Take the time to give a respectful, responsible general accounting of your experiences with test preparation and test performance. Conducting a truthful self-assessment now will help you build on skills you have while developing those you lack.

For each of the following items, circle the number that best describes your typical experience with test-preparation and test-taking skills. Here is the key for the numbers:

0 = never, 1 = almost never, 2 = occasionally, 3 = frequently, 4 = almost always, 5 = always

When considering your experience with test preparation and test taking, how often:

1.	Did you prepare for an exam earlier than the night before the exam date?	0	1	2	3	4	5
2.	Did you prepare for an exam a week or more before the exam date?	0	1	2	3	4	5
3.	Did you review your graded exam to seek clarification about missed questions so you could learn from your mistakes?	0	1	2	3	4	5
4.	Did you review your test-preparation strategies for effectiveness or ineffectiveness?	0	1	2	3	4	5
5.	Did understand the test format before exam day?	0	1	2	3	4	5
6.	Could you complete a test without having your mind going blank or freezing up?	0	1	2	3	4	5
7.	Did you read all the directions and quickly survey the exam for its content and format before you started it?	0	1	2	3	4	5
8.	During an exam, did you complete all of the easy items before you attempted the more difficult items?	0	1	2	3	4	5

Add up your scores for items 1, 2, 3, 4, and 5. Divide by 5. Write your answer here: _____

Using the key provided to explain each number (0, 1, 2, 3, 4, 5), complete this sentence: When it comes to test-preparation skills, I _____ prepare for tests effectively.

Add up your scores for items 6, 7, and 8. Divide by 3. Write your answer here: _____

Using the key provided to explain each number (0, 1, 2, 3, 4, 5), complete this sentence: When it comes to test-taking skills, I _____ perform on tests effectively.

Based on your answers, what insights have you gained about your experiences with test preparation and test taking?

TEST PREPARATION: WHAT SKILLS DO YOU HAVE?

If you added up all of the tests you have ever taken—in school, on jobs, for your driver's license, and so on—you would likely come up with a number in the hundreds.

Activity 10.2 gives you the opportunity to build on Activity 10.1. Take a moment to think about your testing experiences. Specifically, examine how you prepared and when you prepared, what worked and what did not work. Identify practices you may want to continue in college—and practices it is time to eliminate.

TEST ANXIETY

Anxiety is a general feeling of unease, uncertainty, anticipation, and even fear about an event. The resulting stress may be positive, helping you stay on your toes and perform well, or it may be debilitating, causing you to freeze up.

There are two forms of stress: positive stress and negative stress. Both physically arouse the body. *Positive stress* helps you remain focused and move toward a goal. This may be similar to having "butterflies in your stomach," but your heightened sense of awareness allows you to perform at a higher level of competence. *Negative stress* goes beyond a few butterflies. You may actually feel as though a boulder is crushing your chest, because breathing becomes difficult. Or you may feel nauseous. Your fight-or-flight response may be triggered.

The same kinds of feelings can occur on test day, resulting in **test anxiety**. Most students are likely to feel a reasonable amount of uncertainty. They wish to perform well, get a high score, maintain a respectable grade-point average (GPA), and feel good about their efforts. But even when well prepared, students may still have nagging doubts: "Did I study the correct material?" "Maybe I should have looked at my notes one more time." "I wonder if a study group or a visit to the professor's office would have been helpful." Whatever may cause their anxiety, these students make their way to class, complete the test successfully, and move on to the next unit of material.

Activity 10.2

What Test-Preparation Skills Do You Have Right Now?

Let's gather some information on your experiences. Reflect on your **test-preparation skills** experiences. Think about the "big picture." That is, don't just concentrate on an exam you completed last week. Moreover, don't concentrate on only the good experiences or only the poor grades. Rather, think about your testing experiences in general as you complete this activity.

1. **Preparation.** How have you prepared for exams? Check all of the following items that apply to you:

   ■ I reviewed my notes nightly.

   ■ I participated in a study group.

   ■ I used instructor study guides when provided.

   ■ I asked the instructor if there were old tests I might be able to use for practice.

   ■ I used the textbook publisher's website to review chapter objectives and take practice quizzes and tests.

   ■ I used a tutor.

   ■ I visited my instructor's office for content clarification.

   ■ I seldom did any preparation for a test.

   ■ I used other methods that included:

   ....

   ....

2. **Timing.** When did you start preparing for a test? Check all of the following items that apply to you:

   ■ At the beginning of a new unit of material, I would study my class notes nightly.

   ■ I would start reviewing my notes and readings at least three or four days prior to the examination.

   ■ I waited until the night before the exam.

   ■ I looked over my notes the morning of the exam.

   ■ Generally speaking, I never studied for exams.

   ■ Is there any other way to describe when I started to prepare for exams?

   ....

   ....

3. **Good results.** What test-preparation strategies have worked well for you in the past? Describe them.

   ....

   ....

4. **Poor results.** What test-preparation strategies have not worked well for you in the past? Describe them.

   ....

   ....

5. **Best practices.** Based on your past successes, which strategies do you believe will continue to work for you in school? Explain how you know these are beneficial strategies.

   ....

   ....

6. **Questionable practices.** Based on your past challenges, which strategies do you need to discontinue? Explain how you know these are not beneficial test-preparation strategies.

   ....

Other students, though, become so paralyzed by thoughts of an examination that they make themselves sick with worry. One unsuccessful testing experience leads to another, which leads to another, and a self-fulfilling prophecy is born: "I never do well on tests!"

Once a student sits down and sees the test paper lying on the desk, his or her reaction might be anything from a mild case of the jitters to full-blown terror. This test-day anxiety, however, can be reduced considerably with effective test-preparation strategies. But first, it's important to understand why test anxiety occurs.

WHY DOES TEST ANXIETY HAPPEN?

One organization maintains that 16 percent to 20 percent of students experience a high level of test anxiety and another 18 percent feel a moderate level (American Test Anxiety Association, n.d.). Among the reasons for this response are fear, feelings of inadequacy, and lack of preparation.

- **Fear.** The consequences of the test or performance may be so great as to cause an unhealthy physical or emotional response. For instance, if one test result will determine whether you get into a particular program (say, nursing or engineering), your level of anxiety may increase from the fear of losing your dream. This type of high-stakes testing heightens your physical and emotional arousal.

    - **Suggestion.** You may be catastrophizing. That is, you may be making too much of this one exam. One opportunity does not (very often) determine your life's direction. Stop, take a breath, and **reframe** the situation. Look at it from another perspective. If you have difficulty doing this, ask a friend, family member, or mentor for input. Failing, while not pleasant, is rarely the end. In many cases, it presents an opportunity to regroup and move forward.

- **Feelings of inadequacy.** You believe that no matter what you do, your lack of ability (perceived or real) will be the reason you cannot perform to an acceptable standard. This may be the case, for instance, when a student enrolls in a course he or she has struggled with in the past.

    - **Suggestion.** What would you tell a good friend if he or she admitted having the same feeling? It is doubtful you would say, "You are right! There is nothing you can do. You will fail!" You would look for something positive to say to help your friend through the anxiety. Do the same thing for yourself. As you prepare for the exam, make a list of all the strengths you have. Build on these positives, and minimize the negative self-talk.

- **Lack of preparation.** The final exam is in one hour—and you have not read the assigned readings, looked at your notes, or reviewed the instructor-provided study guide. No wonder your blood pressure is elevated, your hands are sweating, and your mouth is a little dry!

    - **Suggestion.** This is where priority management has a significant impact. At some point early in your weekly planning, preparing for your math exam has to move up on the list of "Things I Must Do This Week." The more time you spend with the course material before exam day, the more familiar you will be with it—and the more confident you will feel when you enter the testing situation. In this case, test-day anxiety can be eliminated (or at least greatly reduced) by organized and timely preparation. Priority management does rule!

Activity 10.3

Identifying Your Sources of Test Anxiety

Identifying stressors is the first step in learning to overcome them. What are your sources of test anxiety?

1. Do you tend to be anxious about exams because of any of the following? Which of the following apply to you?

Pressuring myself to get nothing but an "A"	Lack of ability (course material beyond my capabilities)	Negative self-talk (convinced myself I would do poorly)
Focusing on the effect the test grade will have on my GPA	Comparing my performance to the performances of other students	Listening to classmates complain about the difficulty of exams
Poor previous testing experiences	Panic brought on by timed situations	Not studying
Fear of how others may judge me	Lack of appropriate effort on my part	Other sources:

2. Share your answers with a close friend or mentor. Brainstorm ideas to lessen your test anxiety.

Activity 10.4

Critically Thinking about Your Test-Preparation Skills

Let's apply the R.E.D. Model for critical thinking to examine your beliefs about your test-preparation skills.

R — Based on your responses in Activities 10.1, 10.2, or 10.3, identify either one of your best or one of your questionable practices.

E — Now apply the R.E.D. Model to examine your belief. You may find it helpful to write your responses in your notebook or journal.

D

Critical-Thinking Step	Application to Your Testing Skills
Recognize Assumptions	Clearly state this particular testing practice. How do you know this assessment of your testing practice is correct?
Evaluate Information	Provide a specific explanation (give examples) of this testing practice. Examine your identified testing practice beyond a superficial (simplistic) explanation, and look at all of the complexities involved. Examine your testing practice from more than one perspective (point of view).
Draw Conclusions	Based on your evidence, does your conclusion about your testing practice make sense? How is your assessment of this testing practice connected to your academic progress?

Based on your answers, what insights have you gained about your testing practice? What is the next step you will take to improve your testing skills?

EVERYTHING IS CONNECTED

Let's pause and examine how the study-skills strategies you already have mastered are related and connected to test preparation. When you connect the strategies together, you will see that test preparation is not a one-time event. Table 10.1 and Figure 10.1 show the interconnectedness of just a few selected study-skill strategies to test preparation. The power of study skills lies in the fact that they all reinforce one another. As you master each skill, your academic foundation becomes stronger—and your academic future brighter!

Table 10.1 **Test-Preparation Strategies: Building on Previous Skills and Strategies**

Study-Skill Strategy	Application to Successful Test-Preparation Strategies
Critical Thinking	■ Use the R.E.D. Model to *understand* your test-preparation problems. ■ Analyze test-preparation difficulties you may have. Go beyond assumptions; examine factors that affect your test performance.
Problem Solving	■ Use the R.E.D. Model to *solve* your test-preparation problem—for instance: 　■ Using the information received from your review of previous exams, your instructor's input, and a tutor's opinion, you may decide to begin a new studying program that will set aside time to visit your instructor once a week with specific questions about new material covered in class. 　■ You may consider working with a study group. 　■ At the very least, when you review your notes each day, you may decide to write a brief summary of the day's notes.
Creative Thinking	■ Maybe you feel that you have done absolutely everything to improve your testing practices—but nothing seems to work. The frustration mounts. It's time for creative, outside-the-box, outside-the-lines, novel thinking. For instance: 　■ You recognize that you have not been exercising as you once did. You feel sluggish most of the time. Combining physical activity with intellectual stimulation, you decide to engage in a yoga class once a week. You believe yoga's meditative emphasis will help calm and focus your mind.
Attitude	■ When you examine why you have difficulty with tests (in general or in a particular course), do you use self-defeating words or positive words? 　■ Self-defeating: *I have never done well on math exams. There is no reason to expect that will change this term. I'll hope for the best.* 　■ Positive: *My experience with math has not been positive. I might not earn an A in this course; however, if I use the campus resources available to me, I will do better than I have ever done before.*
Intrinsic and extrinsic motivators	■ Find a motivator that will help move you through the test challenge you have been experiencing. Whether intrinsic or extrinsic, look for motivating incentives that will inspire you to meet and defeat your challenge. 　■ Intrinsic: *I know what I need to do to achieve favorable test results. I've worked hard and owe it to myself to do the very best I can.*

(continued)

Table 10.1 **Test-Preparation Strategies: Building on Previous Skills and Strategies (continued)**

Study-Skill Strategy	Application to Successful Test-Preparation Strategies
	■ Extrinsic: *Regardless of what I have done in the past, my financial aid depends on passing all my courses. Doing well on tests will not only prepare me for other course work, but it will also allow me to continue receiving the funding I need for school.*
Review your notes	■ Every night, reflect on class work through a brief writing activity. Do the following: ■ Maintain an ongoing file of your nightly summary review. Perhaps creating a computer folder labeled "notes review" will make it easier to organize and keep up with your daily reviews. Over the course of a unit's material, you will build a study guide. Reviewing your short summaries will help prepare you for each coming exam.
Reading	■ Use the SQ4R strategy (survey, question, read, recite, record, review) to make sense of your reading assignments and to remember more of what you read. Remember these points: ■ Before reading, understand the purpose of the assignment—why you are reading. ■ Take reading notes, review them, and use them with your class notes. ■ Continue to build your vocabulary.
Learning preferences	■ We all have unique ways to process information. Make sure you understand your learning preferences, and practice strategies to make your learning preferences work for you. ■ Understand how you take in information effectively. ■ As best as you can, create a study environment that complements your learning preferences.
Memory	■ Remember the three components of an improved memory: Notice the material, store the material, and reclaim the material. Consider the following: ■ Use organizational charts to help you make connections. ■ Schedule your study time in regular intervals. (Do not cram.) ■ Understand why you forget, and then review strategies to help you more effectively store and retrieve information.

PREVIOUS TEST RESULTS

Effective test preparation requires continual review and practice. Effective preparation for your exam next week should begin immediately after you complete your most recent exam.

A common reaction by many students following the completion of an exam is to forget it and concentrate on the next opportunity. Although this is an understandable reaction, you need to pause and reflect on the exam. Consider this the first step in preparing for the next exam.

Completing Activity 10.5 will help you get ready for the upcoming exam. It requires you to anticipate the exam. But also notice that the last portion is a **post-exam analysis.** This type of activity accomplishes a couple of things. While the material you

Figure 10.1

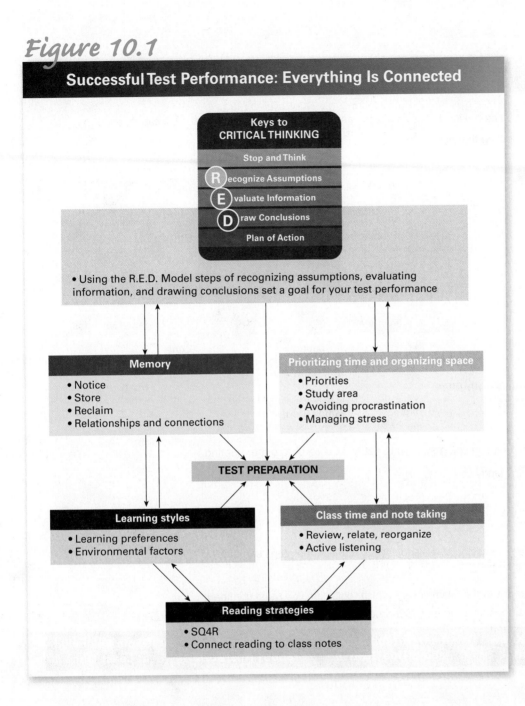

Successful Test Performance: Everything Is Connected

Keys to CRITICAL THINKING

Stop and Think

(R)ecognize Assumptions

(E)valuate Information

(D)raw Conclusions

Plan of Action

- Using the R.E.D. Model steps of recognizing assumptions, evaluating information, and drawing conclusions set a goal for your test performance

Memory
- Notice
- Store
- Reclaim
- Relationships and connections

Prioritizing time and organizing space
- Priorities
- Study area
- Avoiding procrastination
- Managing stress

TEST PREPARATION

Learning styles
- Learning preferences
- Environmental factors

Class time and note taking
- Review, relate, reorganize
- Active listening

Reading strategies
- SQ4R
- Connect reading to class notes

were just tested on is still fresh in your mind, review the content. You may see some of this information again on a midterm or final examination (or in another course). Make sure you have it correct now. If you answered an item incorrectly on this exam, you do not want to get it wrong again. It is important to understand what worked and what did not work for you. Use this time to identify your challenges and strengths—and set a goal for the next exam.

If you are getting ready to take the first exam in a class, consider any quizzes you might have taken thus far. Or you can skip this step until you prepare for your second exam.

Activity 10.5

Test-Preparation Checklist

Select one of the courses you are taking this term. Class name? Instructor's name? Test date, location, and time? Check or circle all of the following that apply.

1. Type of exam:

Multiple choice	True/False	Matching
Completion or short answer	Identification	Essay
Lab work	Problems	Other

2. What I need when I study:

Textbook	Notes	Teacher's study guide
Worksheets	Past exams	Supplemental readings
Calculator	Pens, pencils, paper	Other

3. Will I study alone or with a study group?

Alone   Study group

(To get the most from a study group you may wish to set an agenda before the meeting.)

4. Will the teacher lead any study sessions?

Yes   No

If "yes," when and where?

5. When will I study? Make a specific plan—and stick to it. Place the steps and dates on your calendar.

6. Prioritization: What topics will the exam cover? Which topics are you most confident about, and which ones need a lot more of your time?

Topic	I Really Know This Stuff	I am Not Too Sure about This Stuff	I Have No Clue about This Stuff	Topic Reviewed at Least Once
1.				
2.				
3.				
4.				

7. Predict some test questions.

8. Things I need for the test:

Pens, pencils, paper, "blue book"	Calculator	Notes to use during the test
Textbook to use during the test	Ruler	Other

Test preparation does not end when you hand in your test. Start preparing for your next exam by doing a post-exam analysis:

9. For what part of the exam were you the most prepared? Why?

10. For what part of the exam were you the least prepared? Why?

11. The biggest help:

My notes	My study schedule	My study group
My homework	My study environment	Tutoring sessions
Meeting with my instructor outside class	Other	

12. My major challenge(s):

Ran out of time during the test	Did not expect this type of test	Studied the wrong material
Did not start studying early enough	Other	

13. The grade I realistically expect to receive: _____ Grade I actually received: _____

14. My realistic plan to improve for the next exam will include: _____

Completing the following checklist will help you prioritize your preparation activities, reduce your levels of anxiety, do well on your latest opportunity, and prepare for your next testing situation.

BEFORE YOU WALK INTO THE CLASSROOM

Let's assume it is the night before your exam. You have practiced sound study-skill strategies, and there is no need to cram for your exam. In short, you feel confident about the exam you will take the next day. You have prepared. All is good! You have worked hard and are now ready to reap the rewards of your efforts. You would like to see a return (in the form a great grade!) on your investment of study time.

Consider the following suggestions for final reminders and tips to help you maximize the hours of study time you have invested thus far.

- **Know your material.** Don't just memorize it—understand it. More than likely, the wording on the exam will be different from what you found in your book or what the teacher said in class. Timely and organized studying will help you become comfortable, confident, and successful. Your strategies for reviewing class notes will help here. Competence leads to confidence and will help lessen your anxiety.

- **Consider tutoring.** If you have been diligent with your studies but still have difficulty with the subject matter, you may wish to seek help from the instructor or a student tutor. Your academic adviser should have information on peer tutors.

- **Be rested and ready.** Do not sabotage yourself and your good efforts. On exam day, you want to be rested and ready to go. Emotional and physical memory blocks can be minimized (if not eliminated) by getting a restful night's sleep. You know the amount of sleep you need to wake up rested and alert. Get it on the eve of an examination.

- **Set your alarm—and arrive early.** Wake up early enough so you have plenty of time to arrive at the test site. In fact, for test day, arrive 15 to 30 minutes ahead of time. This will give you extra time in case traffic or some other unexpected event causes a delay. Anticipate the unexpected and be ready. Athletes speak of "getting in a zone" or "putting on a game face." This is your time to "put on your test face"!

- **Feed your body appropriately.** After a wonderfully relaxing night's sleep, treat yourself to a healthy meal or snack prior to the exam. Depending on the time of the exam, eat a good breakfast or lunch. But don't overeat—that might leave you groggy. Again, use strategies that fit you. If your exam will be during a night class, consider having a small snack before entering the classroom.

- **Be familiar with format.** Before test day, ask the instructor if he or she has past versions of the exam you can review.

- **Find out if "props" are allowed.** If you have a math test requiring many formulas, can you write the formulas on an index card to use during the exam? Can you use a calculator? How about your notes or textbook? Will the instructor allow you to use them during the exam?

- **Ask your instructor about an alternative testing environment.** If you have a documented disability, the student services office may be able to assist with specific accommodations to help you minimize distractions.

- **Gather your materials.** The night before the exam, gather all the materials you will need for test day. These materials can include paper, pens, pencils, calculators, notebooks, textbooks, and/or take-home essays. Place them where you will find them in the morning: in your book bag, on a table, or by the door. If you will be using a laptop, be sure to charge the battery.

- **Bring extras.** In addition to the usual pen, pencil, and paper you may need for your exam, pack extras. A couple of sharpened pencils with good erasers, a few extra sheets of paper, a spare pen, or extra batteries may come in handy during the exam.

- **Keep accurate time.** Make it your responsibility to keep track of time during the exam. If you use a cell phone to keep track of time, be sure to get your instructor's permission to have your cell phone on your desk during the exam.

- **Avoid negative people.** You want to stay positive, obviously. Avoid classmates who dwell on how hard the test will be. Also, avoid those students who have not prepared and come running in, all anxious and hyped up on caffeine. Because they have chosen not to prepare does not mean you have to be drawn into their drama and self-defeating game.

- **Talk positively to yourself.** Finally, as you prepare for the exam, be kind to yourself. Don't sit there saying, "I am going to fail." Respect your skills, talents, and experiences.

EMERGENCY STUDYING

"Okay," you say. "Organization is great, but what can I do if I have not kept up? What can I do to survive a test when I'm down to the night before, and I'm not ready?"

Here are some pointers for last-minute or **emergency studying**. This is not a desirable situation, but if it's all you have, then know how to get the most from it.

Do not …

- Be tempted to read quickly everything you have not read yet. If you read a large quantity of information too fast, you probably will have poor recall of the details.
- Panic. Okay, so you didn't study as you wish you had. Test day is no time to panic.

Do …

- Accept the fact you will not be able to study everything.
- Relax as best you can.
- Start by anticipating your teacher. What type of questions (format and content) will he or she ask?
- Go to your notes and text to find the most important material. Use the SQ4R strategy to guide you.
- Follow these steps when you find important information:
  - Read it.
  - Create a question for which the information is the answer.
  - Say the information to yourself.
  - Check to see whether you are correct.
  - Do it until you get it correct twice.
  - Find and study some important information from every chapter that was assigned.

Next time, plan ahead and establish a study schedule.

TEST TAKING: WHAT SKILLS DO YOU HAVE?

Test-taking skills can be organized into two categories: skills for efficient test taking and skills for handling different types of tests.

EFFICIENT TEST PERFORMANCE

You are prepared and sitting in the classroom, and the test is placed in front of you. It's time for all of your preparation efforts to pay dividends for you. But effective test preparation can be hampered by inefficient behaviors during the test. If this is your problem, consider the following test-taking strategies:

- **Review the entire exam.** Before you begin writing answers, review all of the items in the exam. Get a "feel" for the test. How long will you need to do page 1? Page 2? In other words, establish a pace for yourself. Use your SQ4R reading strategy here. Do this quickly.

■ **Do the easy items first.** If you do run out of time, you don't want to have missed the easy points. "Easy" in this case refers to content as well as item type. Obviously, make sure you answer all the questions you know. You may wish to do the types of questions you are most comfortable with before you tackle the more challenging ones. If matching is easy for you, do the matching items first.

■ **Watch for so-called trigger words.** Don't get an item wrong because you failed to see a trigger (key or important) word. Underline, circle, and/or box key words. (We will discuss trigger words again later in this material.)

■ **Block your test paper.** If your eyes tend to drift from one item to another during an exam, use a blocking technique to help you focus. Use two blank pieces of paper to cover the items immediately above and below the item you are working on. For example, if you are working on problem 3, block out problems 2 and 4. Use this technique to force your eyes to focus on only one item.

■ **Remove yourself from distraction.** If possible, sit as far away from any distractions as you can. Get away from windows, open doors, noisy students, and the like. In a large lecture hall, this may be difficult, but your instructor may be able to suggest some alternatives.

SPECIFIC EXAMS REQUIRE SPECIFIC STRATEGIES

There are several **types of exams**: multiple choice, true/false, matching, completion, essay, and so forth. But no matter what type of test you are taking, you need to read all instructions carefully. And regardless of the type of test, you should not start until you know what you are expected to do. More than likely, the wording on the exam will be different from what you found in your book, what is on the website, or what the teacher said in class. (That is why it is important to know your material. Do not just memorize. Relate concepts to concepts.)

Here are descriptions and examples of the common types of tests and basic strategies for taking them.

Multiple-choice tests This kind of test provides a stem, distracters, and an answer. The *stem* is the beginning of the item. It may be in the form of a question or a statement. Following the stem, you will find four or five possible answers.

Unless otherwise stated, one answer is correct and the others are incorrect. The incorrect items are known as **distracters**.

Here is an example of a multiple-choice item:

The best way to prepare for a test is to: [Stem]

a. depend on your study partner to give you her notes. [Distracter]
b. review your notes nightly. [Correct answer]
c. pull an all-night study session and drink a lot of caffeine. [Distracter]
d. pray the test will be cancelled. [Distracter]

Follow these suggestions to help improve your performance on multiple-choice tests:

■ Read carefully. Look for words such as *not, except, which is incorrect, best, all, always, never,* and *none.*

- <u>Underline</u> key words (if you are allowed to write on the exam) to help you focus.

- Treat each item like a fill-in-the-blank question. Cover all the answer choices before you look at them. Then come up with the answer on your own.

- If you are not sure of the correct answer, use the process of elimination to arrive at it or at least to narrow your options so you can make an educated guess.

- Answer the easy questions first. Save the tough ones for last.

- If you are using an answer sheet, make sure you mark your answers correctly. Match up each answer and question.

Matching tests Matching items usually are organized in two columns. The items in the first column are to be matched with the items in the second column. One column may have more items than the other may. That is, one or more choices may not be used, or some choices may be used more than once. Read the test directions carefully.

Keep the following suggestions in mind when taking a matching test:

- Read all the answer choices first.

- Cross out the items as you use them (if you are allowed to write on the exam).

- Answer the easy items first. Save the tough ones for the end.

Here is an example of a matching item on a test:

Directions: For each item in Column A, choose its best match from Column B. Write the letter from Column B in front of the item in Column A.

Column A	Column B
_____ 1. This memory block may be caused by a lack of sleep.	a. Physical
_____ 2. Feelings of inadequacy may bring about this memory block.	b. Mental
_____ 3. Improperly storing information will cause this memory block.	c. Emotional
	d. Lazy

True/false tests True/false items can be tricky. Pay attention to "all or nothing" phrasing, which should give you a clue. Words such as "always" and "never" are clues that a statement is "false." Words such as *sometimes, maybe, occasionally,* and *frequently* usually accompany "true" statements.

Here are some examples of true/false items:

SQ4R is a reading strategy.

True False

Never study the night before an exam.

True False

Sometimes a study partner will help you prepare for an exam.

True False

If you can define the word *priority*, you will have no problem organizing yourself.

True False

Completion/fill-in-the-blank/short-answer tests A completion item will provide either an incomplete sentence or a brief question for you to answer. Look for key words or clues within the sentence. Unless the instructions say otherwise, the length of the blank does *not* indicate the length of the word or words needed to complete the item correctly.

Here are some examples:

1. Forming a word from the first letters of the words in a series is called a(n) _____.
2. When we establish an order of importance for doing a list of activities, we are said to be _____ our day.
3. Briefly explain one memory strategy to help you effectively store information.

Essay tests Taking essay tests requires both knowledge of the material and the ability to communicate that knowledge. Essay items can appear as questions or statements. The question or statement sometimes is called the *prompt*.

Here are examples of essay test questions:

1. Explain two ways that knowledge of learning preferences can help you be more successful in class. [This prompt is a statement and specifically asks for two items to be addressed.]
2. What did the colonists do between the years of 1763 and 1776 to show their displeasure with the British government? [This prompt is in the form of a question and restricts the answer to a particular period of time.]

Follow these suggestions for improving your answers to essay questions:

- Read the question carefully so you know exactly what you are being asked. Refer to the list of trigger words later in this section.
- Underline, circle, box, or in some way highlight important words in the prompt.
- Look for dates and other types of words that will direct or limit your topic.
- Develop a main idea (thesis).
- Support your thesis with substantial facts. All words need to have a purpose.
- Pay attention to grammar and sentence structure. Yes, English does count!
- Organize your response clearly so that your instructor can identify your main points easily as he or she reads your paper. You may even consider underlining your main points to make them stand out.
- Never leave an essay item blank. Make an educated attempt at an answer. You might get some credit.
- Know what your task is. At the very least, know the following **trigger words** (or key words):

analyze: to divide a topic or issue into its parts; to show the relation of one part to another

apply: to use your knowledge in a new or different situation

assess: to judge the merits of some issue; to evaluate

classify: to put things into categories

compare: to provide similarities (see *analyze*)

contrast: to provide differences (see *analyze*)

criticize: to judge critically (see *assess*)

defend: to argue for a particular issue

describe: to explain an event, issue, topic; to explain the main characteristics

discuss: to explain in detail; to go beyond mere description

evaluate: to judge, criticize, establish standards

identify: to show how something is unique or individual

illustrate: to provide examples

interpret: to describe the meaning of an issue

motivations: to suggest what caused something to happen

relative importance: to explain how two or more factors compare with one another

summarize: to restate briefly

trace: to provide an order or sequence of events

TEST TAKING AND ACADEMIC INTEGRITY

Having *integrity* means conducting oneself in an honest, responsible, and respectful manner. When it comes to testing, **academic integrity** means doing and submitting your own work without any unauthorized assistance. Any violation of academic integrity on an exam is broadly classified as cheating and will be punished according to specific guidelines established by your school.

The following examples are violations of academic integrity during an exam, unless the instructor has given permission prior to the exam:

- Copying from a classmate's paper
- Using "cheat sheets"
- Using class notes, the textbook, and/or any other supplemental source
- Receiving assistance from or giving assistance to another student
- Accessing a cell phone or other digital aid
- Listening to recorded material
- Using a laptop computer to access information
- Looking at or otherwise using old copies of the exam
- Removing any testing information from the exam room

Colleges and universities publish academic integrity policies and consequences for violations. They expect students to be responsible for completing their work in a manner that is honest and respectful of their classmates, instructors, and school.

Activity 10.6

Helping Amani Connect Testing with Success Strategies

Review the opening scenario about Amani. For each of the following topics, identify one strategy and briefly explain how it could help Amani improve her test performance.

- Organization: ....
- Motivation and goal setting: ....
- Learning styles: ....
- Note taking and collaboration: ....
- Reading and review time: ....

Chapter SUMMARY

As you reflect on this topic, remember that you have been confronted with tests, in one form or another, your entire life. While the types of tests described in this chapter are academic in nature, you have taken them often in your career as a student. The content and courses may have changed, but you already have test-taking strategies. Remember them, learn from them, and then move to a higher level of competence and success.

Before leaving this topic, keep the following points in mind:

- Test anxiety is common. Even when you are well prepared, you may still have doubts. Recognize them, but don't let them paralyze you.

- You can apply all of your study-skill strategies to improve your test-performance challenges.

- Take time to analyze the reasons you have difficulty with tests. Go beyond a superficial explanation. Move into a deeper examination of the factors that affect your test performance. Use your critical-thinking skills.

- Effective test preparation can be hampered by inefficiency during test taking.

CRITICALLY THINKING
What Have You Learned?

Let's apply what you learned reading this material to help Amani from the opening scenario. However, before you address Amani's problem and propose your solution, take a moment to review your notes, key terms, learning outcomes, boldface headings, figures, tables, and learning outcomes.

TEST YOUR LEARNING

Now that you have reviewed the main points of this chapter and reread Amani's story, what advice do you have for her? Using the R.E.D. Model for critical thinking, help Amani critically review her concerns:

(R)

Recognize Assumptions

Facts: What are the facts in Amani's situation? List them.

Opinions: What opinions do you find in this situation? List them here.

Assumptions: Are her assumptions accurate?

(E)

Evaluate Information

Help Amani compile a list of questions that will help her make the most appropriate decision.

What emotions seem to be motivating Amani?

What, if anything, is missing from her thought process?

Do you see any confirmation bias?

(D)

Draw Conclusions

Based on the facts and the questions you have presented, what conclusions can you draw?

What advice do you have for Amani? What solutions do you propose?

Based on your suggestions, do you see any assumptions?

Finally, based on what you learned about using critical thinking and testing strategies, what plan of action do you suggest for Amani?

CIVILITY

11

LEARNING OUTCOMES

By the time you finish reading this material and completing the activities, you will be able to do the following:

- Identify the stage of group development that you have found most difficult, and practice a strategy to cope with that challenge.

- Explain at least two considerations for forming your own group.

- Identify at least one healthy way to minimize how negative people affect you.

- Use at least three active-listening techniques to improve your communication skills.

- Use at least one conflict management strategy.

The Case of THE GROUP

Hakeem and four other students have been assigned to a group by their psychology instructor. The group's project is to choose one topic from their textbook and develop a 15-minute presentation (complete with PowerPoint slides) to explain the topic.

The group met for the first time today. After class, Hakeem told a friend what happened in the group.

"The instructor passed out one sheet of instructions for each group. No one grabbed for the instructions, so I picked up the paper and read them to the group. There are a number of tasks that our group will have to complete by the end of this four-week assignment. Each member will be responsible for taking on at least one of the tasks.

"So, after I read the instructions and assignment descriptions, no one spoke. No one volunteered to do anything! This is why I hate groups!

Key Terms

Active listening
Aggressive
Assertiveness
Boundaries
Bullies
Civility
Collective monologue
Communication
Conflict
"Elephant in the corner"
Emotional intelligence
Interpersonal skills
Limits
"Nutritious people"
Passive
"Toxic people"
Trust

INTRODUCTION *Chapter*

"Class, please form a group with three other people, and complete the assignment by the end of the hour."

How many times have you heard something similar from one or more of your instructors? Group work—or collaborative learning, as some call it—can be one of the most challenging experiences for students.

Instructors will tell you that real life—careers, relationships, and the like—requires that you learn how to interact with all types of people. That may be true, but in the classroom, where your grade-point average (GPA) is

"I then asked whether anyone wanted to be the group leader. Jamesha looked at the floor; Rhonda pointed at John; Tony had his head on the desk! Thank goodness, John (reluctantly) agreed to take charge.

"John quickly broke down the assignment into bite-sized tasks. And before we left class for the day, we all agreed to meet in the campus cafeteria 30 minutes before the next class to discuss the project further. Each person is to think about which part of the assignment he or she wants to tackle."

"Unfortunately," Hakeem sighed, "I did not notice anyone but John and me write down the time and place of the next meeting. I am not feeling good about this at all."

CRITICALLY THINKING about *the group* situation

What is going on with this group? Does Hakeem have reason to worry, or is his group displaying typical group dynamics that will play themselves out?

at stake, you may prefer to be responsible for your own work and not have to depend on the person in the back of the room, who is either late to class or sleeping through the lecture!

The reality is that unless you plan to live the life of a hermit, you will interact with people for the rest of your life. You will have intimate relationships, casual friendships, and important professional associations. Your ability to communicate a message of confidence, competence, and civility will affect how people perceive you. Developing effective interpersonal

MyStudentSuccessLab

MyStudentSuccessLab (www .mystudentsuccesslab.com) is an online solution designed to help you "Start strong, Finish stronger" by building skills for ongoing personal and professional development.

relationships can be the difference between a group that maximizes its resources and one that squanders its opportunities.

Maximizing relationships does not equate to "using" people or "taking advantage" of their good graces. It refers to how you and the people you interact with can enjoy a rewarding experience. Whether the association is a short-term group project or one of enduring intimacy, showing respect for yourself and others will help you make meaningful connections.

Not all of your relationships will be harmonious. If you interact with people long enough, conflict will present itself. It is part of the human drama—but it can be a positive force in your life. The key to dealing with conflict successfully is first to recognize when and why it is happening and then to develop a healthy plan for managing and resolving it. Doing so requires practice, patience, and persistence.

More than likely, when you were a young child, you were told by parents, grandparents, aunts and uncles, or teachers to "play nice" with the other children. That simple piece of advice still holds true now that you are an adult—probably even more so. For that reason, this topic will address the concepts of civility, healthy interpersonal relationships, effective communication, and conflict management.

Students choose their classes, but for the most part they do not decide who else will register for the same class and sit in the same classroom. Thus, all sorts of personalities converge each day in campus classrooms. This convergence creates challenges, as the quiet student deals with the loud student, the obnoxious student offends the contemplative student, a student's rude e-mail insults an instructor, or a demanding instructor intimidates an anxious student.

Civility—polite and courteous behavior—will make the classroom and college experience more enjoyable for everyone. **Interpersonal skills**—your strengths and challenges when interacting with other people—are as important during your school years as your academic skills.

EMOTIONAL INTELLIGENCE

We have all heard stories of intelligent people who never seem to be able to "make it." While they may have scored well on an intelligence test and can boast a high IQ (intelligence quotient), they never realize their potential. How can that be?

Daniel Goleman, in his book *Emotional Intelligence*, states that traditional IQ is a small contributor (about 20 percent) to life success (Goleman, 1997, p. 34). He and other psychologists believe a person needs more than a high score on an IQ test to be successful. For instance, Robert Sternberg (1997) suggests there are three types of intelligence: analytical, creative, and practical. And Howard Gardner's theory of multiple intelligences maintains that interpersonal intelligence allows someone to recognize what motivates others and how best to work with them (Gardner, 1983).

Emotional intelligence, says Goleman, is a more accurate predictor of success in life. In particular, the emotionally intelligent person displays these qualities (Goleman, 1997, p. 43):

- Is aware of his or her emotions as they occur
- Can soothe himself or herself appropriately and not let anxiety, gloom, and doom consume his or her life
- Delays gratification and controls impulses
- Has the ability to "tune in" to the emotions of others
- Is skilled at helping others manage their emotions.

As you work with people, be mindful of how you manage your emotions and impulses, how you respond to disappointments, and how well you work with others. The emotionally intelligent person practices civility even when the circumstances are not what he or she would like them to be. To be successful, "book smarts" must be complemented with "people smarts."

Activity 11.1

Reflecting on Your Current Level of Interpersonal Skills

Before you answer the following items, reflect on your current level of interpersonal skills. Think of how well (or poorly) you have related to classmates, co-workers and instructors in past classes.

Write from your heart. This exercise is not meant for you to answer just like your classmates—or to match what you may think the instructor wants to see. Take the time to give a respectful, responsible general accounting of your experiences with interpersonal relations. Conducting a truthful self-assessment now will help you build on skills you have while developing those you lack.

For each of the following items, circle the number that best describes your typical experience when relating to other people. Here is the key for the numbers:

0 = never, 1 = almost never, 2 = occasionally, 3 = frequently, 4 = almost always, 5 = always

When considering your past strengths and challenges with interpersonal skills, how often:

1. Have you been able to identify and appropriately deal with the feelings of a group member?   0 1 2 3 4 5
2. Have you been able to soothe and calm yourself when you have become angry?   0 1 2 3 4 5
3. Were you able to work effectively with a group on a class project?   0 1 2 3 4 5
4. Have you been able to distance yourself from people who continually drain your energy?   0 1 2 3 4 5
5. Are you able to associate with people who energize and excite you?   0 1 2 3 4 5
6. Have you let a speaker know, either by body language or verbal response, that you were truly listening?   0 1 2 3 4 5

7.	Have you asked questions of the person speaking to you?	**0**	**1**	**2**	**3**	**4**	**5**
8.	Have you been an energizing force for another person?	**0**	**1**	**2**	**3**	**4**	**5**

Add up your scores for items 1 through 8. Divide by 8. Write your answer here: _____.

Using the key provided to explain each number (0, 1, 2, 3, 4, 5), complete this sentence: When it comes to relating to other people, I _____ effectively relate to other people.

Based on your answers, what insights have you gained about your experiences with interpersonal skills?

CIVILITY AND COMMUNICATION

THE ART OF COMMUNICATION: Are You Really Listening or Just Talking?

Effective **communication** is an art form. One person constructs and passes along thoughts, information, and feelings about a particular subject to another person. This can occur one to one, as when a friend sends you an e-mail, tweets, posts a status update, engages you in a face-to-face discussion, or gives you a heartfelt hug.

Communication can take place on a larger scale, as well. The term *mass communication* refers to the transmission of information to large numbers (thousands and millions) of people. This occurs via Twitter, Facebook, blogs, newspapers, cable network news programs, and radio talk shows. When mass communication is done well, a connection develops between the sender and the receiver. One conveys a message, while the other listens (or reads).

DIALOGUES VERSUS COLLECTIVE MONOLOGUES

It has also been said that communication is a lost art. The thought here is that people have lost the ability to exchange meaningful ideas with one another. When done poorly, there is no communication, no connection—just words passing in space.

Tune in to a television or radio talk show, and chances are great that you will hear *talking*—but not *conversation*. One person talks, and the other interrupts. The first person interrupts the second person by raising his or her voice. Inevitably, a shouting match results, leaving the listener with a headache. Just because two people are in the same room and talking *at* one another does not mean they are communicating or conversing *with* one another.

A dialogue presupposes that two people have engaged in a conversation, in which one person speaks and the other listens (not merely hears). The second person then appropriately responds to the first with comments relevant to the conversation. This exchange continues back and forth—one person listening and the other person speaking.

Unfortunately, what passes for conversation most times is not dialogue. Think of a recent time when you either observed a group of people talking or you were involved in a conversation with a few friends. Was there true communication? While one person was talking, were the other people quietly listening? When the person talking finished his or her thoughts, did the others respond to those ideas, or did they start talking about something else, not even recognizing what the other person had just said? Did people continually interrupt one another to get their own opinions into the conversation? Were many people talking but no one listening?

Or maybe you witnessed two or three people have a "conversation"; however, while one was speaking the others were busy checking their phones for text messages. (One study refers to this as being "alone together." [Levine and Dean, 72])

If so, what you experienced was a **collective monologue**. When one person speaks without any expectation of an answer from someone else, he or she is presenting a monologue. The air vibrates with words, but not much communication takes place. When two or more people do this together, it is a collective monologue.

It is probably safe to say that you have engaged in a collective monologue at one time or another. Most times, it just passes as typical conversation. But at other times, it can be frustrating and even border on being disrespectful.

Like any action that is repeated often enough, communicating in this way can become a habit—a bad habit. A person who continually engages in collective monologues will eventually be considered a bore, at the least. And while this may be irritating in a social setting, it can be disastrous in a group or professional setting.

ACTIVE LISTENING

An antidote to participating in a collective monologue is **active listening**. It requires the listener to pay attention to what the speaker is saying. Active listening cannot be done halfheartedly. It is work. Listening to the actual words, as well as paying attention to verbal clues (tone of voice) and nonverbal clues (posture, eye contact), requires a degree of focus you may not typically use in daily conversation. But practicing active listening is worth the effort. Active listening is one of the characteristics of "nutritious people," which will be discussed later in this material.

As you read the following characteristics of an active listener, conduct a mental review of how you measure up:

- **An active listener has to be quiet and focus on the speaker.** It becomes increasingly difficult to listen to another person if you are talking yourself. Quiet your mouth. An old saying reminds us that "We have two ears and one mouth," so we should listen twice as much as we talk.

- **The active listener needs to quiet his or her mind.** Attending to the chatter in your own mind will make you miss what the speaker is saying.

- **An active listener pays attention to what is said.** In a face-to-face conversation, maintain eye contact, do not interrupt, and work to understand what the speaker wants to convey. Show respect to the speaker.

- **The active listener lets the speaker know that he or she is listening.** Nod your head, say "I see," or in some other way indicate that you hear what is being said. The key is to be sincere. Nodding and saying "I understand" while really thinking about what you will be doing tonight is not actively listening. It is preparing for a collective monologue.

- **Active listeners not only hear the words but "listen" to the body language.** Look for clues in the speaker's body position to help you understand the message being delivered.

- **The active listener often asks questions about what the speaker has just said.** The questioning is not meant to be confrontational; rather, it is an attempt to make sure the message has been understood. Asking questions indicates your interest in the other person's comments.

- **Finally, the active listener attempts to repeat what he or she has just heard to ensure the message has been understood.** Paraphrasing the message makes the speaker feel affirmed. You do not have to agree with the speaker but only convey you have correctly understood what he or she said.

Activity 11.2

Critically Thinking about Your Interpersonal Skills

R E D

Let's apply the R.E.D. Model for critical thinking to your ability to relate to and work with others in a civil manner. Activity 11.1, which you completed earlier, may be helpful for this activity.

Identify one of your interpersonal strengths or challenges.

Critical-Thinking Step	Application to Your Interpersonal Skills
Recognize Assumptions	Clearly state your strength or challenge with relationship skills. How do you know this assessment of your interpersonal skills is correct?
Evaluate Information	Provide a specific explanation (give examples) of your strength or challenge with interpersonal skills. Examine your strength or challenge with relationship skills from more than one perspective (point of view).
Draw Conclusions	Based on your evidence, do your conclusions above make sense? How is your assessment of your strength or challenge with interpersonal skills connected to your academic progress? What is the next step you will take to improve your interpersonal skills?

CIVILITY AND GROUP DYNAMICS

By the time you find your way to college, you will have already been involved in group work on various levels. Whether collaborating on a community project or doing a school assignment, group work is a common experience for all students. Some groups last for a very brief time. For instance, teachers commonly assign students to groups for in-class activities. Other groups may last for an entire school term. Being involved in groups helps the participants develop communication, collaboration, and conflict-resolution skills.

UNDERSTANDING GROUP DYNAMICS

Whether you work with a group on a short-term classroom assignment or become the member of, say, a sports team for a longer period, you will find that certain stages of group development are present. Merely knowing about these stages will not eliminate the potential for interpersonal problems, but being familiar with common group dynamics can help you anticipate what is to come and, consequently, be better prepared for what lies ahead.

Groups present an opportunity for two, three, or more people to share their talents and develop a better product than any of them could produce alone. But human behavior can be unpredictable and create some challenges along the way (Lencioni, 2002, p. vii).

A common model views group development as a predictable, systematic process. That model was created by Bruce W. Tuckman, who published "Developmental Sequence in Small Groups" in 1965. He described the stages groups progress through, from development to conclusion. His initial model included only four stages, but in a later article, Tuckman and a colleague added a fifth stage. Table 11.1 describes these five stages and provides examples. (For more on Tuckman's research, see Smith [2005]).

While there is a certain predictable unpredictability about groups, the five stages are common to all of them. Depending on the purpose of the group, the stages may take place over months or years. Or in the case of a short-term group, all five stages may be exhausted in less than an hour.

Table 11.1 Stages of Group Development

Stage of Group	Common Dynamics	Example from Hakeem's Group (beginning of this topic)
1. FORMING	■ Group members introduce themselves to one another and learn about the task they are to address. Apprehension and anxiety may be present.	■ The instructor distributes the guidelines sheet to group members.
2. STORMING	■ Conflict (tension) typically arises as members struggle to find a leader, assign tasks, and agree on roles. Groups can end up splitting up at this early stage.	■ Students are reluctant to commit to the tasks at hand.
3. NORMING	■ Members become more comfortable and tackle their tasks. Trust may start to develop.	■ John volunteers to lead the group.
4. PERFORMING	■ This is the productive stage, as members work on their assignments.	■ The group agrees on a time and place to meet.
5. ADJOURNING	■ The group's task is finished, and the group ends.	■ Not yet. This group is just beginning.

FORMING YOUR OWN GROUP

At times, you may be assigned to a group by the instructor, and you will have no choice in determining your group members. The instructor may group students randomly or according to some preset criterion, such as career or co-curricular interests. On other occasions, you will be able to form your own groups. For instance, you may form a study group with a few classmates when you decide to study for a test together. In this situation, there is the desired way to choose members—and then there is the college reality.

In reality, study groups are made up of friends or, if not friends, acquaintances from the same class. The only criterion for group membership, in most cases, is that the students have the same test, essay, or project to prepare for. Perhaps a student who scores well on exams will be asked to join the group. Some members will look for friendly faces to provide comfort until the task is completed.

In fact, this informal method of selecting group members can produce the needed results on short-term assignments. The suggestions that follow, however, may maximize the productivity of a group—especially for a long-term group project (Lencioni, 2002; Katzenbach and Smith, 2003; Stevens, 2002). And even if you are not part of a class or study group, you might find yourself a member of another group—perhaps the homecoming committee, the campus speakers' bureau, a community action group, or the student government issues committee.

Whatever the purpose of the group, when you have the option to choose your own members, consider the following points:

- Size matters. Keep the group at a small, workable number.

- Team members need to have complementary skills. If you have a four-member team, the ideal composition is to have a full-of-ideas creative person, a facts-based thinking person, an organizer who can pull together all the ideas and research, and a "people" person who has a talent for helping others work together.

- Know why you exist. Just as with a reading or writing assignment, everyone in the group needs to agree on your common purpose as soon as possible. Know your direction.

- Disagree. A passionate exchange, in which all speakers and views are respected, can energize a group.

- Accountability is necessary. Ensure that all team members have specific tasks to perform and that they are held accountable to the group for completing their assigned tasks.

- Don't ignore the **"elephant in the corner."** The "elephant" is a metaphor for a problem so big that it is impossible to miss. The elephant's being in the "corner" indicates the problem is being pushed to the side, because no one wants to talk about it. Address and deal with the problem before it sabotages your group.

TRUST: Building on a Shared Experience

All successful groups share at least one key quality: **trust**. Having meaningful, passionate, and respectful discussions—as opposed to shouting matches—will be fostered when members recognize that their main shared concern is arriving at a reasonable answer. This cannot happen when members are worrying whether someone in the group will attempt to undermine them with personal attacks and hidden agendas. You can disagree and argue about an issue, but do not launch a personal assault on another member. Attacking others in this way will undermine trust.

How do you come to trust people you don't really know?

The simple answer to this complex question is that you must build trust over time. It cannot be built by giving money to people, it cannot be built with glitzy technology, and it cannot be built with motivational pep talks. Trust will be built when group members share an experience. The experience can be positive, like winning a volleyball championship for the college. Or the experience can be harrowing, such as surviving a natural disaster with the help of a neighbor. The commonality in both situations is that the people involved came to rely on one another. They anticipated each other's needs—they supported one another.

Members of an effective study group or class project team, for instance, will experience such trust building. When one student is having a difficult day, the others will come to his or her assistance. Each person comes to the group meeting having prepared the material for which he or she is responsible. They work toward a goal, and they do what they can to make sure each member of the group is successful. Trust naturally develops among the members of this kind of group.

Activity 11.3

Whom Do You Trust—and Why?

Take a moment and reflect on the people in your life whom you trust. Your initial thoughts might be of a family member, a church leader, a close friend, or a sports teammate. For this activity, however, please picture someone you have met *since you have been on campus.* It might be a classmate, an instructor, a counselor, an office worker—or anyone else.

1. Write the first name of this trusted individual.

2. Why do you trust this person? What shared experience led to the formation of this trusted relationship?

When you meet and must work with new classmates or instructors during the remainder of your school career—and beyond into the world of work—remind yourself that while it takes time to develop trust, the results are energizing.

CIVILITY AND CONFLICT

Conflict describes a state of disharmony in which one set of ideas or values contradicts another. A conflict can be fairly minor—a roommate who rises for morning jogs and disturbs your sleep. Or it can be quite serious—two group members getting into a shouting and shoving match about the group's work. At times, you will have to confront conflicts of various degrees of severity.

ARE YOU HAVING A DISAGREEMENT OR A CONFLICT?

A conflict is not necessarily the same as a disagreement. For our purposes, an argument about which college football team should be the national champion does not constitute a conflict. It is a difference of opinion, to be sure, but this type of disagreement does not pit one person's core system of values and beliefs against that of another.

Conflict, on the other hand, occurs when deeply held ideas, values, or perspectives are contradictory (McNamara, 1997–2008). The conflict can be between two or more people—or it can be an internal conflict between your own values and actions.

Suppose a young man or woman has been reared with the deeply held value that having sexual relations before marriage constitutes a violation of personal integrity. If either finds themselves in a situation that challenges the deeply held beliefs, they will experience a period of conflict as they attempt to reconcile the contradictory signals.

CONFLICT IS NOT ALWAYS A BAD THING

Earlier in this topic, you read about the dynamics of group formation. Storming is a real and necessary stage that groups and teams will encounter. Conflict about the exact purpose for the team, who has the best talents to be the leader, and what tasks should be assigned to whom can expose contradictory values and perspectives.

One of the dysfunctions of teams occurs when passionate debate does not take place (Lencioni, 2002). So while an absence of conflict may seem heavenly, it is an unrealistic goal in most human relationships—and it may even be unhealthy. The required ingredient is a mechanism to discuss why the conflict exists and how it can be managed and resolved without loss of trust.

When two or more people come together for any length of time, the risk for conflict presents itself. You do not need to enter every relationship with the dread of impending conflict. But it may be healthy to understand that when conflict does occur, it can produce a positive outcome for you and the other person or people involved.

WAYS PEOPLE DEAL WITH CONFLICT

There are many ways to deal with conflict. If five people are involved in a conflict, there will be probably *at least* five solutions presented. If ten people are present, there is a good chance you will find at least ten ideas.

Given this, any list of strategies to manage conflict will be necessarily incomplete. As you read the following strategies and examples, think about how you might handle each situation (McNamara, 1997–2008):

- **Ignore the issue.** Some people will do anything to avoid a confrontation. They believe that peace at all costs is better than arguing and raising their voices. However, this avoidance could lead to a lose-lose situation, in which the initial flame of conflict gets worse because it has not been controlled. Eventually, the conflict will consume all parties in an inferno of controversy. That may result in ill feelings and resentment. This is where the "elephant in the corner" will be found.

    - **Example:** One member of your group always complains about the project at hand. He drags down your energy each time you are around him. Rather than say anything to him or her, your group quietly goes about its work, many times taking on tasks that the "complainer" was to do. You all hope this person will change his or her ways or leave the group, but none of you directly addresses the problem.

- **Refusing to see another side.** In this scenario, as the conflict increases, people may become more entrenched in their views. Depending on the severity of the disagreement, this lose-lose situation can bring a relationship or team to a grinding halt.

    - **Example:** There are four members in your group. Each person believes his or her direction for the group is the best, and no one is willing to concede on anything. No work gets done, and the deadline for the group product gets closer.

- **Give in to the "demands."** In the interest of peace, once again, one person decides to do whatever the other person wants. This is a win-lose situation: Someone gets his or her way, and someone does not. It may leave the underlying issue of the conflict unresolved.
  - **Example:** Your roommate likes to party late into the night. Unfortunately, his or her late hours have been interfering with your sleep patterns. Each day, you awaken tired. When you talk to your roommate about this, he or she begins to whine about how you do not appreciate what he or she does around the apartment. In fact, you are told, your early-morning routines have bothered him or her. Your roommate threatens to move out and leave you to pay the entire monthly rent. You give in—and buy some earplugs.

- **Compromise.** You give a little, the other person gives a little, and the conflict is minimized if not totally resolved. This creates a modified win-win situation, as each person has not been able to achieve all that he or she had hoped for. But for the sake of harmony, a middle course has been agreed on. Because all situations do not reach the synergy level (see the next strategy), compromise sometimes represents a very positive resolution.
  - **Example:** Your late-night roommate has agreed to enter the apartment quietly and not turn the television on when he or she returns after midnight. You agree to be quieter when you arise early for your 8:00 a.m. class.

- **Synergy.** When two or more people hit on a solution that is actually better than any of the previous ideas, synergy has been achieved. A win-win situation results. Although highly desirable, this outcome requires considerable effort to achieve.
  - **Example:** You and your late-night roommate have discovered that two of your good friends are having the same problem: One is an early riser, and one is a "night owl." The four of you decide to switch roommates. The two early risers will live together, and the two night owls will live together. All friendships have been maintained, all four individuals are happier than they were prior to the new arrangement, and you are now able to get a great night's sleep.

AGGRESSIVENESS, ASSERTIVENESS, AND PASSIVENESS

Being able to communicate a message of confidence, competence, and civility will have an impact on how people perceive you. Not only does what you say influence people, but so does *how* you say it (tone of voice) and how you *look* (body language) while saying it. Whether you are speaking to one person or 100, your communication is the sum of many interrelated parts.

One key to successful communication is to speak with an air of confidence. A self-assured person captures attention better than someone stammering for the correct words. Self-confidence underlies an assertive communication style. People who communicate with **assertiveness** can stand up for themselves. They can face demands and can make requests in a nonaggressive manner (Marano, 2011).

Aggressive behavior, on the other hand, represents a harsher attitude. It can border on hostility or a bully-like approach to dealing with other people. Bullies take advantage of **passive** individuals: people who submit to verbal and, in some cases, nonverbal attacks without resistance. Although every situation presents unique circumstances, generally speaking, assertive behavior is seen as the favored road to travel.

DEALING WITH BULLIES

Mention the word *bully*, and people tend to think of the elementary school playground. A larger boy seeks out and finds a smaller fellow, whom he proceeds to verbally and/or physically assault. However, school-age children do not have a monopoly on bullying behavior. It exists in the workplace, and it exists on college campuses (Domonell, 2013; Saillant, 2005).

Bullies repeatedly seek to control other people by means of physical or verbal aggression. Bullying can arise in any situation where one person holds power over or intimidates another. Supervisors and coworkers can bully people, for instance. A student can be bullied because of his or her sexual orientation. A boyfriend can bully his girlfriend, and a girlfriend can bully her boyfriend. Domestic violence is bullying taken to a more extreme level. Faculty can bully students, and even students can bully faculty.

If you suspect a friend is being bullied—or if you are the victim of a bully—seek assistance as quickly as possible. Find someone—a friend, a faculty member, a counselor, or a family member—you trust, and get help.

WHO ARE THE "TOXIC PEOPLE" OF YOUR LIFE?

"Toxic" people "poison" our lives. They can affect us on various levels. A toxic person can be a bully who perpetuates a physically abusive or psychologically demeaning relationship. Or, rather than abusive, the person may act continually in ways that you find to be irritating. In whatever manner they come to us, these toxic people seem to take the life right out of us. Like a balloon losing air, we can almost hear our energy leaving our bodies.

In the book *Positive Energy*, Judith Orloff (2004) writes of "energy vampires"—the toxic people in our lives who continually drain us of energy (pp. 288–320). They whine about their lives, berate us for our actions, and monopolize our interactions. They do not typically engage in conversations, because that would involve a two-way exchange. Rather, you will usually hear monologues about their ailments, opinions, or prejudices. When they finish with us, *they* feel more energized—but *we* feel exhausted, having had our energy zapped.

The metaphor of an energy vampire is powerful (Goldberg, n.d.). The same concept is sometimes referred to as "psychic parasitism." After draining us and leaving us tired and wasted, these people move on. Perhaps you have experienced this with a roommate, a classmate, an instructor, a friend, a co-worker, or even a family member. The experience may be subtle. You are not really sure what happened. But after talking with this person, you feel more tired than you did before. Moreover, in some cases, you can feel the energy draining from your body as the person moves closer to you and begins to speak. In short, these people spread "toxins" into your life.

Two cautionary notes must be added to this discussion of toxic people:

1. As with many things in life, there are shades of gray. Not every situation is black or white. Obviously, a friend who comes to you in distress about a traumatic event that just occurred is not the same as the person who continually seeks you out to complain or criticize and drains energy from your relationship.
2. Every relationship is a two-way street. If you continually find yourself in draining relationships, you should evaluate your actions. Do you do something that draws these types of people to you and encourages their behavior?

HOW TO GUARD AGAINST TOXIC PEOPLE

After you identify the source of your energy loss, what can you do to plug the hole? Orloff provides a number of prescriptions—"antidotes" to the toxin, in effect—including redirecting the conversation, setting limits, and simply spending less time with the person (Orloff, 2004, Chapter 9). See Activity 11.4.

Activity 11.4

How Do You Interact with People?

Pause for a moment and reflect on how you interact with other people. Then answer the questions that follow. Ask someone who really knows you well to share his or her perception of your interaction with others.

Remember: If you ask someone for honest feedback, be prepared to accept what he or she says. Do not request information and then argue with the person because you disagree. Consider feedback a wonderful gift.

1. When talking with people, do you continually "replay" your same stories over and over?

   ❏ Yes   ❏ No

2. Do you hold a conversation with people, or do you engage in a self-centered monologue about your life?

   ❏ Yes   ❏ No

3. When someone speaks with you, do you avoid asking meaningful and substantive questions? Do you lack interest in the other person's "stories"?

   ❏ Yes   ❏ No

4. When describing events that have occurred, do you typically describe things as being devastating and particular only to you? That is, do you believe no one could ever experience the hardships that you have experienced?

   ❏ Yes   ❏ No

5. Do you start most of your conversations with "You are never going to believe what happened to me!" or something similar (Orloff, p. 299)?

   ❏ Yes   ❏ No

6. When in a group, do you always have to be the focus of attention?

   ❏ Yes   ❏ No

7. Do you find your conversations peppered with insults, anger, and attempts to make others look bad?

   ❏ Yes   ❏ No

8. Any "Yes" answers may indicate that you have a tendency to drain energy from others. Think of the list you made of people who drain your energy. Do you think your name will appear on anyone else's list of toxic people (energy vampires)?

   ❏ Yes   ❏ No

9. Based on your answers, what do you plan to do to make sure you do not drain energy from those around you? What will you do to be a "nutritious person"?

   Dealing with energy-draining individuals may be tiring and counterproductive to group results. If you feel ill equipped or not up to the task, draw on support and advice from trusted friends and mentors. And remember never to place yourself in a dangerous or compromising position. Your emotional well-being is important, as is your physical safety.

Basically, if you can establish boundaries and limits, you have a better chance of protecting yourself from the toxins.

BOUNDARIES AND LIMITS

This strategy lets people know just how far you will go—and how far you will let them go. Setting boundaries and understanding limits allows for having a more satisfying life (Lee, 2009, pp. 125–142).

Boundaries show where we begin and end. They let others know what is acceptable and unacceptable. They tell people how far they can go with us. When our boundaries are clearly established, there is no question. People know where they can and cannot go as it relates to you.

Limits, on the other hand, let people know how far you will go. Your limits clearly tell people what you will or will not do. If you establish your limits correctly, people will not be left guessing about what to expect from you. People without clearly established limits end up giving more—physically, emotionally, occupationally—than they want to give. This can result in resentment, hurt feelings, exhaustion, and even rage.

Boundaries and limits can be adjusted along the way, as additional information is learned. However, for boundaries and limits to be effective and healthy, they have to be clear to both you and those you live and work with. You should not get upset when someone breeches a boundary if you have not been clear on what your boundaries are. The same goes for limits. If you do not set—and respect—your own limits, you may find yourself overstretched and ready to snap.

FINDING "NUTRITIOUS PEOPLE" FOR YOUR LIFE

One way to protect your energy and sanity is to associate with **"nutritious people"** (see Leider, 1997, p. 64; Leider and Shapiro, 1995, Chapter 7). These people help to ward off the poison spewed by the energy-draining toxic people you may encounter.

A nutritious person has three main characteristics:

1. When this person sees you, he or she is genuinely glad to see you. His or her face brightens with a smile.
2. When you speak, this person *listens* to you. He or she asks questions about what you say and about what matters to you. He or she exhibits a genuine interest in what you have to say.
3. The nutritious person accepts you as you are. This individual does not attempt to make you into someone he or she would like you to be.

The more nutritious people we have in our lives, the better. It is almost as though we can feel our energy level rising when we see their faces.

Identify the nutritious people in your life. Thank them for being there for you. Finally, ask yourself, "Am I nutritious for other people?"

Chapter SUMMARY

Before leaving this topic, keep the following points in mind:

■ While groups present opportunities for people to share talents and develop better products than one person could produce alone, they can be unpredictable and create challenges.

■ Beware of people who constantly drain energy from you—the toxic people.

■ Seek out nutritious people, who will help energize you.

■ If you want to be considered a nutritious person, listen to and acknowledge what others have to offer.

■ Effective communication is an art form that has no room for collective monologues.

■ Conflict can be positive, when appropriately managed.

CRITICALLY THINKING
What Have You Learned?

Let's apply what you learned in this material to help Hakeem's group from the opening scenario. However, before you address the group's situation and propose your solution, take a moment to think about the main points of the material. Review your notes, the key terms, learning outcomes, boldface headings, and figures and tables.

TEST YOUR LEARNING

Now that you have reviewed the main points and reread the group's story, what advice do you have for Hakeem and his group. Using the R.E.D. Model of critical thinking, help Hakeem critically review any concerns he might have:

Recognize Assumptions:

Facts: What are the facts in the group's situation? List them.

Opinions: What opinions do you find in this situation? List them.

Assumptions: Are Hakeem's assumptions accurate?

Evaluate Information:

Help Hakeem compile a list of questions that will help him and the group make the most appropriate decision.

What emotions seem to be motivating Hakeem?

What, if anything, is missing from Hakeem's thought process?

Do you see any confirmation bias?

Draw Conclusions:

Based on the facts and the questions you have presented, what conclusions can you draw?

What advice do you have for Hakeem? What solutions do you propose?

Based on your suggestions, do you see any assumptions?

Finally, based on what you learned about using critical thinking and interpersonal skills, what plan of action do you suggest for this group?

Treating YOURSELF with RESPECT

12

LEARNING OUTCOMES

By the time you finish reading this material and completing its activities, you will be able to do the following:

- Make two positive changes in your physical activity program and make two healthy dietary adjustments.

- Commit to two actions that will keep you healthy and safe in your relationships.

The Case of NICOLE

Nicole makes physical exercise a cornerstone of her life. Whether it is resistance training in the gym, jogging, riding a bike, or walking her dog, this college student does some type of activity every day. "It helps to keep me physically fit and emotionally grounded," she told a friend recently.

One day, as she was nearing the end of her college semester, she sat down to lace up her running shoes for her morning jog. She did not have much energy on this particular day. She had been up all night completing a term project for her psychology class; her history class study group ended in an argument yesterday afternoon;

Key Terms

Aerobic exercise
Binge drinking
Body Mass Index (BMI)
Date rape
Eating disorder
Habit
Obesity
Recommended daily allowance
Reframe

INTRODUCTION *Chapter*

We all have multidimensional lives. You, your friends, your classmates, and your family have six dimensions: Social, occupational, spiritual, physical, intellectual, and emotional (Hettler). If you want to excel in school, relationships, work, and life, you will benefit by examining the habits you have developed in each dimension of your life. Do you live a healthy and balanced life—or do you find yourself at times to be physically exhausted, mentally stressed, and emotionally drained? A weakness or challenge in one area will have an impact on others; they are all interconnected.

and she was overwhelmed just thinking about her upcoming final exams. This morning she just wanted to finish the run and grab a double espresso to face the day.

"I am not sure where I am going to get the time to do all I need to do," she said to herself. "I'll just have to suck it up and skimp on sleep and forego my jogging for the next two weeks. The good news is that since I have been working out regularly, I don't need to exercise again until the exams and projects are completed."

As she walked out the door, she read the poster on her apartment wall that said, "This too shall pass!"

CRITICALLY THINKING
about *Nicole's* situation

What do you think about Nicole's decision to skimp on sleep and forego her exercise activities for the coming weeks?

Some people spend 25 percent or more of their week at work. Some students spend that much or more time in classes and doing homework. About one-third of your week may be in sleep. But how many of your weekly hours have you set aside for health-related activities? Do you pay attention to what you eat? Did you know that you can start a worthwhile exercise and diet program with as little as a 2 percent investment of your time?

Your social sphere will have a major impact on your physical and emotional well-being. Caring, nurturing, and encouraging relationships can

MyStudentSuccessLab

MyStudentSuccessLab (www.mystudentsuccesslab.com) is an online solution designed to help you "Start strong, Finish stronger" by building skills for ongoing personal and professional development.

Figure 12.1

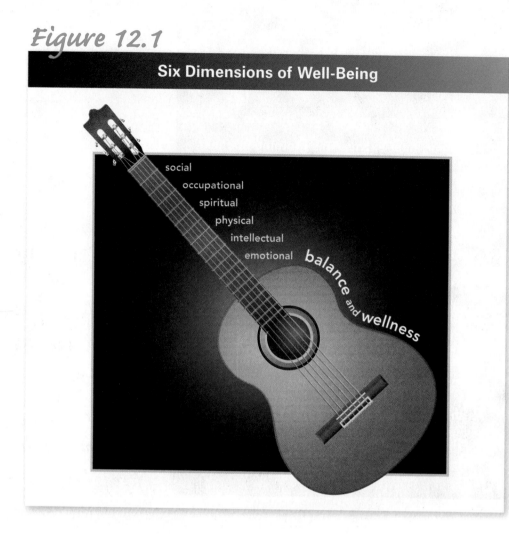

Six Dimensions of Well-Being

social
occupational
spiritual
physical
intellectual
emotional

balance and wellness

augment your physical health. But unfortunately, risky behaviors (alcohol, drugs, and sexual activity) can jeopardize not only your education but your life as well. A healthy life is about well-thought-out and balanced choices.

When you live a balanced life, you have a better chance to experience contentment by being intellectually alert, emotionally stable, and physically strong.

Activity 12.1

Reflecting on Your Current Level of Balance and Well-Being[*]

Before you answer the following items, reflect on your current level of balance and well-being. Think of how well (or poorly) you have taken care of the various dimensions of your life.

Write from your heart. This exercise is not meant for you to answer just like your classmates—or to match what you may think the instructor wants to see. Take the time to give a respectful, responsible general accounting of your experiences with health and well-being. Conducting a truthful self-assessment now will help you build on skills you have while developing those you lack.

For each item, circle the number that best describes your typical experience when attempting to maintain a sense of health and well-being. Here is the key for the numbers:

0 = never, 1 = almost never, 2 = occasionally, 3 = frequently, 4 = almost always, 5 = always

When considering your past and present experiences with health and well-being, how often do you:

1.	Engage in healthy activities each week?	0	1	2	3	4	5
2.	Eat a variety of healthy foods each day?	0	1	2	3	4	5
3.	Maintain a healthy weight—not overweight or underweight—for your body type?	0	1	2	3	4	5
4.	Abstain from any tobacco products?	0	1	2	3	4	5
5.	Avoid using alcohol or illegal drugs?	0	1	2	3	4	5
6.	Not put yourself in dangerous or compromising situations?	0	1	2	3	4	5
7.	Not put others in dangerous or compromising situations?	0	1	2	3	4	5
8.	Have a social network of at least one person you can talk to about challenges you face?	0	1	2	3	4	5
9.	Get enough restful sleep each night so that you wake up energized and clear headed?	0	1	2	3	4	5

Add up your scores for items 1 through 9. Divide by 9. Write your answer here:_____

Using the key provided to explain each number (0, 1, 2, 3, 4, 5), complete this sentence: When it comes to leading a life of balance and well-being, I _____ engage in healthy habits.

Based on your answers, what insights have you gained about your experiences with your health and well-being?

*A Health Risk Assessment (HRA) is a common tool used by healthcare professionals to determine the level of risk individuals have in their lives. The Pre-Assessment activity in this material uses some typical items found in HRAs. See the following for an example: "Stress Management for the Health of It," *Clemson Extension* (Appendix I, Healthstyle Quiz), April 2002, www.nasdonline.org/docs /d001201-d001300/d001245/d001245.html (accessed May 24, 2013).

SIX DIMENSIONS OF WELLNESS

EVERYTHING IS RELATED

Nicole's story at the beginning of this topic reminds us that each dimension of life affects all the others. In some cases, they may blend and meld so closely that you may not know where one ends and another starts. The more you remain aware that each dimension needs attention and care, the better your chances of living a healthy life—a life of balance.

However, this requires the development of healthy habits. A **habit** is something you have repeated so often that it is a behavior you do automatically. It has become second nature.

Paying attention and caring for each life dimension must become a habit. The stronger your life dimensions are, the better you will be able to withstand the various stresses and pressures of life. When you develop and practice a healthy lifestyle, you become a stronger person. Additionally, when you act honestly, responsibly, and respectfully within each dimension toward yourself and others, you act with integrity. Table 12.1 describes this relationship.

Table 12.1   **Connection Between Integrity and the Six Dimensions of Well-Being**

Dimension of Your Well-Being	Connection to Your Integrity (selected examples)
Social	You do not gossip or spread rumors about others. You speak with honesty when talking with or about other people. You respectfully enter—and maintain—relationships.
Occupational	On the job (or in the classroom) you take care of your responsibilities in an honest fashion. You are honest with yourself about why you do what you do for work. You do not use others' resources (without their permission) for your own gain.
Spiritual	You respectfully attempt to understand differing spiritual beliefs. You seek to live your life according to a higher purpose. You see yourself as part of a larger world force.
Physical	You treat your body with respect. You follow a responsible diet and exercise regimen. You get quality sleep each night.
Intellectual	You do not engage in acts of academic dishonesty. You continuously feed your mind with responsible, thought-provoking material. You respectfully listen to and discuss differing points of view.
Emotional	You find healthy and responsible ways to handle stressful situations. You are respectful of your emotional needs as well as the needs of those around you. You understand how your emotional well-being affects other dimensions of your life.

Honesty, respect, and responsibility. When talking about the condition in which you maintain your body, mind, and emotions, can you think of anything that is more important? If you abuse yourself, you are not living with integrity. For that reason, let's first examine the impact the physical dimension has on your life.

EXERCISE

The Centers for Disease Control and Prevention (CDC) reports that the leading cause of death in the United States is cardiovascular disease (CVD). And the leading causes of heart problems (as well as other health problems) are poor diet, weight problems, and physical *inactivity* (Kochanek, 2013). Thirty-eight percent of all deaths have been attributed to CVD.

Moderate cardiovascular activity of just thirty minutes per day can help reduce heart disease, lower cholesterol, control blood pressure, and relieve stress. Daily exercise will also enhance sound and restful sleep at night. Although there is no guarantee that physical activity will prevent health problems, research indicates that even moderate levels of activity produce beneficial results (American Heart Association, 2013). Remember, no matter what you do for physical activity, make sure it is safe for you. Always seek professional and/or medical guidance before starting any physical regimen. A personal trainer (easily found at most neighborhood gyms), a coach (located on campus), and your personal physician can provide you with appropriate conditioning information.

The CDC recommends both aerobic and muscle-strengthening activities to improve physical conditioning. The CDC suggests the following physical activity guidelines for adults to receive "important health benefits" (Centers for Disease Control, 2011).

The CDC says that greater health benefits will come if you are able to increase your activity in duration as well as intensity. Once again, your level of activity must

Activity for Health Benefits

Activity	Duration
Aerobic exercise	
Moderate (which means you can still talk while doing the exercise, but you "break a sweat"). Examples include fast walking, water aerobics, biking, and lawn mowing.	150 minutes per week
Vigorous (which means you breathe hard and fast and can only speak a few words without pausing for breath). Examples include jogging, running, bicycling fast, swimming laps, and playing basketball.	75 minutes per week
Muscle-strengthening concentrating on the major muscle groups	2 or more days per week

OR

be appropriate for your state of conditioning. Information of this sort can be found in a wide variety of sources. Your student center or campus health center might offer fitness programs. Consider consulting a health care professional about the best physical fitness activity for you.

As you research the healthiest physical activities for your condition and goals, consider how the following might meet your needs:

- *Aerobic exercise.* Typically, **aerobic exercise** is defined as activity that increases your heart and breathing rates, as well as working your muscles. Like the CDC, the American Heart Association (2013) touts the benefits of physical activity for 30 minutes per day. Depending on your current level of physical conditioning, you may need to begin at 5 or 10 minutes a day and then increase that as your body acclimates to this exertion. Swimming, kickboxing, biking, and jogging are examples of aerobic activity. Find one that excites you, and you will have a better chance of making the activity a habit.

- *Strength or resistance training.* Whether it is Pilates, weight lifting, or yoga, when done appropriately a couple of times per week, this form of activity helps to strengthen muscles and bones. There may be community or campus classes you can take for appropriate instruction. Check with your student activities center for information. If you have access to a gym, ask a staff member to help orient you to the gym equipment and class schedules. Remember, slow and steady wins the race. Don't overdo any exercise.

- *Flexibility training.* Injury can occur when muscles are not sufficiently warmed up and stretched. Flexibility training will not only reduce the possibility of injury, but it will also keep your muscles and joints flexible. Whether you engage in simple, gentle stretching or take part in a more vigorous yoga practice, flexibility training limbers the muscles and quiets the mind.

Physical conditioning does not just occur in the gym or on the athletic field. Incorporate it into your everyday life. When feasible, use the stairs instead of the elevator; park a little farther from the door; walk or bicycle instead of driving; walk around campus between classes. If the thought of finding 150 minutes per week for regular exercise seems like a fantasy, it may help to **reframe**—look at from a different viewpoint—the situation. Once you make the decision that your physical health is a non-negotiable priority, it will be time to make some appropriate and healthy choices.

- *Think action steps.* Break your goal of 150 minutes of moderate-intensity physical activity into smaller action steps.

- *Think 10 minutes.* Think of your activities for a week. Some of them are high priority (non-negotiable); others can easily be rated as non-priority items (negotiable). Perhaps you find yourself watching television two or three hours a day, or maybe you devote two or three hours a day to a social network site or text messaging. Now, think "10"—10 minutes. The CDC states,

  > *You don't have to do [150 minutes] all at once. Not only is it best to spread your activity out during the week, but you can break it up into smaller chunks of time during the day as long as you're doing your activity at a moderate or vigorous effort for at least 10 minutes at a time (2011).*

- *Think 2 percent.* This strategy provides a way to begin a new routine and build a healthy habit. Within five days, at 30 minutes per day, you will have completed your 150 minutes of activity. Your health is worth 10 minutes in the morning, 10 minutes in the afternoon, and 10 minutes in the evening. So each day, take three 10-minute chunks of time from your non-priority activities. Build and maintain a healthy habit.

Thirty minutes per day represents about 2 percent of your entire day. Two percent! Your health is worth at least a 2 percent investment.

Activity 12.2

Personal Well-Being: Establishing a Personal Exercise Plan

At the beginning of this topic, you read about Nicole and how she was considering her exercise and health to be negotiable during the final hectic weeks of the semester. Model for Nicole—using this activity—how to develop a reasonable and achievable plan for the coming week.

Establish your physical exercise goal for the coming week.

- In column (1) list all of the activities you plan to do this week as part of your exercise program.
- In column (2) write the day(s) you will complete each activity.
- In column (3) write the number of minutes you will do each activity this week.
- Complete columns (4), (5), and (6) as you finish the activities.

(1) Exercise I *Will* Do This Week	(2) When	(3) Duration (in minutes)	(4) Exercise I *Did* Do This Week	(5) When	(6) Duration (in minutes)
1.					
2.					
3.					
4.					
5.					
6.					

At the end of the week, write a statement about your week of physical activity. Did you do what you said you would do? What is your plan for next week?

SABOTAGING YOUR PHYSICAL CONDITIONING—TOBACCO

According to the Centers for Disease Control ("Smoking and Tobacco Use," 2012), more than 400,000 Americans die each year due to smoking and "secondhand smoke exposure." In addition to cost factors and health issues, it is becoming increasingly difficult for smokers to find public places where they can light up their cigarettes legally. Because secondhand smoke can also be harmful, more and more states have passed laws limiting where people can smoke. If you use tobacco, organizations and programs exist to help you quit. Check with your campus wellness office or your community health department for referral information.

Quitting any habit can be difficult, but attempting to kick a nicotine habit has additional challenges. The critical period is the first three months. During that time old "triggers" will prove tempting (Smokefree.gov, n.d.). If you used to smoke a cigarette each morning with a cup of coffee, breakfast will be a trigger time. If you used to meet friends who smoked between classes, you may have to alter your routine. If you fail on your first attempt, don't beat yourself up. You will be that much stronger and well prepared for your next attempt. It *will* be difficult, but your emotional willpower (a dimension of life) and a strong support system (another dimension of life) can help you move to a tobacco-free lifestyle.

DIET: It Can Be Hard to Eat Healthy Foods!

One of the key strategies to minimize weight gain—and probably the simplest to comprehend—is to balance your caloric intake (what you eat) with caloric expenditure (what you do). More intake than expenditure, on a regular basis, will eventually lead to weight gain. Likewise, if a person regularly does not consume enough calories to fuel activity, other problems can develop. The Dietary Guidelines established by the U.S. Department of Health and Human Services provide simple, common-sense strategies. Referencing the impact of ill health on the individual and the nation, the USDHH maintains that a slimmer waistline not only reduces risks for disease but is also good for our nation as a whole (2011).

WHAT DOES A HEALTHY DIET LOOK LIKE FOR YOU? AVERAGE DAILY RECOMMENDATIONS

For convenience purposes, many of us may rely on fast foods or "processed foods." Fast food can be found on most any corner in your town or city. Processed foods are foods that have been altered from their fresh or natural state, either by canning or freezing. Additionally, be mindful of boxed and bagged items found on the grocery shelves. Although these convenience products can be delicious, they may also carry health concerns (for instance, high salt content). For our purposes here, we will concentrate on four items: calories, total fat, sodium, and sugar. Being aware and taking responsibility for your choices are the first steps to a healthy diet—and healthy lifestyle. A person should develop a diet geared to his or her needs and in conjunction with his or her healthcare provider's advice.

Most food products contain some type of nutrition facts label listing the ingredients. Often you will also see a notation like "percentage of **recommended daily allowance**." Table 12.2 gives broad information for three categories of food ingredients. The amount of calories a person eats is dependent on variables like intensity of daily activity, age, height, and medical condition. These general figures about the ingredients of the product are included to help the consumer make informed decisions about what he or she eats (U.S. Food and Drug Administration, 2013).

Note that nutrition fact labels generally give amounts per serving. If you eat the contents of the entire can, bag, or package, the amounts (usually) increase considerably.

What Does a Healthy Diet Look Like for You? The Reality (for Many). Most people probably do not eat according to recommended daily allowances. Table 12.3 has information on a few selected fast food choices you, your friends, and your family may make. Note the numbers and compare to Table 12.2.

A couple of observations are worth noting. One burrito with beef contains more than the total amount of sodium (salt) recommended for an entire *day*. (That means no more salt for the rest of day—if you want to live according to the daily recommended allowance.) Look at the Caffe Mocha. In one cup, you will receive more than 15 percent of your total fat intake for an entire day (on a 2,000-calorie diet)—and more than 10 percent of total caloric intake for the day.

Calorie-Cutting Tips. The first calorie-cutting tip is to be aware of what you put in your mouth. Table 12.3 graphically shows that even what we might consider a good choice—a vegetarian burrito, for instance—can clobber us with calories, fat, and sodium, a disheartening trifecta for any health-conscious person. Consider the following basic tips as you go about your menu selection:

■ *Know what is in your food.* In the grocery store, read the package labels. Before you go to a coffee shop or restaurant, check the Internet to see if they list their menu and nutrition facts. See the footnotes in Table 12.3 for some of those sites.

Table 12.2   Daily Dietary Recommendations

Dietary Intake	Maximum Recommended Total Fat Per Day	Maximum Recommended Total Sodium Per Day
2,000 calories per day	65 grams	2,400 milligrams
2,500 calories per day	80 grams	2,400 milligrams

Table 12.3 **Actual Nutrition Numbers**

Food	Total Calories	Total Fat (grams)	Sodium (mg)	Sugar (g)
Hamburger[1]	250	9	480	6
Medium french fries[2]	380	19	270	0
Chicken McNuggets? (6 pieces)[3]	280	18	540	0
Diet Coca-cola® (small)[4]	0	0	10	0
Sweet tea (small)[5]	150	0	10	36
Minute Maid® Orange Juice[6] (small)	150	0	0	30
Salad (vegetable, tossed, no dressing, 1.5 cups)[7]	33	0.1	54	0
Ranch dressing (2 tbsp)[8]	148	15	287	1
Vegetarian burrito[9]	690	20	1030	2
Super burrito (beef, refried)[10]	1180	44	2790	8
Original Recipe® KFC chicken breast (1)[11]	360	21	1080	0
KY Grilled Chicken® (breast, 1)[12]	220	7	730	0
Ham, egg, cheese on croissant[13]	560	31	1440	5
Double whopper ™ with cheese[14]	990	65	1480	11
1 slice medium cheese only pan pizza[15]	240	10	530	2
1 slice medium meat lovers' pan pizza[16]	320	18	820	2
Caffe latte with 2% milk (12 oz)[17]	150	6	115	13
Caffe mocha (12 oz, soy milk and whipped cream)[18]	260	11	95	26
Iced black coffee (12 oz.)[19]	3	0	5	0

[1] McDonald's, "McDonald's U.S.A. Nutrition Facts for Popular Menu Items" (May, 2013), http://nutrition.mcdonalds.com/getnutrition/nutritionfacts.pdf (accessed May 25, 2013).

[2] Ibid.

[3] Ibid.

[4] Ibid.

[5] Ibid.

[6] Ibid.

[7] Calorie Count (2013), http://caloriecount.about.com/calories-salad-vegetable-tossed-i21052 (accessed May 25, 2013).

[8] Calorie Count (2013), http://caloriecount.about.com/calories-kraft-foods-ranch-dressing-i4115 (accessed May 25, 2013).

[9] Calorie Count (2013), http://caloriecount.about.com/calories-moes-southwest-vegetarian-burrito-i301708 (accessed May 25, 2013).

[10] Calorie Count (2013), http://caloriecount.about.com/calories-taco-del-super-burrito-beef-i66475 (accessed May 25, 2013).

[11] Kentucky Fried Chicken, http://www.kfc.com/nutrition/ (accessed May 25, 2013).

[12] Ibid.

[13] Burger King, "Ham, egg, cheese CROISSAN'WICH®" (2013), http://www.bk.com/en/us/menu-nutrition/breakfast-menu-201/combo-meals-211/ham-egg-and-cheese-croissan-wich-meal-v4032/index.html (accessed May 25, 2013).

[14] "Burger King Nutrition Facts" (May 2013), http://www.bk.com/cms/en/us/cms_out/digital_assets/files/pages/MenuNutritionInformation_April2013_1.pdf (accessed May 25, 2013).

[15] "Pizza Hut Nutritional Information," http://www.pizzahut.com/nutritionpizza.html (accessed May 25, 2013).

[16] Ibid.

[17] MyFitnessPal, "Calories in Starbucks Caffe Latte Tall" (2013), http://www.myfitnesspal.com/food/calories/starbucks-caffe-latte-tall-2-milk-50503048 (accessed May 25, 2013).

[18] MyFitnessPal, "Calories in Starbucks Caffe Mocha" (2013), http://www.myfitnesspal.com/food/calories/starbucks-caffe-mocha-tall-soy-milk-with-whipped-cream-136737 (accessed May 25, 2013).

[19] MyFitnessPal, "Calories in Starbucks Iced Brewed Coffee Black" (2013), http://www.myfitnesspal.com/food/calories/starbucks-iced-brewed-coffee-black-tall-72600435 (accessed May 25, 2013).

- *Do not supersize your meals.* More is not necessarily good. It may fill you—but fill you with fat- and salt-laden calories that can cause weight gain and other health issues.

- *Go easy on the salad dressing.* You may find more calories, fat, and sodium than you thought in your favorite prepared dressing. Even when a salad is healthy, the dressing can tack on 100 to 200 *additional* calories.

- *Increase fresh food items in your diet.* Be a smart eater. Compare nutritional facts for fresh and processed foods.

- *Read food nutrition labels carefully.* Again, read what you eat. One number that may be overlooked is the "servings per container" (near the top of the label). The nutrition numbers on a label typically represent one serving. So if you were to eat the entire container (Figure 12.2) you would need to double all of the numbers. Instead of 280 calories, 13 grams of fat, and 660 milligrams of salt, you would be taking in 560 calories, 26 grams of fat, and 1,320 milligrams of salt. When you compare those figures to the daily recommendations in Table 12.2, you can see the impact this one container of food would have on your diet for the day.

Figure 12.2

Nutrition Facts

Serving Size: 1 cup (228g)
Servings per Container: 2

Amount Per Serving

Calories 280 | **Calories from Fat 120**

	% Daily Value*
Total Fat 13g	20%
Saturated Fat 5g	25%
Trans Fat 2g	
Cholesterol 2mg	10%
Sodium 660mg	28%
Total Carbohydrate 31g	10%
Dietary Fiber 3g	12%
Sugars 5g	
Protein 5g	
Vitamin A 4%	Vitamin C 2%
Calcium 15%	Iron 4%

*Percent Daily Values are based on a 2,000-calorie diet. Your daily values may be higher or lower depending on your calorie needs.

	Calories:	2,000	2,500
Total Fat	Less than	65g	80g
Sat Fat	Less than	20g	25g
Cholesterol	Less than	300mg	300mg
Sodium	Less than	2,400mg	2,400mg
Total Carbohydrate		300g	375g
Fiber		25g	30g

Calories per gram:

Fat 9   Carbohydrate 4   Protein 4

These basic guidelines offered here are for informational purposes. A person should develop a diet geared to his or her needs and in conjunction with his or her healthcare provider's advice.

Activity 12.3

Personal Well-Being Calorie Counting: How Do You Measure Up?

Budgets (or logs listing what you do) are useful tools to determine how we use a particular resource. A priority management budget, for instance, helps keep track of how time is used (and possibly misused). A money budget shows how much money is earned, spent, and saved. Once the facts of the budget are known, then it becomes easier to determine ways to improve the use of that particular resource.

For this activity, you will keep track of (log) your calorie intake for seven consecutive days. You may wish to keep a small pad with you to record the information throughout the day and then transfer to a computer worksheet at the end of the day. A small notebook will work as well. You can dedicate one page of your worksheet to each day of the week. For this to be meaningful, you must list *everything* you eat. Whether it is a full meal, a small bag of pretzels, a can of soda, or a piece of candy, write it down.

1. Using your information literacy skills, find a credible resource that has information about the appropriate healthy caloric intake for a person of your age, gender, and height. You may even find a site that allows you to keep your food log online.

2. Write your healthy target calorie budget for a 24-hour period at the top of each day's page.

3. Find a site that provides information about the calories contained in various food items.

4. Enter your food choices in your pad, notebook, or spreadsheet for seven consecutive days.

5. What steps do you need to take in order to achieve (or maintain) a healthy caloric intake?

ISSUES OF WEIGHT AND OBESITY

In a 2009–2010 study, the CDC found that more than one-third of U.S. adults are obese ("Overweight and Obesity," 2012; Ogden et. al., 2012) and that since 1980, obesity in children and adolescents has nearly tripled ("Overweight and Obesity," 2013). How can a wealthy nation like the United States end up with such a weight problem? Some say it is precisely because of the lifestyle we lead (Hellmich, 2002). Junk food is readily available (and widely marketed). Cars and elevators replace bicycles and walking. "Virtual" physical activities substitute for participation in physical activity. And although genetics and medications may have an impact on weight gain, other controllable factors such as method of food preparation (frying), size of portions ("supersized" and/or all-you-can-eat), and lack of self-discipline can contribute to obesity.

When one is overweight, he or she has extra body weight from body fat, muscle, bone, and water. **Obesity** refers to the condition of having a body mass index (see Table 12.4) of 30 or higher (Centers for Disease Control and Prevention, April 27, 2012). Obesity has become an American health crisis. In 2000, no state had an obesity prevalence of more than 30 percent. In 2010, 12 states weighed in with obesity

rates above 30 percent of the population (Centers for Disease Control and Prevention, August 13, 2012). The CDC warns that increased body fat increases chances for heart disease, high blood pressure, type 2 diabetes, breathing problems, and some types of cancer.

Body Mass Index for Adults. A traditional way to measure your level of fat is to calculate your body mass index (BMI). Use Table 12.4 to check your BMI. First, find your height on the far left column. Next, move across the row to find your weight. Once you've found your weight, move to the very top of that column. This number is your BMI (National Heart, Lung, and Blood Institute, 2012). Table 12.5 will help you interpret your BMI number. Although the BMI chart can be used for most men and women, it does have some limits:

- It may overestimate body fat in athletes and others who have a muscular build, as muscle weighs more than fat.

- It may underestimate body fat in older persons and others who have lost muscle.

Eating Disorders. On the other end of the spectrum from obesity are **eating disorders** that result in unhealthy—and even fatal—weight loss. Millions of Americans suffer from life-threatening eating disorders like anorexia and bulimia while millions more struggle with bouts of binge eating. The National Eating Disorders Association (NEDA, n.d.) says that eating disorders are not to be taken lightly as they are "devastating conditions" that can be "potentially life-threatening." They are serious and not just a passing phase in one's life.

In other words, the causes of eating disorders go beyond mere individual willpower. Although choice remains an important component in avoiding or

Table 12.4 BMI Calculation

Height/BMI	21	22	23	24	25	26	27	28	29	30	31
4'10"	100	105	110	115	119	124	129	134	138	143	148
5'0"	107	112	118	123	128	133	138	143	148	153	158
5'1"	111	116	122	127	132	137	143	148	153	158	164
5'3"	118	124	130	135	141	146	152	158	163	169	175
5'5"	126	132	138	144	150	156	162	168	174	180	186
5'7"	134	140	146	153	159	166	172	178	185	191	198
5'9"	142	149	155	162	169	176	182	189	196	203	209
5'11"	150	157	165	172	179	186	193	200	208	215	222
6'1"	159	166	174	182	189	197	204	212	219	227	235
6'3"	168	176	184	192	200	208	216	224	232	240	248

Table 12.5 **Interpreting Body Mass Index**

BMI	
18.5–24.9	Normal weight
25.0–29.9	Overweight
30.0–39.9	Obese
40.0 and above	Extreme obesity

Note: Weight is measured with underwear but no shoes.

addressing a disorder, psychological and societal factors play a crucial role as well. Anorexia nervosa and bulimia nervosa are two disorders that are frequently discussed:

- *Anorexia nervosa.* People with this serious disorder are most often female, but males can suffer as well. They have an extreme aversion to weight gain—and perceive themselves as fat, overweight, or obese when, in reality, they are severely below normal weight. This serious disorder can be fatal.

- *Bulimia nervosa.* This potentially fatal disorder mixes frequent periods of binge eating with self-induced vomiting or the use of laxatives and fasting to purge the food from the body. Like the anorexic person, the bulimic person is fanatically concerned about body image.

For a more complete listing, visit NEDA's website. If you or a friend suffers from an eating disorder, seek assistance immediately. A first stop might be a campus counselor or the wellness center.

REJUVENATE WITH REST

An appropriate and regular exercise program combined with wise dietary choices are steps to a healthier lifestyle. Another proactive step is to visit your doctor regularly. Whether you use campus resources, personal health insurance, or a community agency, see a doctor for periodic checkups. Such regular visits can help detect problems before they escalate into major health crises. National Women's Checkup Day (typically around Mother's Day) and National Men's Health Week (week leading up to Father's Day) are reminders of the importance of regular checkups. Prepare for the exam by reviewing your family medical history and writing a list of questions you wish to ask the doctor.

It is also important to avoid fatigue and sleep deprivation. More than 40 million Americans suffer from a sleep disorder of some type. Research suggests that the lack of deep sleep on a regular basis can have a negative impact on blood pressure and heart health. Often caused by juggling too many items in a day, lack of appropriate sleep can create irritability and even depression (U.S. Department of Health and Human Services, National Institutes of Health, 2011). Consider the following tips for a restful night's sleep:

- Avoid caffeine, nicotine, and alcoholic beverages before bedtime.
- Avoid large meals and large quantities of any type of beverage before bedtime.

- Avoid late afternoon naps as they can disturb your sleep pattern at night. Of course, timing of naps also depends on your daily schedule. A person who rises late in the morning and stays up until late at night (a musician for example) will have a different "clock" than a person who rises early each morning for class and turns into bed before 10:00 p.m.
- Add physical activity to your daily routine—but not immediately before bedtime.
- Consider discontinuing the use of electrical devices (computers and tablets) immediately before bedtime to help your mind unwind and slow down.
- Unwind before going to bed by reading something relaxing or listening to soothing music.
- See your doctor if you experience sleep problems on a recurring basis.

THE EMOTIONAL AND PHYSICAL SIDE OF SOCIAL RELATIONSHIPS

NUTRITIOUS RELATIONSHIPS

A strong social dimension in your life will provide support and encouragement. In times of emotional turmoil—stress—your social relationships can prove to be a key base of stability. It is estimated that more than 20 million Americans suffer from depression, which can affect their physical, social, and emotional states. Depression can negatively influence performance on the job (occupational dimension) or in the classroom (intellectual dimension). Talking with someone you trust (a friend, faculty member, family member, church leader, or a health care professional) can help you sort through what may seem like impossible circumstances. Leave the lines of communication open between you and your support network. Not only might you benefit, but also someone else with an emotionally challenging issue might benefit from you. (National Institute of Mental Health, 2013; CDC, 2012).

NOT ALL RELATIONSHIPS ARE NUTRITIOUS

Nutritious relationships help build our self-confidence and love for life, but other relationships can be less satisfying. Some such encounters may be only irritating; others can be dangerous and life-threatening.

Alcohol—Binge Drinking. Social drinking can lead to any number of unhealthy situations. For instance, the National Institute on Alcohol and Alcohol Abuse defines **binge drinking** as drinking that raises blood alcohol content to 0.08 grams or more. For men, typically five drinks within two hours will generate this result. For women, four drinks can have the effect (Centers for Disease Control and Prevention, 2012). The number of binge drinkers has continued to increase on college campuses, and the harmful effects of such behavior have not diminished. Binge drinkers, and those around them, suffer from physical and behavioral side effects. Besides the obvious symptoms of loss of consciousness, vomiting, and irregular breathing, secondary effects also have a negative impact.

Binge drinkers can use abusive language, engage in physical altercations, drive while intoxicated, or interfere with the study habits of nondrinkers. The National Institute of Alcohol Abuse and Alcoholism found the following sobering statistics regarding college students (18 to 24 years of age):

- Nearly 2,000 die each year from alcohol-related injuries.
- More than 690,000 students have been the victim of an assault by a drinking student.
- More than 97,000 students experience alcohol-related sexual assault or date rape.
- 599,000 students suffer injuries while under the influence of alcohol.
- Almost one-quarter of college students report academic consequences (like poor grades or poor attendance) due to drinking.
- More than 150,000 students develop an alcohol-related health problem, and a small number report attempting suicide due to drinking or drug use.

If you or a friend has an alcohol problem, seek help immediately. Whether you talk with a counselor, residence hall assistant, member of the clergy, or family member, find someone who can direct you to the appropriate services.

Sexual Violence. Date rape—nonconsensual intercourse with a friend or acquaintance—is one form of sexual violence. One source holds that alcohol is a major factor in date rape and that women between the ages of 16 and 24 have a greater chance of being raped by an acquaintance. The following suggestions offer help on how to avoid date rape ("How to Avoid Date Rape," 2006).

- Be vigilant. Be wary of flirty and casual intimacy; 84 percent of rape victims know their attackers.
- Group dates offer safety in numbers.
- Consider carrying pepper spray or mace to use in the event you are attacked.
- Limit your alcohol intake; 90 percent of date rapes occur when the victim is drunk. If you are drinking, pay attention to your open drink, which can be an invitation for an unscrupulous person to try to slide in a drug undetected.

THE HEALTH RISKS OF SEXUAL ACTIVITY

Years ago, the term *VD* (venereal disease) was used to describe diseases passed on because of sexual activity. VD then became known as *STDs*—sexually transmitted diseases. Today, you may hear the label of *STIs*—sexually transmitted infections. The CDC reports that there are nearly 20 million cases in the United States today. And people between the ages of 15 and 24 have the highest incidence for gonorrhea and Chlamydia. The CDC warns that "in addition to increasing a person's risk, for HIV infection, STDs can lead to severe reproductive health complications, such as infertility" (CDC, March 2013).

At one time, the main concern with unprotected sex was an unplanned pregnancy. Today, as the statistics just cited indicate, the stakes have increased. Perhaps you are sexually active now or are thinking of being sexually active. Maybe you are practicing the "Just say no" method, but you have a friend who is active. Whatever situation you find yourself in, it is wise to be aware of some of the many physical and emotional consequences of sexual activity in today's society.

While a detailed description of these infections is beyond the scope of this book, STIs include Chlamydia, Gonorrhea, Syphilis, genital herpes, genital warts and human papillomavirus (HPV), HIV/AIDS, and Vaginitis. Abstinence is the surest way to prevent the spread or contraction of STIs; if you are sexually active, seek competent medical advice to protect you and your partner. If you, a family member, or a friend has contracted any STI, seek medical care as soon as possible. Your health-care provider can also provide counseling concerning prevention of STIs. The CDC website can provide further information.

Chapter SUMMARY

Pause for a moment and reflect on the balance—or lack of balance—in your life at this point in the school term.

In particular, before leaving this topic, do the following:

- Reflect on two specific examples of how you have become stronger by acting honestly, responsibly, and respectfully.

- Evaluate the positive changes you have made in your physical activity program and diet during the last week. If you have not yet made changes, consider what positive changes you can make in the next week.

- Evaluate actions you have taken to keep yourself healthy and safe in your relationships.

CRITICALLY THINKING
What Have You Learned?

Let's apply what you learned in this material to help Nicole from the opening scenario. However, before you address her situation and propose your solution, take a moment to think about the main points of the material. Review your notes, the key terms, learning outcomes, boldface headings, and figures and tables.

TEST YOUR LEARNING

Now that you have reviewed the main points and reread Nicole's story, what advice do you have for her? Using the R.E.D. Model of critical thinking, help Nicole critically review any concerns she might have:

R

Recognize Assumptions

Facts: What are the facts in Nicole's situation? List them.

Opinions: What opinions do you find in this situation? List them.

Assumptions: Are Nicole's assumptions accurate?

E

Evaluate Information

Help Nicole compile a list of questions that will help her make the most appropriate decision.

What emotions seem to be motivating Nicole?

What, if anything, is missing from Nicole's thought process?

Do you see any confirmation bias?

D

Draw Conclusions

Based on the facts and the questions you have presented, what conclusions can you draw?

What advice do you have for Nicole? What solutions do you propose?

Based on your suggestions, do you see any assumptions?

Finally, based on what you learned about health and well-being, what plan of action do you suggest for Nicole?

Financial *13*
LITERACY

LEARNING OUTCOMES

By the time you finish reading this material and completing the activities, you will be able to do the following:

- Develop a budget to help you manage your money and minimize your debt.

- Establish a goal to identify and eliminate unnecessary spending.

- Build awareness of spending, borrowing, earning, and saving patterns.

- Recommend strategies for using credit and other borrowing.

The Case of ROYCE

Royce graduated from high school five years ago. He married his high school sweetheart, and they have one child. Royce is working 40 hours per week at a local shipping company. He decided to return to college for his degree and saved enough money to pay for his first year of tuition and books. Beyond that he is not sure how he will fund his education. He has earned a 4.0 GPA his first term in college and believes he is on the right track. Royce decided that he will work double shifts if he has to in order to pay for his degree.

To stretch his money, Royce uses his savings only for tuition and other fees. He paid for his books and supplies with his credit card. Royce told his wife, "By using the card, I only have to pay a few bucks a month

Key Terms

Annual fee
Banking statement
Bankruptcy
Budget
Credit limit
Credit score
Debit card
Debt
Financial literacy
Identity theft
Interest rate
Service charge
Wealth

INTRODUCTION *Chapter*

Financial literacy—having and responsibly using knowledge about money—requires more than memorizing terms or completing charts. What counts is how you put the knowledge into practice. This topic will provide a bare-bones overview of four concepts a financially literate person must understand: personal budgets, checking accounts, savings accounts, and loans. Financially literate people honestly assess their financial needs, responsibly adhere to a realistic budget, and respectfully take care of their financial obligations.

to the credit card company, we can still have some money in the bank, and I can continue my education."

Unfortunately, Royce has had some unexpected expenses come up and had to dig deeper into his savings than he had planned. He just registered for the next term of classes and charged his tuition, fees, and books to his credit card. He feels uneasy about the debt he is building but thinks using his credit card is his only option. Royce also asked his boss for more overtime work.

"I think I earn too much money for any kind of financial assistance," he told his wife last night. "My choices are limited. Either I pull extra shifts or I will need to sit out next term and save more money."

CRITICALLY THINKING
about *Royce's* situation

Is Royce missing anything in his analysis of the situation? Where might he get help concerning financial assistance for his education? What other resources are available? What do you think about Royce using his credit card to finance his education?

Your financial literacy affects life's balance. Money—or the lack of it—can have a profound impact on your physical and emotional health. While it sounds overly simplistic, the choices you make concerning budgeting, earning, spending, and saving will have a major impact upon your standard of living now and in the future. The information that follows in this topic will help you examine your current financial health and consider the course you wish to chart for your financial well-being.

MyStudentSuccessLab

MyStudentSuccessLab (www .mystudentsuccesslab.com) is an online solution designed to help you "Start strong, Finish stronger" by building skills for ongoing personal and professional development.

On any given day, you can read news reports of greed, corruption, and bankruptcies. It is enough to leave you shaking your head and questioning how some people make money their god. While some can become obsessed with money for negative purposes, money is a good thing. When you earn and spend with integrity, money can accomplish great things for you, your loved ones, and your community.

In part, financial literacy addresses how one deals with debt. More specifically, the way you handle your debt indicates a great deal about your character. If you have debt, how do you handle it? That is, do you pay your loans in a timely and responsible fashion? How does your debt affect your ability to save?

As you read the material in this topic, please keep the following thoughts in mind. These strategies and activities are presented for you to reflect on your financial health (now and the future). You would do well to consult with trained financial planners/experts before investing money or incurring debt.

Activity 13.1

Reflecting on Your Current Level of Financial Literacy Skills

Before you answer the items that follow, reflect on your current level of financial literacy skills. Think of how well (or poorly) you have handled your finances to this point in your life.

As you complete this activity, write from your heart. This exercise is not meant for you to answer just like your classmates—or to match what you may think the instructor wants to see. Take the time to give a respectful, responsible general accounting of your experiences with budgets, debt, and savings. Conducting a truthful self-assessment now will help you build on skills you have while developing those you lack.

For each of the following items, circle the number that best describes your typical experience with finances. Here is the key for the numbers:

0 = never, 1 = almost never, 2 = occasionally, 3 = frequently, 4 = almost always, 5 = always

When considering your past successes and challenges with finances, how often did you:

1.	Make and stick to a daily/weekly/monthly budget?	0	1	2	3	4	5
2.	Deposit money in a savings account on a regular (weekly, biweekly, or monthly) basis?	0	1	2	3	4	5
3.	Balance your checking account each month?	0	1	2	3	4	5
4.	Pay off credit card balances each month?	0	1	2	3	4	5
5.	Protect your personal identification information for your financial accounts?	0	1	2	3	4	5
6.	Have enough money to cover your checks or debit transactions?	0	1	2	3	4	5
7.	Know the interest rate, grace period, and annual fee for your credit cards?	0	1	2	3	4	5
8.	File for a free credit report?	0	1	2	3	4	5
9.	Use strategies to avoid **identity theft**?	0	1	2	3	4	5

Add up your scores for items 1 through 9. Divide by 9. Write your answer here: _____

Using the key provided to explain each number (0, 1, 2, 3, 4, 5), complete this sentence: When it comes to financial literacy, I _____ handle my finances with integrity.

Based on your answers, what insights have you gained about your financial literacy skills?

BUDGETS

YOUR PERSONAL BUDGET

Your personal **budget** shows you where your money comes from and where it goes. It is a tool to help you manage your finances.

You might be thinking, "But I'm a college student. I do not have any money! I don't need a budget." True, you may not have a lot of money, but a budget is still a practical idea—if for no other reason than building a sound financial habit. A budget provides a big picture of your financial health. It helps you understand how much money it actually costs to live in your world—with your lifestyle. When used properly, a budget will help you live within your means and build wealth at the same time. Whether you established a budget at the beginning of this school term or have never used a budget, this would be an appropriate time to review your earning and spending habits.

DEBT AFFECTS WEALTH

Sometimes people have great intentions, but by the end of the week or month, they just cannot figure out where their money has gone.

When expenditures exceed income, **debt** is the result. Figure 13.1 offers a simple graphic portrayal of the relationship between income and expenses. For

Figure 13.1

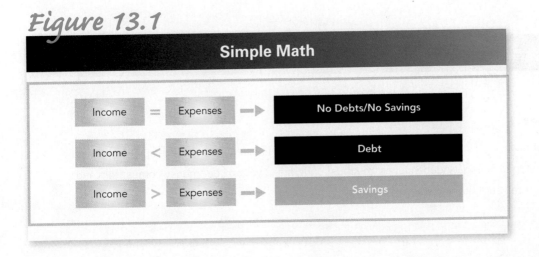

Figure 13.2

Simple Math (Part 2)

PERSONAL FINANCIAL STATEMENT

Assets (what you *own*)

minus

Liabilities (what you *owe*)

equals

Your net worth

many college students, debt is a realistic and necessary part of their lives. Student loans used to finance a college education, however, represent debt you eventually must repay in a timely fashion. If you do not repay a loan (default) or are late with loan payments, your credit rating can be affected. Credit ratings will be discussed later in this material.

A person in debt has a negative net worth (see Figure 13.2). Persistent debt will create long-term financial problems. **Bankruptcy** is the most severe example of debt gone awry. Not only is the bankrupt person in debt, he or she has gone through a legal action stating that the debt is so significant that there is no hope of paying it with current resources. According to the *Third Branch News* of the U.S. Courts (August 2012), there were more than 1.2 million personal and consumer bankruptcy filings between July 2011 and June 2013. Regardless of what led to the bankruptcy, the person's credit rating will likely be affected in one way or another.

If you are consumed by debt, you will face added challenges to become financially independent. The next three sections on checking accounts, savings accounts, and loans will make more sense if you consider each in the context of your personal budget.

Activity 13.2

Your Personal Budget

PRIORITIES

Budget worksheet

A budget keeps track of financial income (earnings) and financial obligations (expenditures). Developing a realistic budget is an important step to financial independence. You must understand where your money comes from and where it goes before you can start building wealth.

Monthly Budget

Income	$	Expenditures	$	How much of a priority is this expenditure to my life? 1 = not at all 5 = huge priority / 1 to 5
Primary employment		Tuition		
Other employment		Books		
Interest from bank accounts		Food		
Investments		Housing		
Spouse's income		Transportation: Bus fare		
Roommate's contributions		Transportation (car): Gas, insurance, repairs		
Parents' contributions		Clothes		
Loans		Phone		
Scholarships		Internet connection		
Other		Debt payments		
Other		Haircuts		
Other		Medications		
Other		Recreation		
Other		Child care		
Other		Other		
Other		Other		
Other		Other		
Other		Other		
Other		Other		
Other		Other		
Total income	$	Total expenditures	$	

Total income: $ _____

Total expenditures: $ _____

Surplus or debt: $ _____

1. If you have a surplus (extra) at the end of the month, congratulations! How do you plan to wisely use or invest this money?

2. If you have a deficit (debt) at the end of the month, what responsible strategies can you use to erase the debt and regain financial integrity?

CHECKING ACCOUNTS

A checking account allows you to deposit your money with a financial institution (typically, a bank or a credit union). The funds remain with the bank or credit union until you need to withdraw them by writing a check or using a debit card (discussed later).

BENEFITS

Checking accounts provide a number of advantages for the account holder.

- *Safety.* Consider the alternatives if you do not have a bank account in which to deposit your funds. When you receive money—say from a paycheck—you will either carry around a wad of cash in your pocket or hide it somewhere until you need to use it. Checking accounts allow you to store your money in a safer manner. Most banks or credit unions will insure their depositors' money. Your bank representative can give you this information.

- *Convenience.* In addition, a checking account will allow you to cash or deposit a check without having to pay a fee for such service. With the use of a check or debit card, you have immediate access to your funds at any time. (There may be a delay when you deposit out-of-state checks.) If you have a computer and Internet connection, you can pay bills or transfer money to other accounts you might have (like a savings account) with online banking. Most financial institutions provide this convenience for their customers.

  If you use online banking, be mindful of your privacy. You will need a personal identification number (PIN) and a password. If you give these identifiers to anyone else, that person can access your money. When logging into your online account, it is best to use a private computer. If you choose to use a public computer (or a friend's computer), be sure to log off from your account when completed and then close out the Web browser. Do not save your password on a public computer.

- *Direct deposit.* Many employers have moved from issuing paper paychecks to directly depositing your earnings into your bank account. Some colleges do this when issuing student work checks or financial aid. Direct deposit saves you a trip to the bank, and your funds are (generally) immediately available when deposited.

- *Proof of payment.* Once you have paid a bill with a check, and the check has been presented for payment ("cashed"), you have proof of payment (a receipt). Most banking institutions provide copies of the cashed checks online so that you can access them anytime.

- *Debit cards.* An alternative to paper checks, **debit cards** (also referred to as bankcards or check cards) look like credit cards and are used like credit cards—with a major difference. A debit card actually represents money you have in a bank account. When used, you are not buying on credit; you are withdrawing money from your checking account at the time of purchase. You cannot make the purchase if you do not have money in your account.

If you do, you will have other problems. See the section on NSF below. You do not pay later in the month, as you would with credit. Vendors give you a record of your purchases (a receipt) at the time you use your debit card. You will also be able to access automatic teller machines (ATMs) with your card at any time of the day or night, seven days a week, in order to withdraw money from your account. Like online banking, take precautions to protect your card, PIN, and money. Some banking institutions will place your photo on the debit card. In the event of card loss or if you find that someone else has accessed your account, contact your financial institution immediately.

CONSIDERATIONS

Although checking accounts provide many benefits, keep the following in mind.

- *Checkbook register.* Whether you use a debit card, handwritten checks, or a combination of the two, keep an accurate accounting of the amount of money you spend and the amount of money you put into the account. You can obtain a checkbook register from your bank (see Figure 13.3), where you can enter the date, amount, and type of transaction you make. Although this sounds very simplistic, it is not unusual to hear about individuals who have not kept track of expenditures—and then "bounced" a check.

- *Nonsufficient funds (NSF).* If you write a check but do not have enough money in the account to cover the amount of that check, it is considered a bad or worthless check that "bounces" back to you like a rubber ball. This creates a few problems. For one, you will have to pay an additional fee to your bank as well as to the vendor to whom the bad check was given. Second, your credit rating can suffer. Third, depending on the severity of the offense, the vendor could decide to bring criminal charges against you. Ask your banking institution about the availability of *overdraft protection* in case you do overdraw your account. Such a service eliminates the bad check to the vendor part of

Figure 13.3

Number	Date	Transaction	Withdrawal	✓	Deposit	$

Checkbook Register

the process as the bank takes money from either your credit card or your savings account, but your bank may still charge you a fee for each overdraft. This can become costly. If the bank tacks on a $35 overdraft fee, then that $5 latte just cost you $40! Just another reminder to keep track of your checking account balance.

- *Blocking.* If you use your debit card to rent a car, reserve a hotel room, or buy gas for your car, ask the company if it engages in "blocking." If the company does, it blocks out more money from your account than the actual cost of the product or service—thus making that money unavailable to you at that time. Once you have returned the car (or checked out of the hotel), if there are no damages, then just the rental fee (or lodging charge) is charged against your account. In the meantime, depending on the amount blocked, you may overdraw your account because you were not aware of the blocking practice (Federal Trade Commission, 2012).

- *Balance your checking account monthly.* Each month your banking institution will mail to you or post on your online banking site a **banking statement** of your account. This will show all money that went into and out of your account during the past month. Compare the bank statement to the register in which you have been keeping track of your transactions. Look for any discrepancies like arithmetic errors or items you may have forgotten to enter. Note too that the balance on the statement might not reflect the actual balance in your account on the day you receive the statement. This can happen either because you wrote checks after the date of the statement, or because some of the checks you had written did not "clear" (or make it to) the bank yet. Do not forget to include these in your calculations, as well as any deposits made after the date of the statement.

- *Service charge.* Your bank may assess a **service charge** each month. This is a small fee charged by the bank for allowing you to have the account. Shop around for the lowest fees, as they can add up over time. Some institutions will waive this fee if you also hold a savings account with them. Inquire about special promotions that may be available.

SAVINGS ACCOUNTS

Money can be a corrupting influence in life. And it can be a liberating force.

For the purposes of this section, let us work with the premise that money is good. Money can be (and is) a powerful motivator for people. Besides basic survival needs, it allows people to travel, experience cultural activities, and help people in their community. It pays for health care and day care. It buys transportation, paves roads, and picks up the garbage. And it pays for a college education. Yes, money is good when used honestly, respectfully, and responsibly.

The next few pages will examine basic ways you can begin to build **wealth** in your life—how you can save and invest money. We are not talking necessarily about being "rich"—having lots of money. And we are not talking about living a high-consumption lifestyle (buying lots of material things). Wealthy people have money but also live within their means (do not spend more than they have) while they build financial independence.

Let's examine how you can begin, even as a "poor college student," to acquire wealth. We will start with the basics—a savings account. Whereas checking accounts are used for immediate access to your funds, savings accounts help manage your funds for the future.

BENEFITS

A savings account provides a number of benefits for the account holder.

- *Pay yourself first.* In their book *The Millionaire Next Door*, Thomas Stanley and William Danko propose a practical way to build your wealth (1996). Once you deposit your paycheck but before you start buying things and satisfying your desires, pay yourself first. Their suggested number is 15 percent of your net pay. That is, once taxes and other deductions have come from your paycheck, place 15 percent of the remainder in your savings account. In this way, you will steadily accumulate savings. For instance, if you earn $100 per week after all deductions, 15 percent would equal $15. Quick arithmetic shows that you will be able to put away $780 a year plus interest. At the end of your four-year college education, you will have more than three thousand dollars waiting for you. If you earn more, you save more with this strategy. Not a bad way to start your post-college career.

Perhaps, though, you are stretched so thin at the end of the month that the thought of 15 percent is a fantasy. Okay. Then look for what you can do. Even if you can only scrape together a spare five dollars every week, start there. While it may seem small, you will be doing two important things: (1) saving money and (2) developing a savings discipline.

Activity 13.3

How Do You Build Wealth? One Penny at a Time!

Perhaps you are saying, "Hey, I work and go to school. And I am barely making ends meet. There is no way I can save. I'd like to, but there is no money left at the end of the month." Or maybe your story is reflected by the statement, "I take a full load of classes and earn a couple of bucks a week. There is *nothing* for savings!"

Review your personal budget (Activity 13.2). Look at everything you choose to purchase. (This is where a clear and accurate budget will help you considerably.) Do you buy soda, coffee, or snacks? Consider the person who buys one large soda in the morning and one large soda in the afternoon. Let's say the sodas cost $2 each. That amounts to $4 each day—or a total of $20 over the course of a five-day work or school week. At the end of four weeks, $80 is spent; for the year, $1,040. By the end of a four-year college degree, more than $4,000 will be consumed on 2,080 large containers of coloring, caffeine, sugar, and carbonation. If the money is instead placed in an account, it will increase each month. If the account adds interest every month, your money grows even faster.

The questions to ask are, "What do I value more, soda or building wealth? Where can I make *at least one* different choice in my weekly expenditures?"

- *Building a disciplined habit.* If you practice the pay-yourself-first principle week after week, you will find it becomes a habit. You will not think twice about putting money in the bank. Although the amount is important, the habit of regular deposits is more significant, especially when you first begin a savings plan. Set a goal, establish savings as a part of your budget, and commit to your action steps. Done over a period of months, it will become difficult for you *not* to save before spending on frivolous items. Moreover, this habit will help you in the future when you will have more money to consider investing in items such as stocks, bonds, mutual funds, and retirement funds. Remember that retirement saving does not begin when you are nearing retirement. It should begin when you get your first job. A modest savings and investment strategy started in your early to mid twenties has the potential to yield *millions* of dollars over the next 40 years. Start early. Remember this simple guideline: You build wealth one penny at a time.

- *Peace of mind.* A common part of financial advice is to have enough money in your savings account to cover at least six to eight months of living expenses. In other words, have enough money saved so that if you were not able to work for six to eight months you would still be able to take care of your expenses for that period. Knowing you can do that will help provide peace of mind in case an emergency arises. Again, this is where an accurate personal budget becomes useful.

CONSIDERATIONS

As emphasized previously, the important point early on is to develop the habit of consistent savings. As you accumulate money in your savings, you may wish to consider the various options available to banking customers. Depending on variables like the state of the economy and specific bank practices, you can find different savings opportunities.

- *Interest rate.* Ask your banker about the **interest rate** for savings accounts. This is the amount of money the bank will pay you for keeping and using your money. Interest rates will fluctuate based on economic conditions and the type of account you have.

- *Balance your savings account regularly.* As with your checking account, your banking institution will provide you with periodic (usually monthly, but possibly quarterly) statements of your savings deposits and withdrawals. Even though this statement will not reflect the same level of activity as your checking account, you still need to examine it closely. At the least, you will be able to keep track of the amount of interest you earn each month.

OTHER INVESTMENTS

Even if you only have a couple of dollars in your savings account, educate yourself about other investment plans. Understand what stocks, bonds, mutual funds, and Individual Retirement Accounts (IRAs) are—and how, eventually, you can become involved if you wish to be. Your campus may have workshops about investing, or perhaps a business or finance instructor on your campus can direct you to appropriate information. Use your information literacy skills to research investing. Educate yourself.

LOANS

Many students receive financial aid in the form of loans or scholarships. Loans provide needed money to attend college, but they also represent debt that must be repaid after graduation. In essence, with every college loan you acquire, you add to the post-college debt you will need to repay. The loans are one of the opportunity costs of attending college. On graduation, you will take your diploma *and* your debt with you. In addition to the credit history that you are establishing, the ways in which you handle that debt after graduation (pay off timely versus default) reflects your integrity.

For instance, soon after receiving your diploma, you may decide to finance a new automobile. The financial institution considering your loan application will rate you as a potential client and credit risk. Generally, the lenders examine your credit history, ability to pay the loan based on your income and other debts you may have, and what valuables you have that could be used to pay the loan if need be (Visa, n.d.).

FINANCIAL AID

Tuition, fees, books, supplies, room, and food add up quickly. Just as all students come to college with varying degrees of experience and academic preparedness, so too do they have varying abilities to pay for their education.

Your campus financial aid office can provide you with information about available sources of money. Chances are if you needed scholarships, loans, grants, or other forms of assistance to attend school this term, you already have some experience with the financial aid process. At the most basic level, make sure you complete all necessary paperwork in a timely fashion. Also, if you receive loans, be sure you understand how much interest you will have to pay for the use of the money.

- *Finding the money (part 1)*. Be proactive and seek out information months in advance of when you will actually need the money. Follow through at all points of the process.
- *Finding the money (part 2)*. Look beyond your school for available aid. Many community organizations sponsor annual scholarship awards based on scholastic achievement, service to the community, essay submission, or some other non-financial-need-based criteria. Your school's financial aid officer will have the latest listing of available funding sources. You also can check your college's website for available assistance. Financial aid packages differ from state to state, campus to campus, and student to student.

- *Satisfactory academic progress (SAP)—time to completion.* Check with your counselor or financial aid officer about limitations on the total number of credits financial aid will fund over the course of your college career.

- *Satisfactory academic progress (SAP)—grade point average.* Generally, a 2.0 cumulative average must be maintained in order to remain eligible for financial aid. Specific scholarships may have higher requirements. Check with your financial aid officer for specific information.

- *Satisfactory academic progress (SAP)—completion percentage.* Understand any requirements concerning how much of your course work you have to complete satisfactorily in order to remain eligible for financial aid.

CREDIT CARDS

Your student loans may be only one part of your debt. If you do not yet have a credit card, be prepared for card offers. Go to a campus sporting event, and you may find representatives at a credit card table willing to give you a free T-shirt if you sign up for a credit card. When you buy clothes, you may be asked by cashiers if you would like to apply for a store credit card. "Sign up now, and we'll automatically deduct 5 percent from your bill today" may be a pitch you will hear. Credit can be quite enticing and intoxicating.

Benefits. Credit cards, when managed well by a self-disciplined individual, can be beneficial.

- *Immediacy.* Credit cards allow you to buy a product or a service right when you need or want it. For instance, if you take your car in for an oil change and find out that you also need $400 worth of tires, a credit card can help you purchase them. Because the tires are needed for safe transportation and you need them immediately, you can use the credit card company's money (for typically a month) with no charge—providing you pay your debt in full and do not carry a balance. This immediacy, if not controlled with discipline, can lead to significant problems. (See Considerations below).

- *Similar advantages to debit cards.*
  - Give you the option of carrying less cash on your person.
  - Eliminate the need to carry a checkbook. Credit card purchases can be completed with the swipe of the card at the cash register.
  - Provide written proof of your purchases. You can view these on your monthly statements and on your online account.
  - Allow for online purchases. Since the vendor does not have to wait for the check to arrive, you receive your product more quickly.
  - Give you the option to pay for everything purchased in a month with one single check at the end of the month.

- *Additional protections and services.* Credit card companies may offer different services such as product protection or reward points (hotels) or miles (airlines). Check with your credit card company to be sure what you will receive with your card.

- *Credit history.* With each purchase and timely payment (or late payment), you build a credit history and a credit rating. This will have an impact in the future when it comes time to buy a car, apply for a home mortgage, seek a business loan, or apply for a job.

Considerations. Unfortunately, credit cards can lead to problems. One study found that 70 percent of undergraduates have credit cards and more than 90 percent of these cardholders fail to pay off their balance each month. And the vast majority has no idea what the interest rate is on the cards in their pockets. They are building debt, paying interest on accumulated balances, and establishing habits that may create difficulties in their financial futures (White, 2012).

Although there are benefits to credit cards, they *have* to be used judiciously—and within your budget to make timely payments. Some things to consider before applying for a credit card are:

- *Credit card fees.* It is not unusual for a credit card company to charge an **annual fee** to use its card services. Read the fine print in your credit card agreement for information about penalty fees for late payments, fees for exceeding your credit limit, and cash advance fees. Be a smart consumer. Know what fees you will have to pay for services you use.

- *Interest rate.* The interest rate calculated for loans and credit cards represents the cost to use someone else's money. Sometimes this is stated as APR—annual percentage rate. This is how much it will cost to carry balances on your credit card. Rates can change. For instance, there might be an introductory offer that escalates to a higher rate after six months. You could be charged for daily balances or monthly balances that you do not pay. It is not unusual for rates to be 18 percent or higher. Know what the fine print states.

- *Compound interest.* Also, understand that when you carry a credit card balance from month to month, you end up paying interest not only on the amount of the purchase price but also on the interest charge from previous months. You will end up paying more for the product or service than the original purchase price. Although compound interest will help your money grow in a savings account, it can drain your wealth when applied to your credit cards.

- *Calculate first.* Before you purchase an item on credit, do a quick calculation of exactly how much the purchase will cost if payments are stretched over time. Your credit card company may have a payment calculator on its website. (Or use your information literacy skills to find an online calculator.)

Activity 13.4

Calculating the Real Cost

For this activity, locate an online credit card calculator. You can use your favorite search engine to locate this information. Once you find the calculator, use the scenario below to help you understand how long it will take to pay off a credit card debt. Enter the purchase price, the interest rate charged by the card, and the minimum payment you plan to make.

Here is your problem: You found a great deal on a new laptop computer. It has everything you want for just $800. You decide to buy it with your credit card and pay $25 per month until your debt is paid. If the credit card rate is 18 percent, how long will it take you to totally repay the debt? How much interest will you have paid by that time? How much will the laptop actually cost you (add the interest paid to the $800 price tag)?

- *Earning versus debt: The 70/20/10 rule.* Type "savings 70/20/10 rule" into your favorite search engine and you will find information on this simple formula for building your wealth. According to this "rule," you should use no more than 70 percent of your income for basic living (survival) expenses like rent, utilities, and food. You need to set aside 20 percent of your income for wealth-building purposes (savings and investments). Finally, 10 percent goes to paying off any debt you have (You Can Deal With It, 2010).

  So, according to this formula, if you earn $10,000 a year doing part-time work, your annual debt should not exceed $1,000 and $2,000 should be going into your wealth building plan. Review your personal budget in Activity 13.2.

- *Minimal payment trap.* Paying only the minimal payment each month on your credit card balance can drastically increase the cost of your purchases. If you have to carry a balance from month to month, pay as much as you can so that your debt will be retired as soon as possible.

- *Credit limit.* This number indicates how much money you can charge on your credit cards. The limit should not be viewed as a challenge for you to spend that much. If, however, you have a very low limit, be mindful of that as well. It could be an embarrassing situation if you attempt to pay for a product or service (especially in a business situation), only to have your card rejected. And credit limits (sometimes referred to as credit lines) can be reduced by the card company because your credit score drops or due to late payments to your creditors (Santiago, 2008).

- *Protecting your credit history.* Your credit history follows you through life. Late payments or nonpayment of loans (student loans "count") will have an adverse effect when you attempt to borrow money, finance an automobile, or mortgage a home. A poor credit history may even have a negative impact when you seek employment as prospective employers see it as a reflection of character (integrity). The first way to protect your credit history is to avoid reckless spending habits. If you do incur a debt, paying your obligations in a timely manner will reflect well on you in the future.

- *Credit score.* As of this writing, three consumer reporting companies—Equifax, Experian, and TransUnion—will provide a free copy of your credit report, at your request, once every twelve months. Make this a priority; place it on your calendar. Space each request out by four months, and you will be able to have three reports a year. For instance, in January request from Equifax; May from Experian; and September, TransUnion. Additional information may be found at the Federal Trade Commission's website. When you request your free credit report, you can also request your **credit score** (generally for a small fee). This three-digit number reflects your credit history—and is used as a predictor of your risk to a creditor. In short, it reflects the financial choices you have made in the past (for instance, paying your credit cards on time), and the score may affect your future financial options. Lenders, landlords, employers, and even cell phone companies may access your credit score to determine your financial responsibility and personal integrity. Late payments can negatively affect credit scores. Applying for or having a large number of credit cards may also cause a decrease in your credit score (McFadden, 2010).

- *Emergency purposes.* Consider keeping your credit card for emergency purchases only. A trip to the hospital emergency room is an emergency; a late-night pizza party is not.
- *Cancelling cards.* As stated, you can use credit cards in a beneficial manner; however, if you lack self-discipline in credit purchases, you may want to consider cancelling your account with the credit card company. Call and write the company to cancel your card(s).

Activity 13.5

Managing Credit Card Debt

The reality (supported by statistics) is that many college students will plunge into the world of credit card debt. Credit cards can be beneficial *if* you know how to use them responsibly—and for some people that is a very big *if*. In the preceding section, you read suggestions to manage, if not totally avoid, credit card debt. Now, with a classmate, brainstorm at least three other suggestions to manage or avoid credit card debt and write your ideas here.

IDENTITY THEFT

The FBI found that identity theft has affected millions of people (2006). Identity theft is not new. As long as unscrupulous people exist, identity theft can happen to any of us. Thieves can steal your social security number, driver's license number, checking account information, credit card or debit card numbers and PINs, and other personal information like your birth date. They can literally steal your identity. Although no one is immune, there are steps you can take to help limit the threat of identity theft.

- Request credit reports regularly (see above). Read the reports carefully.
- Protect your debit and credit cards. Never give your PIN to anyone.
- Ask your bank if you can have your photo placed on your debit or credit cards.
- When paying by credit card or debit card, do whatever you can to make sure you actually see the store employee "swipe" your card in the store's machine or cash register.
- Because your credit card number may appear on the receipt, be sure to take that with you. (It has become almost standard practice for vendor receipts only to record the last four digits of your card number. But be safe.)
- When you pay your credit card bill by mailing a check, consider personally delivering the envelope to the post office. Leaving an envelope in an unlocked residential mailbox for the postal carrier to collect carries risk. If someone were to take the envelope, he or she would not only have your checking account information, but also your credit card information.
- When discarding receipts, be sure to shred them into tiny pieces.
- Beware of people looking over your shoulder when using automated teller machines (ATMs) and checkout line credit/debit "swipe" machines at the store.

- Do not hold your credit or debit cards in any way that someone near you can see and take note of the numbers.

- Do not answer "phishing" e-mails that offer you large sums of cash after you forward personal information. Beware of unsolicited e-mails telling you that an account will be cancelled unless you provide personal information.

- When shopping online, be aware of the vendor's reputation. Also, know your protection coverage. In some cases, you may have better protection against loss from a credit card that is fraudulently used than a debit card that is used by a thief.

- When reordering checks, do not have them mailed to your house. Ask your banker if you can pick them up at the bank. This limits the possibility of a mailbox thief riffling through your mail, stealing your checks and your bank account number.

- Research what a reputable credit monitoring service company can do for you. If you decide to pay for this service, carefully check the company's reputation and know exactly what you are purchasing.

- If you suspect your identity has been stolen—or if it has in fact been stolen—contact your financial institution immediately. Challenge any charges you did not make. Notify your local police. Consider closing any accounts that have been tampered with; ask your financial representative for advice and strategies.

In short, be mindful of your finances and your identity.

Chapter SUMMARY

Money—or the lack of it—can have a profound impact on your physical and emotional health.

Although it sounds overly simplistic, the choices *you* make concerning budgeting, earning, spending, and saving will have a major impact on your standard of living now and in the future. This topic helped you to examine your financial health, focusing on the importance of a personal budget and the need to begin a wealth-building strategy for your future.

CRITICALLY THINKING

What Have You Learned?

Let's apply what you learned in this material to help Royce from the opening scenario. However, before you address Royce's problem and propose your solution, take a moment to review your notes, key terms, learning outcomes, boldface headings, and figures and tables.

TEST YOUR LEARNING

Now that you have reviewed the main points and reread Royce's story, what advice do you have for him? Using the R.E.D. Model for critical thinking, help Royce critically review his concerns:

R

Recognize Assumptions:

Facts: What are the facts in Royce's situation? List them.

Opinions: What opinions do you find in this situation? List them.

Assumptions: Are Royce's assumptions accurate?

E

Evaluate Information

Help Royce compile a list of questions that will help him make the most appropriate decision.

What emotions seem to be motivating Royce?

What, if anything, is missing from his thought process?

Do you see any confirmation bias?

D

Draw Conclusions

Based on the facts and the questions you have presented, what conclusions can you draw?

What advice do you have for Royce? What solutions do you propose?

Based on your suggestions, do you see any assumptions?

Finally, based on what you learned about financial literacy, what plan of action do you suggest for Royce?

Exploration *14*
of MAJORS
AND CAREERS

LEARNING OUTCOMES

By the time you finish reading this material and completing the activities, you will be able to do the following:

- Identify personal interests and how they relate to coursework (majors) and potential careers.

- Conduct research to determine skills, experience, and education needed for a career area.

- Explain two positive and two negative consequences of changing a college major.

- Gather information to help you build an effective résumé and portfolio.

The Case of MIYOKO

Miyoko's mother is a nurse. So was her grandmother. Two of her cousins have just graduated—and will be nurses. Miyoko has been "primed" since childhood to be a nurse. Her family talks about how good she is with people and what a great nurse she will be. Her mother is even talking about getting Miyoko summer work at her hospital for experience; she is excited about the potential to have her daughter work with her.

For her part, Miyoko is *not* excited about nursing. She wants to be an artist. She has a talent

Key Terms

Ambition
Declare a major
General Education
    Requirements
Groupthink
Initiative
Passion
Portfolio
Potential
Risk
Undeclared

INTRODUCTION
Chapter

Some students enter college knowing exactly what they want to do after graduation. Arriving on campus with a clear career vision, these students know what courses they need to complete by graduation day. Focused and set on a particular outcome, they declare a major as soon as possible.

Other students have a vague idea of what they would like to study and what they would like to "become" upon graduation. They may not be as clearly focused as the first group of students just described, but they know

and passion for creating visual arts. Her family keeps telling her she needs to do something practical, something that has a future. Art, Miyoko has been told, is a great hobby—not an occupation to pay the bills.

Miyoko has an appointment with her advisor today to discuss declaring a major. She does not want to disappoint her family; however, she wants to pursue her passion. She is frustrated and confused.

CRITICALLY THINKING
about *Miyoko's* situation

What suggestions do you have for Miyoko? Should she follow her heart, her family, or something else?

their interests and what courses they want to explore before the end of their first term in college.

Then there are students who are just as committed to their college studies as their declared classmates, but they have yet to match their interests and abilities to a course of study or a long-term career commitment. Some major universities report 75 to 80 percent of their entering first-year students do

MyStudentSuccessLab

MyStudentSuccessLab (www.mystudentsuccesslab.com) is an online solution designed to help you "Start strong, Finish stronger" by building skills for ongoing personal and professional development.

not have a declared major (Simon, 2012; Cuseo, 2005). Additionally, it would not be unusual to find nearly 50 percent of declared majors changing their academic major at least once (Simon, 2012; Orndorff and Herr, 1996). In essence, for every student you meet on campus who is pursuing a declared major, statistically another has declared and then changed to a different major area of study.

College allows students to explore new ideas. The exploration can lead to questions that challenge your fundamental belief system. So what happens if, after you declare a major, your explorations lead you down a new path, *away* from your major? Can you change direction? The short answer is yes. However, such a change needs careful consideration.

Whether or not you have chosen a major, this topic's reflective activities will help you make (or reinforce) one of the most significant academic decisions you will confront in college.

Choosing a college major is a three-level decision. There is the what—as in *what* will your major course of study be in college? There is a time component—*when* in your college career do you need to declare a major? And finally, there is the process— *how* will you go about making this critically important decision? The material of this topic will examine the resources that will help you with the *what*, *when*, and *how* of choosing a major. This material will also examine the connection between your choice of major, your passion, and a future career.

Activity 14.1

Reflecting on Your Current Level of Knowledge about College Majors and Career Possibilities

Before you answer the items that follow, reflect on your current level of information about majors and careers.

As you complete this activity, write from your heart. This exercise is not meant for you to answer just like your classmates—or to match what you may think the instructor wants to see. Take the time to give a respectful, responsible general accounting of your experiences and knowledge in this area. Conducting a truthful self-assessment now will help you build on skills you have while developing those you lack.

For each of the following items, circle the number that best describes your typical experience. Here is the key for the numbers:

0 = never, 1 = almost never, 2 = occasionally, 3 = frequently, 4 = almost always, 5 = always

When considering your knowledge of majors and careers, do you:

1.	Understand what it means to "declare a college major?"	0	1	2	3	4	5
2.	Realize which assessments you can take that may help you identify a major or career?	0	1	2	3	4	5
3.	Establish and keep appointments with an advisor about your potential college major?	0	1	2	3	4	5
4.	Know someone who can serve as a mentor for major and career information?	0	1	2	3	4	5

		0	1	2	3	4	5
5.	Have plans to interview someone in a career field that interests you?	0	1	2	3	4	5
6.	Recognize what questions to ask when you interview someone in a career field that interests you?	0	1	2	3	4	5
7.	Have an appointment with, or have already visited, your campus career development center?	0	1	2	3	4	5
8.	Understand the positives and negatives of changing from one college major to another?	0	1	2	3	4	5
9.	Collect information and material for your resume and portfolio?	0	1	2	3	4	5

Add up your scores for items 1 through 9. Divide by 9. Write your answer here: ....

Using the key provided to explain each number (0, 1, 2, 3, 4, 5), complete this sentence: When it comes to majors and careers, I _____ gather and evaluate information about majors and careers.

Based on your answers, what insights have you gained?

MAJOR MISCONCEPTIONS

Whether because of misinformation or misinterpretation, students many times hold more myths than truths about college majors. The following are 10 of the major misconceptions about college majors (Leonard, 2013; Plattsburgh State University, n.d.; University of South Dakota, 2009).

1. *Once I have my major, I have my career.* It is not always true that completing a major commits you to a particular career or job.

2. *Once I have a major, I am locked into it.* Most students come to college without a major—and half will change their major at least once.

3. *Once I have my major, there is no looking back; there should be no second thoughts.* This is closely connected to the preceding item. There will be times and courses that cause you to reflect on your choice. This is healthy. It may lead to a change in major—or it may lead to a deeper commitment. Embrace the uncertainty and grow from it.

4. *There is no need to stress about majors—I can keep changing until I find what I like.* Yes, you can (and statistically speaking, will) change your major, but you are limited by resources of time and money. Your college may even have restrictions.

5. *Students without a declared major lack focus and commitment.* College is a time for learning—and that includes exploring your passions and options. Not having a major does not mean you lack commitment.

6. *Students who change majors lack dedication.* As stated, more than 50 percent of college students will change majors. To be sure there are disadvantages—but there are a number of advantages as well.

7. *Find and eliminate majors by taking introductory courses.* Enrolling in an introductory course can be an excellent way to get basic information about

a field of study. But it is not necessarily an efficient method. This requires a commitment of time (and money). And if you find you do not like the course or major, you have only eliminated rather than chosen a major.

8. *I can worry about my major after I complete all my general requirements.* If you know your major, you may be able to satisfy a specific academic major requirement by taking a specific general education requirement. Working with an advisor will help you with this information.

9. *Before deciding on a major, I need to know what the market forecast is for jobs.* The jobs outlook (forecast) is important information but not necessarily the determining factor in choosing a major. You have to consider your abilities (such as what you can do well), your desires (such as where you want to live), your time to graduation (when you will enter the job market), and your passions (the interests that energize you).

10. *My advisor or my campus career development center has tests that will tell me what my major should be.* Measuring your preferences for types of activities, tasks, and careers may help you to focus on a particular area. Or it may raise more questions in your mind. Do not wait for a test to say what you need to major in or the career you should prepare for. You will need to make the ultimate choices.

CHOOSING A MAJOR: MAKING AN INFORMED CHOICE

College life presents one choice after another. So far this term you have made decisions concerning course selections, study methods, and personal relationships. Some choices may have been excruciatingly difficult, whereas others required little effort. One of the most important, and perhaps most perplexing, decisions for first-year students involves choosing a college major. The difficulty may only be procedural, as you learn which bureaucratic hoops to jump through. You may only need answers to typical questions. "Who can help me?" "Where do I get information?" "Are there forms to complete?" "Is there a deadline?"

More commonly, though, students simply do not know what they want to study in college. The college determines the **general education requirements (GER** or "Gen Ed")** that students must complete for a degree. Beyond that core of courses, however, students may not know what to take—or even what their college or university has to offer. The vast listing of available courses can seem overwhelming to a first-year student.

DECLARING A MAJOR

The word *major* in its most general sense refers to something that ranks high in importance or concern when compared to other things. A major event—like graduation from high school or a marriage proposal—represents a transitional moment in a person's life. What follows differs from what has just happened. When students choose or **declare a major,** they commit to a particular course of academic preparation. Once the academic major has been declared, course work becomes more focused and more specialized. These courses will provide a depth of reading and discussion not found in the general education requirements of the college or university.

WHAT SHOULD YOU DO IF YOU ARE "UNDECLARED"?

It can be easy to fall into the trap of thinking that uncertainty about what you want to be for the rest of your life means you must be deficient as a student. Nothing could be farther from the truth (see Major Misconception 5).

Students who have not decided on a major fall into the category of "undecided," or **undeclared**. That is, they have not declared their college course of study. Undeclared does not mean uncommitted. It means what it says—this student has yet to declare or decide on a field of study. Nor does undecided mean indecisive. Undeclared students have not made a decision, but that does not mean they are incapable of making a decision.

Reasons for not declaring a major abound (Cuseo, 2005). Perhaps the undeclared student sees the college and university experience as a time for exploration, a time to investigate many areas of interest. Some students are, by nature, very deliberate in their thinking and decision making. Reflection is a prized quality for these students. They want to gather as much information as possible, mull it over, and then make a decision. They are committed to making an informed decision—one they can live with. Like a singer searching for the right song to match her voice, these students want a major that will match their passions and desires.

Not all entering students require a prolonged period of thought and reflection. You will share classes with students who have had dreams of being a teacher, a doctor, an accountant, or a fashion designer since they were in elementary school. They see no need for further exploration. They *know* what they want to do with their lives—and they want to move toward their dreams immediately.

However, it is possible that some of these "I-already-know-what-I-want-to-be-after-graduation" students may have made either an uninformed or a premature decision (Cuseo, 2005). Coming in with hard and fast ideas on careers may indicate narrow thinking or a decision heavily influenced by someone else.

For instance, the concept of **groupthink** refers to what happens when group thinking overshadows individual concerns. In order to get along with the others, a member agrees with what the group as a whole thinks; individual disagreement is stifled. A similar situation can occur when a family decides the best major for a son or daughter, leading the student to declare a major without a full exploration of alternatives. Refer to the story of Miyoko at the beginning of this material.

Please do not misinterpret the foregoing paragraph. Simply because a student comes to college knowing what he or she wants—or has a family deeply involved in his or her education—does not indicate a problem. Such confidence, coupled with a family support circle, can be truly energizing and inspiring.

The point remains, though, that many first-year students may not be ready to make a quick decision concerning their major. They need to explore their talents and passions before making a meaningful commitment. These students—and you might be one of them—need time to grow into their major.

WHAT ARE YOU PASSIONATE ABOUT?

Identifying your **passion**—what you are committed to and what you love to do with your days—can help you understand why you get up in the morning. This *what* provides the purpose for your day. Sometimes, though, people pursue goals that do not connect to their passions, talents, and desires (see Major Misconceptions 2 and 3).

Completion of a goal does not ensure that it furthers your life or otherwise has a positive impact on you or those around you. The same is true for your major. Once you

Figure 14.1

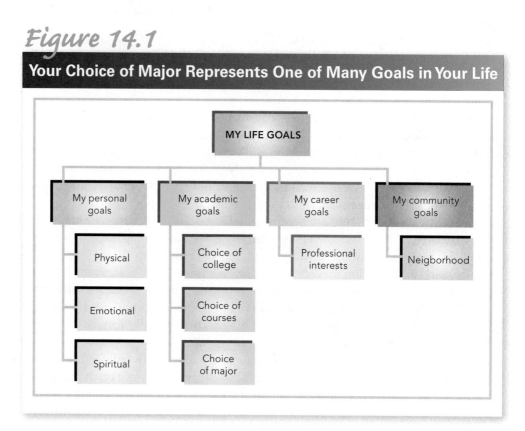

Your Choice of Major Represents One of Many Goals in Your Life

have declared a major, how do you know it is the correct choice *for you?* Will it contribute to your overall balance and wellness? As depicted in Figure 14.1, your choice of a college major represents one of many life goals. Think of how rewarding each goal will be when you connect it to what you love to do—what gives you purpose.

Activity 14.2

Why Do You Want To Do?

List three academic majors you would like to explore. For each of the possible majors, reflect on and then write why you want to pursue that major.

SOURCES OF INFORMATION ABOUT ACADEMIC MAJORS

Self-assessment. A sense of purpose is energizing. It gives direction to life (Leider, 1997). Any time you have wondered "What am I going to do with my life?" the question of purpose comes to the forefront.

Your professors, counselors, family, and friends can provide critical input about what they see as your strengths, weaknesses, abilities, and possibilities. And you are a source as well. Ask yourself, "What are my desires, abilities, and passions?" Although your choice of an academic major is not irreversible (see Major Misconceptions 2 and 3), it *is* a critical decision that cannot be taken lightly. The choice involves more than just picking a department and enrolling in courses. If done without thought and planning, it can be frustrating, time-consuming, and costly.

Activity 14.3

Choosing What Is Right for You

In the four quadrants below, you will find questions to help you assess your own likes, dislikes, strengths, and challenges. Think of these as starting questions. Feel free to add more. Record your answers in a journal, in your notebook, or in a document on your computer.

My Likes	My Dislikes
What classes, tasks, and activities do you enjoy?	What classes, tasks, and activities do you *not* enjoy?
What is it about these courses and activities that you like?	What is it about these courses and activities that you dislike?
With what types of people do you like to associate? What do you like about these types of people?	With what types of people do you find it difficult to associate? What do you dislike about these types of people?
When working, what type of physical environment energizes you?	When working, what type of physical environment is the least energizing for you?
Do you like spontaneity and flexibility—do you like to make spur of the moment plans?	Does flexibility scare or irritate you—would you rather know what is going to happen and when it is going to happen?
Do you like to work alone, or would you rather work with other people?	Do you avoid speaking in front of people?
Are you tolerant and accepting of other people's challenges?	Do shortcomings in other people bother you?
What types of books, magazines, or movies do you enjoy?	What types of books, magazines, or movies do you avoid?
If money were not a factor, what career would you choose to enter?	What type of career field do you think you would avoid at all costs?
List other *likes*.	List other *dislikes*.

My Strengths	My Challenges
Which of your traits, characteristics, and strengths have *helped* (or which do you believe will help) you create opportunities for yourself?	Which of your traits, characteristics, and strengths have *hindered* (or which do you believe will hinder) you in creating opportunities for yourself?
What types of tasks do you have a talent for?	What types of tasks do you have difficulty doing or completing?
Are you realistically confident about your abilities?	Do you tend to be unrealistically confident? That is, do you overstate your abilities?
Are you usually able to focus clearly and persist until a goal is completed?	Do you usually procrastinate?

My Strengths	My Challenges
Are you effective at "thinking outside of the box" (creative thinking)?	Is it difficult for you to be a creative thinker?
Are you optimistic?	Are you pessimistic?
Do you work well in groups?	Do you have difficulty working with certain types of people? If so, which types of people?
Are you usually a self-starter?	Do you usually wait for directions or orders before beginning a task?
List other *strengths*.	List other *challenges*.

Based on what you like to do and based on your strengths, complete this sentence: *I would like to study* a college major that allows me to _____.

Based on your dislikes and challenges, complete this sentence: *I would like to avoid* a college major that requires me to _____.

This activity draws from Ken Kragen, *Life Is a Contact Sport* (New York: Morrow, 1994), 41–45.

Campus advisors. Your campus advisor will be one of your most useful resources. This person knows the guidelines and bureaucratic steps needed to declare a major and register for the correct classes. While the "do-it-yourself" mentality does show fortitude and initiative, at times it can be foolish. That is especially true when it comes to the academic advising and counseling services your campus has to offer. Some students may view a visit to the counselor's or advisor's office as a time-consuming task. Other students may view course selection as something they can do themselves. You might have heard a classmate say, "All I have to do is read the catalog, look at the current term's class offerings, and fill in the blanks. It is not exactly rocket science!"

It might be helpful to view counseling and advising differently. In fact, establish a goal to visit a counselor *voluntarily* at least two times per term. A mid-term meeting gives you a head start on preparing for the next term's registration process. You and the counselor can review the requirements that direct your course of study. This allows you to make sure you are taking the correct courses. Maybe a course you need will be offered only once per year. Without the help of your counselor you might not know this—and you may end up waiting additional time to take a required course. This mid-term visit would also be an appropriate time to discuss your grades, successes, and challenges.

An end-of-the-term meeting gives you an opportunity to review what has happened during the academic term. Did you make satisfactory progress? Have your goals changed concerning your major? Or maybe you have been undeclared, and now you have decided to declare your major. This would be the time to discuss the requirements of the particular degree or certification program you would like to pursue. The academic counselor or advisor can answer your questions and direct you to appropriate sources in your career development center (see Major Misconceptions 3 and 10).

College Catalog. You can find a listing of the majors that your college or university has to offer by searching the school catalog (either a printed copy or online).

Four-year schools generally provide extensive information matching academic offerings to potential careers.

A two-year college's list of majors will not be as extensive, but you still have options from which to choose. While differences may exist from state to state and institution to institution, at a two-year college, you may be able to earn an Associate of Arts (AA) degree, an Associate of Science (AS) degree, or an Associate of Applied Science (AAS) degree. Your college catalogue will explain what is offered and the benefits of each offering. Again, your advisor will be a valuable resource.

Campus Career Center. A visit to a campus career center can lead you to print resources, Internet sites, and contact with people in your areas of interest. Here you can find brochures, flyers, books, computer software, and specific websites designed to help you make an informed decision about your future course work.

Career and Personality Inventories. The career center may also have specific computer programs (and trained staff) that allow you to complete career, personality, and interest inventories. Personality assessments will not tell you what you *should be*. Rather, they can help you better understand yourself, how you relate to people, and how you handle specific tasks (see Major Misconception 10). Check with your advisor or counselor for more information. Two such inventories, the MSSL Golden Personality Inventory and the Thinking Styles Inventory, can be found in the MyStudentSuccessLab (**www.mystudentsuccesslab.com**).

Career Information. Choosing a major is not always synonymous with committing to a particular career. A major in history, for instance, does not mean you have to be an archivist in a museum; you could be a teacher, lawyer, or journalist. A sociology major does not have to prepare for a life of social work; it might lead you to criminal justice, law, or marriage and family counseling.

It is possible, however, to look at specific careers to help with your decision about a major. Think of this as working *backward*. Rather than choosing a major and then moving forward to the outcome (see Major Misconception 1), starting with the end in mind (the career) may help focus your choice of a major. For instance, broadcast journalism might intrigue you. That may lead you to explore course work in writing, literature, history, or political science.

The U.S. government annual publication the *Occupational Outlook Handbook* (2013), which lists specific career areas, can be found online. Clicking on a career link will lead to information about the nature of the work, employment statistics, qualifications needed, working conditions, job outlook for the future, earnings potential, related occupations, and other sources of information about a given career area.

In addition to online and print information about prospective careers, consider the following (Duncan, 2008):

- *Find a mentor.* Establish a personal relationship with someone who can provide objective advice on the selection of a major, as well as meaningful career advice.
- *Utilize extracurricular activities.* Frequently, outside college activities such as organizations and clubs will provide opportunities and experiences to help you determine if you have accurately gauged your interest and aptitude for a particular field of study.

■ *Pursue internships and summer employment.* Vocational exposure to the real-world work environment remains one of the most effective ways to determine if a career choice is a good match. Look for opportunities or contacts that can assist you in obtaining practical experience in your selected field of study.

Specific Departments and Instructors. In addition to your counselors and advisors, take time to visit your instructors and ask them about specific majors, including the preparation needed and the future career possibilities with such an academic background. Some college departments may have literature already printed and ready for distribution.

Activity 14.4

Preparing for an Information-Gathering Interview

Find a person in your career field of interest—and set up a time for an interview about his or her career. Your advisor, instructor, family, friends, and work connections can help you locate an appropriate person. After contacting the person for an interview, but before the actual meeting, type a list of questions you want to ask. Here are a few categories you may want to explore with someone knowledgeable about your career interest:

1. Emotional rewards/drawbacks of the career?
2. Financial rewards/drawbacks of the career?
3. Education/training needed to prepare for the career?
4. Best major to prepare for this career?
5. What do you find most satisfying about this career?
6. "Typical" day in this career field?
7. Necessary skills and talents for this career field?
8. Sources for more information about this field?
9. In one sentence, how would you best describe this career?
10. What else do I need to know at this point?

Before you go to your information-gathering interview, purchase an appropriate thank you card. After the interview, write a few lines of appreciation to the person you interviewed and mail it. With each interview, you are building a network. You could do the same with an e-mail or text—but a neatly handwritten note on a card you picked out indicates you have taken a little extra time to show appreciation and gratitude.

Using Multiple Intelligences. The theory of multiple intelligences may provide additional information as you seek help choosing your major. Occupations typically require the skills and talents of two or more intelligences. For instance, a teacher needs linguistic intelligence and interpersonal intelligence—and also logical-mathematical intelligence if she wishes to be a math teacher. You may believe that an accountant only needs to have a highly developed mathematical intelligence. But in the course of her job, she might need to meet with clients—and thus would benefit from interpersonal intelligence skills. Look for opportunities to sharpen as many of your intelligences as possible. You never know when you will have to draw on two or more of them at one time (Morris, 2011; Armstrong, 1994).

YOUR COURSE WORK

The decision you finally make will have an impact on your course work and scheduling. Colleges and universities have a prescribed number of courses needed for a degree or certificate. The exact number and nature of these courses may vary from institution to institution, but your course work will generally fall within three areas:

- *General education requirements* (called *core* at some colleges): Courses your school believes to be important for *all* students, no matter their major
- *Major requirements:* In-depth study of your chosen academic area
- *Electives:* Courses that you "elect" (or choose) to take in addition to the GERs and those required for your major

Your college may have additional course work, as well as restrictions on types of elective courses allowed (if any). Completing the requirements in a timely fashion moves you closer to the academic goal of graduation. As usual, your school's catalog and academic advisors will be resources.

Activity 14.5

Critically Thinking about Your Options

Once you have gathered appropriate information, it is time to begin narrowing your choices. Your goal will be to move closer to a declared major.

1. As a review, list the possible majors you have been seriously contemplating.

2. Of those listed, which ones can you *eliminate?* Perhaps you have realized that a particular major no longer holds your interest; or perhaps one of your courses kindled such a strong interest that it has overshadowed all other choices. List the eliminated majors, and next to each one briefly indicate why—at least at this time—you have decided to eliminate it.

3. Which major now has the most attraction for you?

4. Briefly explain the reasoning for your choice.

CHANGING YOUR MAJOR

A certain amount of risk is involved with everything we do. Obviously the level of **risk** depends on the activity; some risks can be deadly, others merely a momentary thrill. When we risk, we step outside our comfort zone; we take a chance.

Declaring a major has a certain amount of risk associated with it. Many students make this decision with less than half of their college education completed. Then, after a semester or two of study, they may find that their chosen academic area is not what they had hoped. For whatever reason, the major neither fulfills nor excites them.

THE REALITY OF CHANGE: What Can You Do If You Are Not Satisfied with Your Major?

If, because of new explorations and insights, you find yourself looking at an alternative course of study, welcome the new direction. You have not "failed" or "lost focus." You have not necessarily even made a mistake. Consider any detours as *learning opportunities* (see Major Misconceptions 2, 3 and 6).

MAJOR CHANGE: The Positive Side

Consider the following positive points regarding a major change:

- When you made your initial major decision, you may not have fully explored other areas of interest. You may have entered college with a childhood dream of pursing a certain career that you actually knew very little about—and then, on deeper inspection, you discovered that the career does not inspire you after all. If you are "guilty" of anything, it would be premature articulation—you committed before you had all the facts.
- Changing your major may reflect a maturing mind rather than an indecisive personality (Cuseo, 2005).
- Pursuing a goal does not always move in a straight line. A change in direction may simply mean you have adjusted your goal to a more realistic and satisfying outcome.

Changing a College Major: A Positive Story

Steve graduated from high school, left home, and entered his first year of college. For as long as he could remember, Steve was going to "become a teacher." It was all he had ever wanted to be.

During his first year in college, he worked toward completing his GERs. He looked forward to diving into teacher preparation. Steve had declared his major—history—and was moving closer to his goal.

During the summer between his freshman and sophomore years, he attended a picnic at his godfather's home. There he had an enlightening conversation with a man who had enjoyed a long and satisfying career in the federal criminal justice system. By the end of the day, Steve was thinking about a new direction for his education.

When he returned to campus in the fall, he changed his major from history to sociology. Three years later, he graduated as the valedictorian of his class and quickly landed a job. The academic major change had led him to a new career.

But the story does not end there. Six years after his college graduation, not satisfied with his career, he returned to college. He earned his teaching credentials—and landed a job as a high school history teacher. Though the route had been circuitous, Steve found himself now enjoying the career he had initially pursued. It was a ten-year journey from college acceptance, to declaring a major, to changing a major, to beginning a career, and then to changing careers. His outcomes changed along the way, but his initial intent to help people discover their own talents and intentions was achieved.

A couple of graduate degrees later, Steve now teaches college students, facilitates national workshops, and writes books—including this book you are now reading.

MAJOR CHANGE: The Downside

As with most choices, of course, there can be negative repercussions as well (see Major Misconception 4):

- Depending on when the decision is made, changing your major may lengthen your time in college—thus becoming more costly in terms of time and dollars.

- In some schools, changing your major can count against you, as there may be a restriction on the number of credit hours a student may attempt or earn. Know your school's policies.

- If you do not have a new major to embrace, you will fall back into the undeclared category. This may mean more trips to the career center, more assessments, and more research into a major—procedures that you have been through at least one time already. (This "downside" may turn into a positive, however, as a second look may sharpen your academic and career focus.)

- You may feel pressure to quickly declare a new major—and once again make a less-than-informed decision.

FIX WHAT? A FINAL THOUGHT ABOUT CHANGING MAJORS

If you find yourself considering a major change, think carefully about the situation. Is changing your major the *only* answer? Perhaps a discussion with an instructor or advisor might clear up some concerns you have—concerns that may seem large and forbidding if you have not gathered correct information. Understand what you can "fix" with a major change—and what you cannot.

For instance, you may be able to fix the problem of content comprehension by moving from a math-oriented major to one that focuses on literature. But if you are having trouble because you are homesick, you can change your major monthly but the real problem—homesickness—will remain. You have to know what to address.

Perhaps you have come to the conclusion that there are more students in your major area than potential jobs. For that reason, you consider a change of major (Gordon and Sears, 2004). Before adopting that fix, though, take advantage of another opportunity to talk with the department chair, an academic advisor, someone in the career field, or a career counselor. They might have job placement information that surprises you (see Major Misconception 9).

A LOOK TO THE FUTURE: BUILDING A PORTFOLIO

A *résumé* is a summary of your professional and work qualifications. It oftentimes accompanies an application for employment. Generally speaking, it helps the prospective employer answer the question, "Why should I hire you?" Or even more pointedly, "Why should I pay you money to do work for my company?"

Consider résumé writing a terminal (ending) activity, one that generally has more urgency at the conclusion of your college career. Of more importance at this point in your education is the collection of material to eventually include with your résumé. This collection about your background will be the beginning of a personal **portfolio**—and it is part of what will "sell" you to an employer.

A PORTFOLIO CHECKLIST

When the time comes for résumé writing and job interview preparation, you will already have a wealth of material to consult if you start working now on the items that follow. For our purposes here, keep it simple and look at the essentials you can collect now. To begin the process, purchase five large envelopes. You could also do this on your computer with a document folder. Label the envelopes or folders as follows:

1. *Résumé material.* In this envelope or folder place:
   - Copies of your college transcripts.
   - A list of jobs you have had (include start date, end date, supervisors, and your duties).
   - Copies of any certificates or awards you have received.

2. *Letters of recommendation.* In this envelope or folder place:
   - Any letter or commendation you have received from teachers or employers. Ask for a letter of recommendation when you complete a significant activity such as an internship.
   - An ongoing list of people you will be able to use as references for prospective jobs.

3. *Products.* In this envelope or folder place:
   - Information or samples of anything you have created that might favorably impress an employer (written work, software programs, artwork, writing, videos, and so forth). These items should show how you stand out in a positive way.

4. *Skills.* In this envelope or folder place:
   - An ongoing list (update it as you gain expertise) of your salable skills and talents. Again, what makes you indispensable to a future employer? Why do they need you?

5. *Biography.* In this envelope or folder place:
   - Personal information that one day might help on a job interview. Who significantly influenced your life or helped create an interest in a certain career? What types of books do you like to read? What are your career and personal goals? How do you handle challenges?

THE CHOICES YOU HAVE MADE

Have you ever shopped at a retail store and noticed a sign that announced, "Please pardon our dust—we are working hard to serve you better"? Renovations take time—and at times, they create chaos. In some ways, this school term may have been a time for *your* renovation and renewal—changes for the better. You *are* a work in progress.

Because of your academic successes, social networking, and career explorations, you have become a more self-aware person. Self-aware people reflect on their actions, understand how those actions affect themselves and others, and assume responsibility for their choices.

Self-aware people do not have all the answers. None of us do. In fact, as you make decisions about your major area of study, you may have more questions now than when this term started. Self-aware people are, at least, more alert to circumstances around them—and how those circumstances may have an impact on themselves and their surroundings.

PRIORITIES AND CHOICES

Even as you have become more attentive to what works for you and what does not work, you still may feel a bit confused or apprehensive about your future. As you complete this school term and move into the next phase of your life, ask yourself two questions:

- What have I been doing to get what I desire from college and life?

- Am I satisfied with the choices I have made this term?

Whether you reached your goals in full or in part, you have moved closer to your destination. Even if that destination has changed, one thing is certain: you have changed and grown.

These changes reflect the choices you have made. Now, as you near the end of a successful term, it is time to look to the future. What have you learned that will affect the choices you will make next term, next year, and the rest of your life? Choices change lives, and with these choices you create the opportunity to master your life.

You probably have heard someone say that "He has so much potential." Or perhaps someone made the observation that "She will definitely go far. She has so much ambition."

While **ambition** (a desire to reach a goal) and **potential** (the possibility of becoming something greater than you are) are important characteristics, they are useless without **initiative**. Responsible decision making and follow-through are needed to put potential and ambition into action. Ambition is the desire, potential is the ability, and initiative is the doing.

Throughout this school term, you have had to make choices every day to put your ambition and potential into action. Your choices reflect what you consider important in your world. They reflect your priorities—the paths you have decided to take. Activity 14.6 will help you put your choices in perspective.

Activity 14.6

Reflections on Your Priorities

A. List the five people, issues, or things you value the most in your life at this time.

B. List the five activities that take most of your time in a typical week.

C. Compare the two lists (A and B above). Do your activities reflect what you say are your priorities? That is, what you say you value, is that where you spend your time?

D. What changes, if any, do you need to make as you look to your future?

Adapted from Hal Urban. *Making Choices that Change Lives: 15 Ways to Find More Purpose, Meaning, and Joy.* New York: Simon & Schuster, 2006. 155)

Respect where you have been; reflect on where you would like to go. Then continue to make responsible choices.

I would like to leave you with two suggestions to guide your days to come:

1. You will be confronted with situations that are not of your choosing. Recognize that you *do* have the choice on how you respond to those situations in a balanced and healthy manner.

2. Living a life of wellness and balance is a lifestyle choice. Recognize that you have that choice—and make it. When you pay attention to, and take care of, your life dimensions (social, occupational, spiritual, physical, intellectual, and emotional), you increase the likelihood of living the life you want to have for yourself.

Embrace your ability to choose and live each day honestly, responsibly, and respect-fully! The following 14-step guide provides key strategies for your life of integrity.

A 14-STEP GUIDE TO A LIFE OF BALANCED PRIORITIES

1. *Transitions, Balance, and Organization* Organized planning and action will help you navigate each new phase of your life, enhance your academic success, maintain balance, and reach your dreams.

2. *Critical Thinking* Critical thinkers demonstrate command of basic information about an issue as they logically, precisely, and systematically examine the issue from many sides.

3. *Priority Management* Organization will not only improve your study habits, but it will also allow you to feel in control of your life and remain healthy and balanced. You cannot manage time. You can, however, manage your priorities.

4. *Information Literacy* You need to know how to navigate through, evaluate, and use information available from print *and* digital resources. Additionally, use social networking sites with personal integrity.

5. *Motivation and Goal Achieving* It will be up to you to stay motivated, set goals for success, and take action. Goals provide purpose and meaning to life. Make choices to put forth persistent effort to achieve those goals.

6. *Learning Styles* One way to become an engaged student is to know as much as possible about the way you learn—and then apply that knowledge to your academic tasks (and beyond).

7. *Class Time Listening and Note Taking* Focus on what is important *inside* the classroom, and you increase understanding of (and confidence with) the vast amounts of material your instructors present each day.

8. *Memory and Studying* If you want to improve your memory, do three things: notice, store, and reclaim the material with which you work. Effective study habits will help you master each of these steps.

9. *Reading* Reading is a strategic process. If you follow a few basic steps, you can tackle your assignments more effectively and effortlessly. Practice the SQ4R strategy.

10. *Test Preparation and Test Taking* Test-preparation skills get you ready and comfortable for a test. Test-taking skills build confidence to efficiently and effectively complete different types of tests in different types of situations.

11. *Civility* Interpersonal skills will serve you well in school and beyond. Your ability to communicate a message of confidence, competence, and civility affects how people perceive you.

12. *Treating Yourself With Respect* Develop strategies to be intellectually alert, emotionally stable, and physically strong. Acting honestly, responsibly, and respectfully builds a life of integrity.

13. *Financial Literacy* The choices you make concerning budgeting, earning, spending, and saving will have a major impact upon your standard of living now and in the future. Build wealth one step at a time.

14. *Exploration of Majors and Careers* Understand your passions and use campus, Internet, and community resources to help you make informed decisions about your academic major and career choices. Live a life of purpose!

Chapter SUMMARY

Choosing a major requires time and focus. This material introduced you to strategies, resources, and people you can use to help with the important process of selecting an academic course of study. Use your time in college to explore your passions, interests, and skills. Take each step mindfully and enjoy the journey!

Before leaving this topic, remember to:

- Identify questions you have concerning college majors and potential careers.
- Find campus, community, and Internet resources that will help you make an informed decision about declaring your college major.
- Understand the positive and negative consequences of changing a college major.
- Keep a list of the skills you now have (or are now developing) that an employer will find valuable.

CRITICALLY THINKING
What Have You Learned?

Let's apply what you learned in this material to help Miyoko from the opening scenario. However, before you address Miyoko's problem and propose your solution, take a moment to review your notes, key terms, learning outcomes, boldface headings, and figures and tables.

TEST YOUR LEARNING

Now that you have reviewed the main points and reread Miyoko's story, what advice do you have for her? Using the R.E.D. Model for critical thinking, help Miyoko critically review her concerns:

R

Recognize Assumptions

Facts: What are the facts in Miyoko's situation? List them.

Opinions: What opinions do you find in this situation? List them.

Assumptions: Are Miyoko's assumptions accurate?

E

Evaluate Information

Help Miyoko compile a list of questions that will help her make the most appropriate decision.

What emotions seem to be motivating Miyoko?

What, if anything, is missing from her thought process?

Do you see any confirmation bias?

D

Draw Conclusions

Based on the facts and the questions you have presented, what conclusions can you draw?

What advice do you have for Miyoko? What solutions do you propose?

Based on your suggestions, do you see any assumptions?

Finally, based on what you learned about majors and careers, what plan of action do you suggest for Miyoko?

Achor, Shawn. *The Happiness Advantage: The Seven Principles of Positive Psychology That Fuel Success and Performance at Work*. New York: Crown Business, 2010.

Adler, Mortimer, and Charles Van Doren. *How to Read a Book*. New York: Simon & Schuster, 1972.

American Heart Association, "Get Moving!" 2013. www.justmove.org/fitnessnews/faqs.html (accessed July 1, 2013).

American Test Anxiety Association. http://amtaa.org/index.html (accessed June 30, 2013).

Armbruster, Bonnie B. in Rona F. Flippo and David Caverly. *Handbook of College Reading and Study Strategy Research*. Mahwah, NJ: Lawrence Erlbaum Associates, 2000.

Armstrong, Thomas. *Multiple Intelligences in the Classroom*. Alexandria, VA: Association for Supervision and Curriculum Development, 1994.

Association of College and Research Libraries (a division of the American Library Association). "Information Literacy Competency Standards for Higher Education." 2000. http://www.ala.org/ala/mgrps/divs/acrl/standards/informationliteracy-competency.cfm (accessed July 8, 2013).

——. "Information Literacy Competency Standards for Higher Education." 2006. http://www.ala.org/ala/mgrps/divs/acrl/standards/informationlitera-cycompetency.cfm#ildef (accessed June 29, 2013).

Beck, Martha. *Finding Your Own North Star: Claiming the Life You Were Meant to Have*. New York: Three Rivers Press, 2001.

Bloom, Benjamin. "Major Categories in the Taxonomy of Educational Objectives." 1956. http://faculty.washington.edu/krumme/guides/bloom1.html (accessed June 25, 2013).

Burger King. "Burger King Nutrition Facts." May 2013. http://www.bk.com/cms/en/us/cms_out/digital_assets/files/pages/MenuNutritionInformation_April2013_1.pdf (accessed May 25, 2013).

Calorie Count. 2013. http://caloriecount.about.com/calories-salad-vegetable-tossed-i21052 (accessed May 25, 2013).

Chastain, Ann. "Smart Goals Help You Achieve Success." *The University of Michigan Extension* (May 14, 2012). http://msue.anr.msu.edu/news/smart_goals_help_you_achieve_success (accessed on June 29, 2013).

Centers for Disease Control and Prevention. "Alcohol and Public Health." Centers for Disease Control and Prevention. November 7, 2012. http://www.cdc.gov/alcohol/fact-sheets/binge-drinking.htm (accessed July 2, 2013).

——. "College health and safety. Mental health: Stress, anxiety, and depression." Centers for Disease Control. August 2012. http://www.cdc.gov/family/college/ (accessed July 2, 2013).

——. "How much physical activity do adults need?" Centers for Disease Control. December 1, 2011. http://www.cdc.gov/physicalactivity/everyone/guidelines/adults.html (accessed July 1, 2013).

——. "Overweight and Obesity Statistics: Adult Obesity Facts." Centers for Disease Control and Prevention. August 13, 2013. http://www.cdc.gov/obesity/data/adult.html (accessed July 2, 2013).

——. "Overweight and Obesity Statistics." Centers for Disease Control and Prevention. January 11, 2013. http://www.cdc.gov/obesity/data/childhood.html (accessed July 2, 2013).

——. "Smoking and Tobacco Use." Centers for Disease Control and Prevention. January 10, 2012. http://www.cdc.gov/tobacco/data_statistics/fact_sheets/health_effects/effects_cig_smoking/ (accessed July 2, 2013).

——. "STD Trends in the US." Centers for Disease Control and Prevention. March 2013. http://www.cdc.gov/std/stats11/trends-2011.pdf (accessed July 2, 2013).

Cherry, Kendra. "Memory retrieval." *About.com Psychology*. The New York Times Company, 2013. http://psychology.about.com/od/cognitivepsychology/p/forgetting.htm (accessed June 30, 2013).

Clark, Donald. "The Components of a Clearly Stated Goal" from *The Art and Science of Leadership* from http://nwlink.com/~donclark/leader/leader.html. Copyright © 2011 by Donald R. Clark. Used by permission of Donald R. Clark (accessed on August 1, 2011).

Clark, Donald. "VAK Learning Styles Survey" from *The Art and Science of Leadership* from http://nwlink.com/~donclark/leader/leader.html. Copyright © 2011 by Donald R. Clark. Used by permission of Donald R. Clark (accessed on August 1, 2011).

"College dropout rate climbs as students face challenges." *News Blaze* (September 12, 2007). http://newsblaze.com/story/2007091202000800001.mwir/topstory.html (accessed October 20, 2012).

Collins, Jim and Jerry I. Porras. *Built to Last: Successful Habits of Visionary Companies.* New York: Harper Business Essentials, 2002.

Cuseo, Joe. Conference on the First Year Experience. Dallas, Texas. February 2004.

———. "Decided, Undecided, and in Transition: Implications for Academic Advisement, Career Counseling, and Student Retention." In *Improving the First Year of College: Research and Practice*, ed. R. S. Feldman (New York: Erlbaum, 2005), 27–50.

———. "Universal Principles of Student Success." Keynote for Educational Frontiers Group. Morrilton, Arkansas. May 20, 2013.

Domonelle, Kristen. "Bullying at Work on Campus: Higher Ed Workers Bullied More than General Workforce." *University Business* (February 2013). http://www.universitybusiness.com/article/bullying-work-campus (accessed July 1, 2013).

Duncan, Royce. In *Rhythms of College Success: A Journey of Discovery, Change, and Mastery.* Upper Saddle River, NJ: Pearson Prentice Hall, 2008.

Dunn, Rita and Kenneth Dunn. *Teaching Students Through Their Individual Learning Styles: A Practical Approach.* Reston, VA: Reston, 1978.

Elder, Linda and Richard Paul. "Universal intellectual standards." *The Critical Thinking Community.* http://www.criticalthinking.org/pages/universal-intellectual-standards/527 (accessed June 25, 2013).

Ewert, Stephanie. "What It's Worth: Field of Training and Economic Status in 2009." U.S. Census Bureau (February 2012): 8. http://www.census.gov/prod/2012pubs/p70–129.pdf (Accessed October 20, 2012).

FBI. "Financial crimes report to the public fiscal year 2006." FBI. 2006. http://www.fbi.gov/stats-services/publications/fcs_report2006/financial-crimes-report-to-the-public-fiscal-year-2006#Identity (accessed June 6, 2013).

Federal Trade Commission. "When a company blocks your credit or debit card." Federal Trade Commission. August 2012. http://www.consumer.ftc.gov/articles/0217-when-company-blocks-your-credit-or-debit-card (accessed June 6, 2013).

Ferguson, Christopher. "Not every child is a genius." *The Chronicle of Higher Education-The Chronicle Review* (June 14, 2009). http://chronicle.com/article/Not-Every-Child-Is-Secretly/48001/ (accessed June 29, 2013).

"Fifty Famously Successful People Who Failed at First," *Online College.org* (February 16, 2010). http://www.onlinecollege.org/2010/02/16/50-famously-successful-people-who-failed-at-first/ (accessed July 13, 2013).

Fleming, Neil. "Is VARK a learning style?" VARK. 2001–2006. http://vark-learn.com/english/page.asp?p=faq (accessed June 29, 2013).

"Freshman College Weight Gain." *Freshman 15*. http://www.freshman15.com/ (accessed June 19, 2013).

Fry, Ron. *Improve Your Reading.* Hawthorne, NJ: The Career Press, 1991.

Gardner, Howard. *Frames of Mind: The Theory of Multiple Intelligences.* New York: Basic Books, 1983.

Gardner, Howard and Seana Moran. "The science of multiple intelligence theory: A response to Lynn Waterhouse." *Educational Psychologist* 41 no. 4 (2006): 227–232. http://alliance.la.asu.edu/temporary/students/katie/MultipleIntelligencesGardner.pdf (accessed June 29, 2013).

Gier, Vicki, et al. "Using an electronic highlighter to eliminate the negative effects of pre-existing, inappropriate highlighting." *Journal of College Reading and Learning* 41 no. 2 (Spring 2011): 40.

Glater, Jonathan D. "To: Professor@University.edu Subject: Why It's All About Me." *New York Times* (February 21, 2006). www.nytimes.com/2006/02/21/education/21professors.html?ex=1298178000&en=361f9efce267b517&ei=5090&partner=rssuserland&emc=rss (accessed June 30, 2013)

Goldberg, Bruce. "Energy Vampires." n.d. http://www.drbrucegoldberg.com/EnergyVampires.htm (accessed July 1, 2013).

Goleman, Daniel. *Emotional Intelligence.* New York: Bantam Books, 1997.

———. "Emotional intelligence." *12 Manage: The Executive Fast Track.* http://www.12manage.com/methods_goleman_emotional_intelligence.html (accessed October 20, 2012).

Gordon, Virginia N. and Susan J. Sears. *Selecting a College Major: Exploration and Decision Making*, 5th ed. Upper Saddle River, NJ: Merrill/Prentice Hall, 2004.

Hallowell, Edward M. *Crazy Busy: Overstretched, Overbooked, and About to Snap!* New York: Ballantine Books, 2007.

Harris, Sam. "Stats regarding texting/mobile devices in the classroom and what instructors are doing about it." *Learning Design and Technology* (May 29, 2013). Maryville University. http://blogs.maryville.edu/learn/2013/05/concerning-stats-about-textingmobile-devices-what-instructors-are-doing-about-it/ (accessed June 30, 2013).

Hellmich, Nance "USA Wallowing in Unhealthy Ways: Obesity Expert Points Finger at Fat-City Society." *USA Today* (August 22, 2002). http://usatoday30.usatoday.com/educate/college/firstyear/articles/20020823.htm (accessed July 2, 2013).

Henry, D. J. *The Skilled Reader* (updated edition). New York: Pearson Longman, 2004.

Hettler, Bill. "The Six Dimensional Wellness Model." National Wellness Institute. http://www.nationalwellness.org/?page=Six_Dimensions (accessed June 19, 2013).

"How to Avoid Date Rape." *Ezilon.com* (June 12, 2006). http://www.ezilon.com/information/article_15242.shtml (accessed July 2, 2013).

Jensen, Eric. "Brain-based Learning: A Reality Check." *Educational Leadership* 57 no. 7 (April 2000): 78.

Katzenbach, John R. and Douglas K. Smith. *The Wisdom of Teams: Creating the High-Performance Organization.* New York: HarperBusiness Essentials, 2003.

Keefe, James. *Learning Style Handbook: II. Accommodating Perceptual, Study and Instructional Preferences.* Reston, VA: National Association of Secondary School Principals, n.d.

Kentucky Fried Chicken. http://www.kfc.com/nutrition/ (accessed May 25, 2013).

Kochanek, K.D. "Heart Disease Facts and Statistics." Centers for Disease Control. 2011. http://www.cdc.gov/heartdisease/statistics.htm (accessed July 1, 2013).

Kragen, Ken. *Life Is a Contact Sport: Ten Great Career Strategies That Work.* New York: Morrow, 1994.

Lee, John. *The Anger Solution: The Proven Method for Achieving Calm and Developing Healthy, Long-Lasting Relationships.* Philadelphia: Da Capo Press, 2009.

Leider, Richard. *The Power of Purpose: Creating Meaning in Your Life and Work.* New York: MJF Books, 1997.

Leider, Richard and David Shapiro. *Repacking Your Bags: Lighten Your Load for the Rest of Your Life.* San Francisco: Barrett-Koehler, 1995.

Lencioni, Patrick. *The Five Dysfunctions of a Team.* San Francisco: Jossey-Bass, 2002.

Leonard, Michael J. "Some Common Myths About Choosing a Major." Penn State University. March 12, 2013. http://dus.psu.edu/md/mdmisper.htm (accessed June 19, 2013).

Levine, Arthur and Diane R. Dean. *Generation on a Tightrope: A Portrait of Today's College Student.* New Jersey: John Wiley and Sons, 2012.

Lin, Derek. "Seize the Day." http://www.taoism.net/articles/seizeday.htm (accessed December 15, 2012).

Lyman, Peter and Hal R. Varian. "How Much Information? 2003." School of Information and Management, University of California at Berkeley (October 27, 2003): 1–14. http://www2.sims.berkeley.edu/research/projects/how-much-info-2003/execsum.htm#paper (accessed June 29, 2013.)

McDonald's. "McDonald's U.S.A. Nutrition Facts for Popular Menu Items." May, 2013. http://nutrition.mcdonalds.com/getnutrition/nutritionfacts.pdf (accessed May 25, 2013).

McFadden, Leslie. "What is a credit score?" Bankrate.com. April 22, 2010. http://www.bankrate.com/finance/credit-cards/what-is-a-credit-score.aspx (accessed June 7, 2013).

McNamara, Carter. "Basics of Conflict Management." 1997–2008. http://w3.palmer.edu/osd/process/PDF/Basics%20of%20Conflict%20Management.pdf (accessed July 1, 2013).

Marano, Hara Estroff. "Assertive, Not Aggressive." *Psychology Today* (August 3, 2011). http://www.psychologytoday.com/rss/pto-20040206-000009.html (accessed July 1, 2013).

Masnjack, Taylor. "Employers use Facebook in hiring." *Daily Vidette.* Illinois State University, February 23, 2006. http://www.videtteonline.com/index.php?option=com_content&view=article&id=16275:employers-use-facebook-in-hiring&catid=67:newsarchive&Itemid=53 (accessed June 29, 2013).

Matte, Nancy Lightfoot and Susan Hillary Henderson. *Success, Your Style: Right- and Left-Brain Techniques for Learning.* Belmont, CA: Wadsworth, 1995.

Medina, John. *Brain Rules: 12 Principles for Surviving and Thriving at work, Home, and School.* Seattle: Pear Press, 2008.

Mearns, Jack. "The Social Learning Theory of Julian B. Rotter." Department of Psychology, California State University–Fullerton. August, 12, 2012. http://psych.fullerton.edu/jmearns/rotter.htm (accessed June 29, 2013).

Miller, George A. "The Magical Number Seven, Plus or Minus Two: Some Limits on Our Capacity to Process Information." *The Psychological Review* 63 (1956): 81–97. Reproduced at http://www.musanim.com/miller1956/ (accessed June 30, 2013).

Miller, William. "Resolutions That Work." *Spirituality and Health* (February 2005): 44–47.

Minninger, Joan and Eleanor Dugan. *Rapid Memory in 7 Days: The Quick-and-Easy Guide to Better Remembering.* New York: Berkeley Publishing Group, 1994.

Morris, Clifford. "A Few General Occupations Profiting from a Dominance in Each of Howard Gardner's Eight Intelligence." 2011. http://www.igs.net/~cmorris/smo1-8.html (accessed June 19, 2013).

MyFitnessPal. 2013. http://www.myfitnesspal.com/ (accessed May 25, 2013).

National Eating Disorders Association. "Types and Symtoms of Eating Disorders." National Eating Disorders Association. n.d. http://www.nationaleatingdisorders.org/types-symptoms-eating-disorders (accessed July 2, 2013).

National Heart, Lung, and Blood Institute. "How Are Overweight and Obesity Diagnosed?" July 13, 2012. http://www.nhlbi.nih.gov/health/health-topics/topics/obe/diagnosis.html (accessed July 2, 2013).

National Institute on Alcohol and Alcohol Abuse. "College Drinking." n.d. http://www.niaaa.nih.gov/alcohol-health/special-populations-co-occurring-disorders/college-drinking (accessed July 2, 2013).

National Institute of Mental Health. "Depression." National Institute of Mental Health. June 10, 2013. http://www.nlm.nih.gov/medlineplus/depression.html (accessed July 2, 2013).

Ogden, C. L., Carroll, M. D., Kit, B.K., and Flegal, K. M. "Prevalence of obesity and trends in body mass index among U.S. children and adolescents, 1999–2010." *Journal of the American Medical Association* 307 no. 5 (2012): 483–490. http://frac.org/initiatives/hunger-and-obesity/obesity-in-the-us/ (accessed July 2, 2013).

Orloff, Judith. *Positive Energy.* New York: Harmony Books, 2004.

Orndorff, Robert M. and Edwin L. Herr. "A Comparative Study of Declared and Undeclared College Students on Career Uncertainty and Involvement in Career Development Activities." *Journal of Counseling and Development* 74 (July/August 1996): 634.

Pardini, Eleanor A., et. al. "Parallel Note-taking: A Strategy for Effective Use of Webnotes." *Journal of College Reading and Learning* 35 no. 2 (Spring 2005): 1–18. http://www.eric.ed.gov/PDFS/EJ689655.pdf (accessed June 30, 2013).

Pauk, Walter. *How to Study in College,* 5th ed. Boston: Houghton Mifflin, 1993.

Piscitelli, Steve. *Study Skills: Do I Really Need This Stuff, 3e.* Boston: Pearson Education, 2013.

Pizza Hut. "Nutritional Information." http://www.pizzahut.com/nutritionpizza.html (accessed May 25, 2013).

Plattsburgh State University of New York. "Common Misconceptions and Advice for Undeclared Students." Plattsburgh State University of New York. n.d. http://web.plattsburgh.edu/academics/advising/undeclaredadvice.php (accessed June 19, 2013).

Posen, David B. "Stress Management for Patient and Physician." *Canadian Journal of Continuing Medical Education* (April 1995). http://www.mentalhealth.com/mag1/p51-str.html#Head_1 (accessed June 25, 2013).

Procter, Margaret. "How Not to Plagiarize." Writing at the University of Toronto (2006). http://www.writing.utoronto.ca/advice/using-sources/how-not-to-plagiarize (accessed January 7, 2013).

Qualman, Erik. "Social Media Revolution (refreshed): Stats from video." *Socialnomics: World of Mouth for Social Good.* May 5, 2010. http://www.socialnomics.net/2010/05/05/social-media-revolution-2-refresh/ (accessed June 29, 2013).

——. *Socialnomics: How Social Media Transforms the Way We Live and Do Business.* New Jersey: John Wiley and Sons, Inc., 2009.

Riedling, Ann Marlow. *Learning to Learn: A Guide to Becoming Information Literate.* New York: Neal-Schuman, 2002.

Saillant, Catherine. "A Bulwark Against Bullies." *LATimes.com* (December 5, 2005). http://pqasb.pqarchiver.com/latimes/access/936841751.html?dids=936841751:936841751&FMT=ABS&FMTS=ABS:FT&type=current&date=Dec+5%2C+2005&author=Catherine+Saillant&pub=Los+Angeles+Times&edition=&startpage=B.1&desc=A+Bulwark+Against+Bullies (accessed July 1, 2013).

Santiago, Steve. "Coping with lower credit card limits." Bankrate.com. May 22, 2008. http://www.bankrate.com/finance/financial-literacy/coping-with-cut-credit-1.aspx (accessed June 7, 2013).

Sapadin, Linda with Jack Maguire. *Beat Procrastination and Make the Grade: The Six Styles of Procrastination and How Students Can Overcome Them.* New York: Penguin Books, 1999.

Shamoon, Evan. "Texting is preferred communication method for college students." *Switched* (March 29, 2009). http://www.switched.com/2009/03/29/texting-is-preferred-communication-method-for-college-students/ (accessed June 30, 2013).

Shapiro, Elayne. "Brain-based Learning Meets PowerPoint." *Teaching Professor* 20 no. 5 (May 5, 2006): 5. http://www.vcu.edu/cte/resources/newsletters_archive/TP0605.PDF (accessed June 30, 2013).

Shirky, Clay. *Cognitive Surplus: Creativity and Generosity in a Connected Age.* New York: The Penguin Press, 2010.

Sholes, DeLene. "Reading for Different Purposes." Education and Career Suite. March 25, 2013. http://suite101.com/article/reading-for-different-purposes-a91899 (accessed June 30, 2013).

Simon, Cecilia Capuzzi. "Major Decisions." *The New York Times* (November 12, 2012). http://www.nytimes.com/2012/11/04/education/edlife/choosing-one-college-major-out-of-hundreds.html?_r=0 (accessed June 19, 2013).

Smith, Brenda D. *Bridging the Gap: College Reading*, 9th ed. New York: Pearson Longman, 2008.

Smith, Mark K. "Bruce W. Tuckman—Forming, Storming, Norming, and Performing in Groups." In *Infed: The Encyclopaedia of Informal Education.* 2005. http://www.infed.org/thinkers/tuckman.htm (accessed July 13, 2013).

Smith, Melinda, et. al. "Stress Symptoms, Signs, and Causes." HelpGuide.org. May 2013. http://help-guide.org/mental/stress_signs.htm. (accessed on June 25, 2013).

Smokefree.gov. http://smokefree.gov/qg-quitting-quitday.aspx (accessed July 2, 2013).

Stanley, Thomas J. and William D. Danko. *The Millionaire Next Door: The Surprising Secrets of America's Wealthy.* Atlanta, Georgia: Longstreet Press, Inc., 1996.

Sternberg, Robert. *Successful Intelligence: How Practical and Creative Intelligence Determine Success in Life.* New York: Plume, 1997.

Stevens, Jose. *The Power Path: The Shaman's Way to Success in Business and Life.* Novato, CA: New World Library, 2002.

"Stress management for the health of it." Clemson Extension. Appendix I. Healthstyle Quiz. In *National Ag Safety* Database. April 2002. Database. http://www.nasdonline.org/docs/d001201-d001300/d001245/d001245.html (accessed May 24, 2013).

Swartz, Roger G. *Accelerated Learning: How You Learn Determines What You Learn.* Durant, OK: EMIS, 1991.

Tinto, Vincent. "Taking Student Learning Seriously." Association of Canadian Community Colleges, Vancouver, British Columbia. January 29, 2004. http://www.slideworld.com/slideshow.aspx/Taking-Student-Learning-Seriously-Vincent-Tinto-Sy-ppt-421083 (accessed June 29, 2013).

University of Guelph. "SQ4R: A classic method for studying texts." University of Guelph (The Learning Commons). 2007. http://www.lib.uoguelph.ca/assistance/learning_services/handouts/SQ4R.cfm (accessed June 30, 2013).

University of South Dakota. "20 Myths About Majors and Careers." University of South Dakota. www.usd.edu/cdc/genworkshop/mythsaboutmajors.pdf (accessed July 8, 2009).

United States Courts. "Bankruptcy filings continue to decline." *The Third Branch News* (August 2012). http://news.uscourts.gov/bankruptcy-filings-continue-decline (accessed June 3, 2013).

United States Department of Education. "Family Educational Rights and Privacy Act (FERPA)." http://www.ed.gov/policy/gen/guid/fpco/ferpa/index.html (accessed October 20, 2012).

United States Department of Health and Human Services. "In Brief: Your Guide to Healthy Sleep." National Institutes of Health, NIH Publication No. 11-5800 (September 2011). http://www.nhlbi.nih.gov/health/public/sleep/healthysleepfs.pdf (accessed July 2, 2013).

——. "USDA and HHS Announce New Dietary Guidelines to Help Americans Make Healthier Food Choices and Confront Obesity Epidemic." U.S. Department of Health and Human Services. May 2011. http://www.hhs.gov/news/press/2011pres/01/20110131a.html (accessed July 2, 2013).

United States Department of Labor. "Computer Workstations." http://www.osha.gov/SLTC/etools/computerworkstations/index.html (accessed June 25, 2013).

——. *Occupational Outlook Handbook.*, Bureau of Labor Statistics. http://www.bls.gov/oco/home.htm (accessed June 17, 2013).

United States Food and Drug Administration. "How to understand and use the nutrition facts label." United States Food and Drug Administration. March 2, 2013. http://www.fda.gov/Food/IngredientsPackaging Labeling/LabelingNutrition/ucm274593.htm (accessed July 2, 2013).

University Senate of Michigan Technological University. "Academic Integrity Policy." April 6, 2006. http://www.sas.it.mtu.edu/usenate/propose/06/8-06.htm (accessed January 7, 2013).

Urban, Hal. *Life's Greatest Lessons.* New York: Simon and Shuster, 2003.

"USA text messaging statistics." *Text Message Blog.* http://www.textmessageblog.mobi/2009/02/19/text-message-statistics-usa/ (accessed June 29, 2013).

VanderStoep, Scott W. and Paul R. Pintrich. *Learning to Learn: The Skill and Will of College Success.* Upper Saddle River, NJ: Prentice Hall, 2003.

Visa, n.d. "The three Cs of credit." *Practical Money Skills for Life.* Visa. n.d. http://www.practicalmoneyskills.com/personalfinance/creditdebt/history/3cs.php (accessed August 12, 2013).

Watson-Glaser Critical Thinking Appraisal, Forms A/B (WGCTA). Copyright © 2007 by NCS Pearson, Inc. Used by permission of Pearson Education, Inc.

West Virginia University at Parkersburg. "SQ4R Reading Method." West Virginia University at Parkersburg. www.wvup.edu/Academics/learning_center/sq4r_reading_method.htm (accessed June 30, 2013).

Whitbourne, Jonathan. "The dropout dilemma: One in four college freshman dropout. What is going on here? What does it take to stay in?" *Careers & Colleges* 22 no. 4 (March 2002).

White, Martha C. "College students are credit card dunces." *Time Business and Money* (April 12, 2012). http://business.time.com/2012/04/12/college-students-are-credit-card-dunces/ (accessed June 6, 2013).

Williams, Erica. "Students need help combating credit card debt." Testimony before the House Financial Services Subcommittee on Financial Institutions and Consumer Credit. June 26, 2008. http://www.americanprogress.org/issues/2008/06/williams_testimony.html (accessed January 24, 2009).

Wilson, Susan B. *Goal Setting.* New York: American Management Association, 1994.

Winget, Larry. *Shut Up, Stop Whining, and Get a Life: A Kick-Butt Approach to a Better Life.* New Jersey: John Wiley, 2004.

You Can Deal With It. "How to Save." You Can Deal With It. 2010. http://www.youcandealwithit.com/borrowers/managing-money/how-to-save.shtml (accessed June 7, 2013).

Zadina, Janet N. "The mystery of attention." Presentation at the National Association for Developmental Education Annual Conference. Nashville, TN. March 22, 2007.

Academic integrity. Having honesty, responsibility, and respectfulness; doing and submitting your own work without any unauthorized assistance. 72–74, 187

Accuracy. Information is factual. 26–27

Acronym. A word formed from the letters (usually the first letters) of other words; memory strategy. 147

Action steps. Specific, measurable, and responsible movement toward a goal. 88–91, 93

Active learning. Students must do what they can to be engaged—involved—in the lesson; establishing connections during the learning process. 112–113, 117, 121, 128

Active listening. Being engaged in what you hear by focusing and participating in the discussion. 118–120, 128, 143

Active reading. Requires you to *do* something rather than passively seeing the words on the page; includes note-taking, highlighting, scanning, and asking questions. 154

Activation energy. The initial movement needed to either "kick-start a positive habit" or help block a negative habit. Reduces or minimizes the obstacles and increases the chances of doing the task. A way to minimize procrastination. 49–50

Aerobic exercise. Defined as activity that increases your heart and breathing rates, as well as working your muscles. 215

Aggressive. Harsher than assertiveness; can boarder on bullying; violating another person. 203

Ambition. A desire to reach a goal. 265

Analyzing. Compare, contrast, examine, and break down information into its smaller pieces. 26–28

Annual fee. The amount of money a credit card holder must pay the credit card company (typically once per year) for the privilege of using the card. 243

Anxiety. A general feeling of unease, uncertainty, anticipation, and even fear about an event. 173, 175–176, 181, 188

Assertiveness. Acting with confidence yet not aggressive; standing up for one's self. 203

Assumption. Consider an assumption to be a theory, paradigm, or one's view of the world. When we *assume*, we accept something to be correct or incorrrect. We may or may not have actual proof, but we believe the opinion or position to be accurate or inaccurate. 24–25, 28–36

Attention. Concentration; listening, observing, and sorting through the vast amount of information presented in class, in homework, or on a job. 99, 101–103, 105, 118–120, 128

Auditory learning. Prefer taking in and putting out information orally. 100, 105

Balance. A state of well-being when you feel intellectually alert, emotionally stable, and physically strong. Maintaining a healthy lifestyle (balance) will help you adapt and thrive in a new environment. The balance (or lack of it) of your life dimensions will have a major impact on the quality of your life experiences. 11–14, 17

Banking statement. Mailed or posted online monthly by the bank. Shows all money that went either into or out of your account during the past month. Use this to keep track of your transactions. 238

Bankruptcy. A legal action taken when one's debt is so significant there appears little hope of paying it off. Implications for credit score and credit history. 234, 236

Binge drinking. The National Institute on Alcohol and Alcohol Abuse defines binge drinking as drinking that raises blood alcohol content to 0.08 grams or more. For men, typically five drinks within two hours will generate this result. For women, four drinks can have the effect. 224

Blogs. Written pieces posted on websites. They usually include the opinions or observations of the writer (known as the "blogger") about a topic. Often times the blogger will include visuals or links to support his or her thoughts. 67, 69–70, 74

Body mass index (BMI). A traditional way to measure your level of fat; takes both weight and height into account. 221–223

Boundaries. Show where you "begin and end"; let others know what is acceptable and unacceptable behavior toward you; tell people how far they can go with you. 205

Brain-based learning. The brain seeks out meaning. It looks for connections as it establishes patterns that will help it make sense of the world. Studies suggest we can take raw facts and make them mean something.   156

Brainstorm. A process to come up with as many ideas as possible—without judgment. Purpose is to generate and create thoughts.   31–33

Budget. Provides a big picture of your financial health. Shows income and expenditures.   233–236, 239, 243–244, 246

Bullies. Seek to control other people by physical or verbal aggression.   204

C.A.P. principle. An acronym that stands for three people who can help a student successfully navigate the campus and all of its resources: classmate, advisor, professor.   11

Calendar. Divides time into years, months, weeks, and days. It is a way to track activities and commitments over time.   40, 45–48, 51–52

Citation. Providing credit when using the words, statistics, and ideas of other authors. Generally consists of the author's name, the title of the publication, the publisher's name, the place and date of publication, and the page numbers from which the material came. If obtained from the Internet, the URL (www.) will be needed.   73–74

Civility. Acting appropriately, acting with respect; a basic component of a working and respectful relationship; polite and courteous behavior.   120

Clarity. Facts and arguments are clearly and unambiguously presented.   26–27

Classroom success. Achievement that is fostered by attendance, attention, and participation. Connected to active learning and attention.   117, 119

Collective monologue. Many people are talking but few (if any) are listening.   197–198, 207

Communication. Construct and pass along thoughts, information, and feelings about a particular subject to another person.   196–197, 199, 203, 207

Comprehension. Describe what you have read in your own words; you understand it.   155, 157, 159–160, 167

Confirmation bias. When preconceived ideas interfere with an unbiased decision. We would only consider information that confirms our beliefs.   25, 31, 36

Conflict. A state of disharmony where one set of ideas or values contradicts another.   201–202

Connections. Relationships between experiences, textbook readings, and classroom lessons; improves memory recall. Note-taking provides the chance to build these connections.   132–137, 139, 143–145, 147, 149

Context. Words surrounding other words that give it meaning.   163, 167

Creative thinking. Thinking that develops (creates) a *new* or *different* product—requires that we look at situations in new ways, from different angles or unique perspectives.   32–33, 35

Credit limit. Issued by the credit card company. Indicates how much money the cardholder can charge.   243–244

Credit score. This three-digit number reflects your credit history—and is used as a predictor of your risk to a creditor. Indicator of financial choices.   244

Critical thinking. Gathering information, weighing it for accuracy and appropriateness, and then making a rational decision based on the facts that have been gathered.   22–28, 30, 32–36

Data retrieval chart (D.R.C.). A technique to organize information; allows for easy categorization, comparison, and contrast of information; can be used to show how one item impacts another; show connections.   143

Date rape. Nonconsensual intercourse with a friend or acquaintance; one form of sexual violence.   225

Debit card. Alternative to paper checks; used much like a credit card but actually represents money you have in the bank.   237–238, 242, 245–246

Debt. Expenditures exceed income.   233–236, 241–245

Declare a major. Students commit to a particular course of academic preparation. Once the academic major has been declared, course work becomes more focused and more specialized.   254–255, 258

Digital tattoo. Consists of everything you post about yourself and everything you write in response to someone else. All the photos, videos, music, and poetry that you post (or someone posts concerning you) to say something about who you are. Your digital tattoo is your online reputation.   70–71, 75

Distracter. An incorrect answer choice given on a multiple-choice test; it distracts you from the correct answer.   184

Distractions. Anything that hinders concentration; an interruption in thought or action.   118–119, 128

Eating disorder. Results in unhealthy weight loss; examples include anorexia, bulimia, and binge eating.   222–223

Elephant in the corner. Metaphor for a problem that is so big that it is impossible to miss, but the problem is ignored because no one wants to confront it.   200, 202

Emergency studying. Last minute studying; not a desirable strategy.   183

Emotional intelligence. A person needs more than a high score on an IQ test to be successful. The abilities to soothe one's self, to recognize emotions in others, and to delay gratification are signs of the emotionally intelligent person.   195

Environmental factors (affecting learning). Affect how we learn. Includes lighting, temperature, types of furniture being used.   100, 104

Evaluate. A higher-level thinking skill; to judge an assumption for fact or fiction.   25, 29, 31–32, 35–36

Excuse. An attempt to explain a particular course of action in order to remove or lessen responsibility or blame for a result.   86

Extrinsic motivation. An external or outside force that will move a person toward a goal.   82

Financial literacy. Having and responsibly using knowledge about money. Indicates ability and choices regarding debt and wealth building.   230, 237

Forgetting. The failure of a previously learned behavior to reappear.   142

GER. The "General Education Requirements" that schools require students to take as a core course of study. Sometimes called "Gen Ed."   254, 261

Goal. A desired end point; a place one wants to reach; a result one wishes to attain.   87–93

Graphics. Pictures, photos, charts, figures, or tables used by an author to illustrate a point.   164

Groupthink. Refers to what happens when group thinking overshadows individual thoughts and concerns. In order to get along with the others, a member agrees with what the group as a whole thinks.   255

Habit. Something we repeat with such frequency that it becomes an involuntary act. It becomes second nature.   16–18, 215–217, 225

Higher-order thinking skills. When a critical thinker is actively and deeply involved in processing information by applying, analyzing, evaluating, and/or creating information and ideas.   22–23, 28

Highlighting. A strategic reading behavior; marking the major points of a reading; a form of active learning. Can be done with a colored highlighter, pen, or pencil.   160–161

H.O.G.s. Huge Outrageous Goals; they encourage us to stretch and strive for large goals.   88

Identity theft. When your personal information (like social security, drivers license, and checking account numbers) are taken by another and used fraudulently for their purposes.   232, 245

Information literacy. Knowing *what* information to look for, *how to find* that information, *how to judge* the information's credibility and quality once it has been found, and *how to effectively use* the information once it has been found and evaluated.   61–62, 66, 74–75

Initiative. Responsible decision making and follow-through.   265

Instructor styles. An instructor's method of presentation and classroom delivery. May range from lecture, to question and answer, to group work, to lab work, to discussion, to seat work. Each instructor has a set of expectations for student performance.   115

Integrity. Acting with respect, responsibility, and honesty toward others and yourself.   14–15

Intelligence. What we use to reason, solve problems; skills we use to interact with our environment.   104, 106–108

Interest rate. The cost charged for the use of another's money. For credit cards, this is the percentage the cardholder must pay if a balance is carried from month to month. Banks can give the depositor interest for the use of the depositor's money.   240, 243

Interlibrary loans. Requesting and transferring library material from one library to another.   62

Interpersonal skills. One's strengths and challenges when interacting with other people.   194–195, 198

Intrinsic motivation. An internal force (from within a person) that moves a person toward a goal.   82

Portfolio. The collection of information about your education, talents, skills, interests, and work experiences. 263

Post-exam analysis. Upon completion of an exam, review how well (or not) you have done; address challenges before the next exam. 178–181

Potential. The possibility of becoming something greater than you are. 265

Priorities. People, events, and/or things that are important to a person. 40–41, 46–47, 50–51, 54–55

Priority management. Priorities are those things that are important in your life (those things that help you get what you want). When you practice priority management, you critically think about what important things you need to do each day. Effective priority management is an essential life skill. 4, 9, 16

Problem solving. The use of critical thinking skills to examine a dilemma, situation, or person that presents a challenge and then propose a solution. 30, 32, 35

Problem-solving trap. Blinded to *new* alternatives by becoming stuck in routine or trapped by our assumptions. Perhaps we continue to look at a particular problem from old points of view. 31

Procrastination. Avoiding and postponing what should be taken care of now. 48–50

Purpose (for reading). Various reasons for reading: answer specific questions, apply information, find details, get a message, evaluate material, and entertain yourself. 158–159, 167

R.E.D. model. Acronym for three critical thinking steps: Recognize assumptions, Evaluate information, Draw conclusions. 24, 26, 29–31, 33–36

Reclaiming. Retrieving information you have stored; typically refers to what we have remembered or forgotten. 141–142, 144–145, 149

Recommended Daily Allowance. Dietary recommendations for caloric intake. Fats, sugars, and sodium are other items typically listed for RDA. 218

Reference librarian. Can help you navigate the library's holdings, introduce you to various search strategies, and direct you to the most appropriate databases. 62–64

Reframe. To view something (an issue, an event, a person) from a different perspective. 175, 216

Relevance. When information relates to the argument or problem at hand. 27

Repetitive strain injuries (RSI). Also called *repetitive stress injuries.* Commonly occur to people who spend long hours typing at a keyboard and staring into a computer monitor. As the name implies, the injury results from repetitive (continual) motions or actions. 52

Review-relate-reorganize strategy. An active notes-review strategy that helps to translate notes from the instructor's words to the student's words. 136–137

Risk. Stepping outside of one's comfort zone. 261

R.O.I. Stands for return on investment. Here this business concept is used as a metaphor for getting the most return (academic and personal success) for the effort you have put into your class time and study time. 134

Scan. In reading, to get a quick overview of what you are to read; understanding the general idea of the assignment. 157, 159, 164

Search engines. Provide the strategy to move mindless Web surfing to a focused ride. They assist in gathering pertinent information from the many databases on the World Wide Web. 63–64, 70

Service charge. A fee charged by the bank for allowing you to have an account at the bank. 238

Short-term memory. Also known as working memory; can manipulate, or work with, the information for a short time; may or may not eventually be transferred to long-term memory. 142, 146

Six Dimensions of Well-Being. A National Wellness Institute model that reminds us that we have six parts of our life: social, occupational, spiritual, physical, intellectual, emotional. We have to take care of all dimensions as they all affect one another. 12

Social media. Consumer-generated media. 67–71

SQ4R. A six-step reading model: survey, question, read, recite, record, review. 156–158, 160, 162, 164, 167

Status updates. Are like mini blogs. People post short messages about something they have just done or are about to do. They can convey a meaningful message, a funny anecdote, or a question. They may include a photo or video or a website link. 69

Strategic reading. Reading in a planned and thoughtful way to understand your reading. 160

PHOTO CREDITS